China's Strategic Priorities

The People's Republic of China is the world's most populous state and largest consumer of energy, having demonstrated momentous progress on an unprecedented scale. This global power has increasingly shaped international relations as a result of its population size, economic development and political character.

Identifying the most significant new issues and problems that have arisen from China's rapid development, this book examines the evolution of China's contemporary foreign policy and international relations. In doing so, it underlines the global importance of China's management of its own politics and economics, and demonstrates how all nation-states have a vested interest in – and to varying degrees are liable for – the consequences of Chinese actions. The book aims to spark debate by drawing attention to these critical issues, placing them on the scholarly agenda as well as that of the practitioner. It provides factual evidence, progressive findings, justification and a rationale for action, expert analysis, and the resulting policy prescriptions. In addition, the book highlights the liable costs of failing to address China's strategic priorities.

This interdisciplinary book draws attention to the most pressing issues that China must address for universal benefit, and will be of great interest to students and scholars of international relations, Chinese studies and political science.

Jonathan H. Ping is an associate dean and associate professor at Bond University, Australia. He is the founder and a director of the East Asia Security Centre at this university.

Brett McCormick is director of global studies at the University of New Haven, USA and a director of the East Asia Security Centre housed at Bond University, Australia.

Routledge Contemporary China Series

1 **Nationalism, Democracy and National Integration in China**
Leong Liew and Wang Shaoguang

2 **Hong Kong's Tortuous Democratization**
A comparative analysis
Ming Sing

3 **China's Business Reforms**
Institutional challenges in a globalised economy
Edited by Russell Smyth, On Kit Tam, Malcolm Warner and Cherrie Zhu

4 **Challenges for China's Development**
An enterprise perspective
Edited by David H. Brown and Alasdair MacBean

5 **New Crime in China**
Public order and human rights
Ron Keith and Zhiqiu Lin

6 **Non-Governmental Organizations in Contemporary China**
Paving the way to civil society?
Qiusha Ma

7 **Globalization and the Chinese City**
Fulong Wu

8 **The Politics of China's Accession to the World Trade Organization**
The dragon goes global
Hui Feng

9 **Narrating China**
Jia Pingwa and his fictional world
Yiyan Wang

10 **Sex, Science and Morality in China**
Joanne McMillan

11 **Politics in China Since 1949**
Legitimizing authoritarian rule
Robert Weatherley

12 **International Human Resource Management in Chinese Multinationals**
Jie Shen and Vincent Edwards

13 **Unemployment in China**
Economy, human resources and labour markets
Edited by Grace Lee and Malcolm Warner

14 **China and Africa**
Engagement and compromise
Ian Taylor

15 **Gender and Education in China**
Gender discourses and women's schooling in the early twentieth century
Paul J. Bailey

16 **SARS**
Reception and interpretation in three Chinese cities
Edited by Deborah Davis and Helen Siu

17 **Human Security and the Chinese State**
Historical transformations and the modern quest for sovereignty
Robert E. Bedeski

18 **Gender and Work in Urban China**
Women workers of the unlucky generation
Liu Jieyu

19 **China's State Enterprise Reform**
From Marx to the market
John Hassard, Jackie Sheehan, Meixiang Zhou, Jane Terpstra-Tong and Jonathan Morris

20 **Cultural Heritage Management in China**
Preserving the cities of the Pearl River Delta
Edited by Hilary du Cros and Yok-shiu F. Lee

21 **Paying for Progress**
Public finance, human welfare and inequality in china
Edited by Vivienne Shue and Christine Wong

22 **China's Foreign Trade Policy**
The new constituencies
Edited by Ka Zeng

23 **Hong Kong, China**
Learning to belong to a nation
Gordon Mathews, Tai-lok Lui and Eric Kit-wai Ma

24 **China Turns to Multilateralism**
Foreign policy and regional security
Edited by Guoguang Wu and Helen Lansdowne

25 **Tourism and Tibetan Culture in Transition**
A place called Shangrila
Åshild Kolås

26 **China's Emerging Cities**
The making of new urbanism
Edited by Fulong Wu

27 **China-US Relations Transformed**
Perceptions and strategic interactions
Edited by Suisheng Zhao

28 **The Chinese Party-State in the 21st Century**
Adaptation and the reinvention of legitimacy
Edited by André Laliberté and Marc Lanteigne

29 **Political Change in Macao**
   Sonny Shiu-Hing Lo

30 **China's Energy Geopolitics**
   The Shanghai Cooperation Organization and Central Asia
   Thrassy N. Marketos

31 **Regime Legitimacy in Contemporary China**
   Institutional change and stability
   Edited by Thomas Heberer and Gunter Schubert

32 **U.S.–China Relations**
   China policy on Capitol Hill
   Tao Xie

33 **Chinese Kinship**
   Contemporary anthropological perspectives
   Edited by Susanne Brandtstädter and Gonçalo D. Santos

34 **Politics and Government in Hong Kong**
   Crisis under Chinese sovereignty
   Edited by Ming Sing

35 **Rethinking Chinese Popular Culture**
   Cannibalizations of the canon
   Edited by Carlos Rojas and Eileen Cheng-yin Chow

36 **Institutional Balancing in the Asia Pacific**
   Economic interdependence and China's rise
   Kai He

37 **Rent Seeking in China**
   Edited by Tak-Wing Ngo and Yongping Wu

38 **China, Xinjiang and Central Asia**
   History, transition and crossborder interaction into the 21st century
   Edited by Colin Mackerras and Michael Clarke

39 **Intellectual Property Rights in China**
   Politics of piracy, trade and protection
   Gordon Cheung

40 **Developing China**
   Land, politics and social conditions
   George C.S. Lin

41 **State and Society Responses to Social Welfare Needs in China**
   Serving the people
   Edited by Jonathan Schwartz and Shawn Shieh

42 **Gay and Lesbian Subculture in Urban China**
   Loretta Wing Wah Ho

43 **The Politics of Heritage Tourism in China**
   A view from Lijiang
   Xiaobo Su and Peggy Teo

44 **Suicide and Justice**
   A Chinese perspective
   Wu Fei

45 **Management Training and Development in China**
   Educating managers in a globalized economy
   Edited by Malcolm Warner and Keith Goodall

46 **Patron-Client Politics and Elections in Hong Kong**
Bruce Kam-kwan Kwong

47 **Chinese Family Business and the Equal Inheritance System**
Unravelling the myth
Victor Zheng

48 **Reconciling State, Market and Civil Society in China**
The long march towards prosperity
Paolo Urio

49 **Innovation in China**
The Chinese software industry
Shang-Ling Jui

50 **Mobility, Migration and the Chinese Scientific Research System**
Koen Jonkers

51 **Chinese Film Stars**
Edited by Mary Farquhar and Yingjin Zhang

52 **Chinese Male Homosexualities**
Memba, Tongzhi and Golden Boy
Travis S.K. Kong

53 **Industrialisation and Rural Livelihoods in China**
Agricultural processing in Sichuan
Susanne Lingohr-Wolf

54 **Law, Policy and Practice on China's Periphery**
Selective adaptation and institutional capacity
Pitman B. Potter

55 **China-Africa Development Relations**
Edited by Christopher M. Dent

56 **Neoliberalism and Culture in China and Hong Kong**
The countdown of time
Hai Ren

57 **China's Higher Education Reform and Internationalisation**
Edited by Janette Ryan

58 **Law, Wealth and Power in China**
Commercial law reforms in context
Edited by John Garrick

59 **Religion in Contemporary China**
Revitalization and innovation
Edited by Adam Yuet Chau

60 **Consumer-Citizens of China**
The role of foreign brands in the imagined future china
Kelly Tian and Lily Dong

61 **The Chinese Communist Party and China's Capitalist Revolution**
The political impact of the market
Lance L.P. Gore

62 **China's Homeless Generation**
Voices from the veterans of the Chinese civil war, 1940s–1990s
Joshua Fan

63 **In Search of China's Development Model**
Beyond the Beijing consensus
Edited by S. Philip Hsu, Suisheng Zhao and Yu-Shan Wu

64 **Xinjiang and China's Rise in Central Asia, 1949–2009**
A history
Michael E. Clarke

65 Trade Unions in China
The challenge of labour unrest
Tim Pringle

66 China's Changing Workplace
Dynamism, diversity and disparity
Edited by Peter Sheldon, Sunghoon Kim, Yiqiong Li and Malcolm Warner

67 Leisure and Power in Urban China
Everyday life in a medium-sized Chinese city
Unn Målfrid H. Rolandsen

68 China, Oil and Global Politics
Philip Andrews-Speed and Roland Dannreuther

69 Education Reform in China
Edited by Janette Ryan

70 Social Policy and Migration in China
Lida Fan

71 China's One Child Policy and Multiple Caregiving
Raising little Suns in Xiamen
Esther C. L. Goh

72 Politics and Markets in Rural China
Edited by Björn Alpermann

73 China's New Underclass
Paid domestic labour
Xinying Hu

74 Poverty and Development in China
Alternative approaches to poverty assessment
Lu Caizhen

75 International Governance and Regimes
A Chinese perspective
Peter Kien-Hong Yu

76 HIV/AIDS in China –
The Economic and Social Determinants
Dylan Sutherland and Jennifer Y. J. Hsu

77 Looking for Work in Post-Socialist China
Governance, active job seekers and the new Chinese labor market
Feng Xu

78 Sino-Latin American Relations
Edited by K.C. Fung and Alicia Garcia-Herrero

79 Mao's China and the Sino-Soviet Split
Ideological dilemma
Mingjiang Li

80 Law and Policy for China's Market Socialism
Edited by John Garrick

81 China-Taiwan Relations in a Global Context
Taiwan's foreign policy and relations
Edited by C.X. George Wei

82 The Chinese Transformation of Corporate Culture
Colin S.C. Hawes

83 Mapping Media in China
Region, province, locality
Edited by Wanning Sun and Jenny Chio

84 **China, the West and the Myth of New Public Management**
Neoliberalism and its discontents
Paolo Urio

85 **The Lahu Minority in Southwest China**
A response to ethnic marginalization on the frontier
Jianxiong Ma

86 **Social Capital and Institutional Constraints**
A comparative analysis of China, Taiwan and the US
Joonmo Son

87 **Southern China**
Industry, development and industrial policy
Marco R. Di Tommaso, Lauretta Rubini and Elisa Barbieri

China's Strategic Priorities

Edited by
Jonathan H. Ping and Brett McCormick

LONDON AND NEW YORK

First published 2016
by Routledge

2 Park Square, Milton Park, Abingdon, Oxfordshire OX14 4RN
711 Third Avenue, New York, NY 10017

Routledge is an imprint of the Taylor & Francis Group, an informa business

First issued in paperback 2018

Copyright © 2016 Jonathan H. Ping and Brett McCormick

The right of the editors to be identified as the authors of the editorial material, and of the authors for their individual chapters, has been asserted in accordance with sections 77 and 78 of the Copyright, Designs and Patents Act 1988.

All rights reserved. No part of this book may be reprinted or reproduced or utilised in any form or by any electronic, mechanical, or other means, now known or hereafter invented, including photocopying and recording, or in any information storage or retrieval system, without permission in writing from the publishers.

Notice:
Product or corporate names may be trademarks or registered trademarks, and are used only for identification and explanation without intent to infringe.

British Library Cataloguing in Publication Data
A catalogue record for this book is available from the British Library

Library of Congress Cataloging-in-Publication Data
Names: Ping, Jonathan H., editor. | McCormick, Brett, editor.
Title: China's strategic priorities / edited by Jonathan H. Ping and Brett McCormick.
Description: New York, NY : Routledge, 2016. | Series: Routledge contemporary China series ; 138 | Includes bibliographical references and index.
Identifiers: LCCN 2015024461 | ISBN 9780415707343 (hardback) | ISBN 9781315886909 (ebook)
Subjects: LCSH: China—Foreign relations—21st century. | Strategic culture—China.
Classification: LCC JZ1734 .C574 2016 | DDC 355/.033551—dc23
LC record available at http://lccn.loc.gov/2015024461

ISBN: 978-0-415-70734-3 (hbk)
ISBN: 978-1-138-60891-7 (pbk)

Typeset in Times New Roman
by Apex CoVantage, LLC

Contents

Acknowledgements xv
Contributors xvii

Introduction: studying China and strategic priorities 1
JONATHAN H. PING

1 **Myth-busting: challenging the conventional wisdom on Chinese strategic culture** 8
ANDREW R. WILSON

Introduction 8
The Great Wall myth: China's defensive strategic culture 8
The Sunzi *myth: the acme of skill is to win without fighting* 12
The Good Iron myth: the preeminence of the civil over the martial 13
The Zheng He myth: China has no history of overseas colonialism or gunboat diplomacy 15
The myth of shi: *the traditional reliance on the 'propensity of things'* 17
Conclusion 19

2 **Western river civilization and the logic of China's strategic behavior** 24
SU HAO AND CUI YUE

Introduction 24
China's geopolitical center of gravity 25
Western rivers and the Chinese civilization 28
The geopolitical logic behind Chinese strategic behavior 33
Conclusion 39

xii *Contents*

3 **Analyzing China's foreign policy: domestic politics, public opinion and leaders** 43
ERIC HYER, ZHANG QINGMIN AND JORDAN HAMZAWI

Introduction 43
Neorealism 43
Neoliberalism 44
Domestic politics 46
Conclusion 57

4 **Crises as impetus for institutionalization: maritime crisis management mechanisms in China's Near Seas** 62
GAYE CHRISTOFFERSEN

Introduction 62
Defining China's maritime strategy 62
US–China crisis management mechanism 64
Sino-Japanese crisis management mechanisms 66
Conclusion 74

5 **The US factor in China's dispute with Japan over the Diaoyu/Senkaku islands: balancing Washington's 'rebalancing' in East Asian waters** 80
ULISES GRANADOS

Introduction 80
The dispute 81
Reasons for the involvement of the US 83
Dealing with the US and Japan: a Chinese strategic dilemma? 84
The US–Japan alliance factor 86
One of China's strategic priorities in East Asian waters:
  managing the US relationship 87
Future scenarios 89

6 **China's relations with India: great power statecraft and territory** 97
JONATHAN H. PING

Introduction 97
Global political economy and critical theory 99
Why territorial assurance as a strategic priority? 100
Historic realignment in the global political economy
  as a strategic imperative 103

The issues of the stateless territory 104
Back to the 1940s 106
Beyond the 1640s 107
Conclusion 108

7 **US–China cooperation: the role of Pakistan after the death of Osama bin Laden**   114
TIMOTHY D. HOYT

Introduction 114
The US–Pakistan relationship 115
The Sino-Pakistan relationship 116
Chinese and US interests in South Asia 117
Opportunities after Bin Laden's death: an increasing coincidence of interests? 119
Conclusion 124

8 **Chinese regionalism: balancing and constraint in the Shanghai Cooperation Organisation**   129
ALICA KIZEKOVA

Introduction 129
China's regional goals 130
Shanghai Five dialogue processes 131
SCO membership and the Sino-Russian driver 132
Beyond the Five-Day War 135
SCO's reaction to Russia's involvement in the South Caucasus 138
China's perspectives 139
The aftermath of the 2008 Russia–Georgia War and China's regionalism 141

9 **Conclusion**   148
BRETT MCCORMICK

Index   153

Acknowledgements

This has been a global project born from a common interest in China and research for publication. It is only possible to achieve such grand projects through bravery, teamwork and persistence. As editors and authors, we would like to thank everyone associated with this publication for their commitment to pursuing our goals through these characteristics.

Each individual author has been supported by their affiliated institution, as acknowledged in the contributors section. The project is a product of the East Asia Security Centre, Bond University, the University of New Haven and the China Foreign Affairs University. The Centre has been supported by professional staff at the three universities and at Routledge (a member of the Taylor & Francis publishing group).

The Centre's activates have been endorsed and given ongoing support by visionary leaders such as Alan Chan, Raoul Mortley and Lourdes Alvarez. The opportunity provided by these people has been endorsed by the commercial success of the Centre, the publishing association with Routledge, and the confidence and access provided by government, military and party officials from the People's Republic of China.

It is a great pleasure to be able to acknowledge the tireless support for the Centre and the East Asia Security Symposium and Conference provided by Kristen Golimowski since 2003. This has been matched by the indefatigable support from Leng Kiat, Lotus Wei Leng, Gemma Li Xian and Henry Li Jun.

We have done all that has been possible to ensure this book matches the significant support provided. Undertaking research for publication is a unique opportunity and challenge that is made rewarding by the promise of attaining new heights in human perception and leaving a lasting legacy. For this significant experience we are eternally grateful.

Jonathan H. Ping and Brett McCormick
15 June 2015

Contributors

Gaye Christoffersen is resident professor of international politics at the Johns Hopkins-Nanjing Center. She obtained a Ph.D. from the Political Science Department, University of Hawaii. She has been a Fulbright professor, received an East-West Center award, an IREX Travel Award, and a Social Science Research Council Faculty Professional Development Grant. Her research focus has been primarily on transnational, non-traditional security issues such as piracy, energy and other issues on which East Asian nations cooperate in Asian multilateral regimes.

Cui Yue received a M.A. from the University of Hawaii and a Ph.D. from China Foreign Affairs University. She is currently a lecturer at the China-Australia Center, University of International Business and Economics, Beijing, China, and an honorary research fellow at the Faculty of Society and Design at Bond University. She specialises in the study of middle power diplomacy and Australian foreign policy.

Ulises Granados received a Ph.D. in history from the University of Tokyo and is presently associate professor of international relations and Asian studies at Mexico Autonomous Institute of Technology ITAM. As a specialist in East Asian maritime history and security, he is author of *Co-existence and Discord: Analysis of the South China Sea Territorial Conflict, 1902–1952*.

Jordan Hamzawi received a B.A. in international relations and Japanese from Brigham Young University and an M.A. in Japanese studies from the University of Michigan, Ann Arbor, Michigan. He is currently pursuing a Ph.D. in political science at University of California, Davis.

Timothy D. Hoyt is professor of strategy and policy and the John Nicholas Brown Chair of Counterterrorism at the U.S. Naval War College, where he was also co-founder of the Indian Ocean Studies Group. He is the author of over 40 books, articles and book chapters with a particular focus on India, Pakistan and security in the Greater Middle East and South Asia.

Eric Hyer received a Ph.D. in political science from Columbia University. He is presently an associate professor in the Department of Political Science and the coordinator of Asian studies at Brigham Young University in Provo, Utah. He is the author of *The Pragmatic Dragon: China's Grand Strategy and Boundary Settlements*.

Alica Kizekova received a Ph.D. in international relations from Bond University. She is an adviser to the Speaker of Chamber of Deputies at the Czech Parliament in Prague and an honorary adjunct research fellow at the Centre for East-West Cultural and Economic Studies, Faculty of Society and Design at Bond University. She is the author of *Soft Balancing in the Indo-Asia-Pacific: from ASEAN to the Shanghai Cooperation Organization*.

Brett McCormick is an associate professor at the University of New Haven and director of their Global Studies program. He received his Ph.D. from Cornell University. Dr. McCormick is a director of the East Asia Security Centre. He specializes in issues of diplomacy and security in northeast Asia.

Jonathan H. Ping is an associate dean and associate professor at Bond University. He is a graduate of the University of Melbourne and received his Ph.D. from the University of Adelaide. He specialises in the study of statecraft. In this area he has developed the first unifying theory of the middle power concept – hybridisation theory – as presented in his book *Middle Power Statecraft*. His work on statecraft has most recently been applied to China in the book *Chinese Engagements*. Dr. Ping is the founder and a director of the East Asia Security Centre.

Su Hao is a professor in the Department of Diplomacy at China Foreign Affairs University. He received his B.A. and M.A. degrees in history and international relations at Beijing Normal University, and his Ph.D. in international relations at the China Foreign Affairs University. He completed post-doctoral study at the University of London and was a Fulbright scholar at Columbia University and at the University of California, Berkeley. He has published books and articles on China's foreign policy, security issues, international relations in the Asia-Pacific region, and East Asia cooperation. Professor Su is a director of the East Asia Security Centre.

Andrew R. Wilson is professor of strategy at the United States Naval War College. He is a graduate of the University of California, Santa Barbara, and received his Ph.D. in history and East Asian languages from Harvard University. Prior to joining the Naval War College faculty in 1998, he taught courses in Chinese history at Wellesley College and at Harvard University. He is the author of numerous publications on Chinese military history, Chinese sea power and Sun Tzu's *Art of War*. Professor Wilson is a founding member of the War College's Asia-Pacific Studies Group and the China Maritime Studies Institute.

Zhang Qingmin received an M.A. from Brigham Young University and Ph.D. from China Foreign Affairs University. He is currently a professor in the Department of Diplomacy, School of International Studies at Peking University, Beijing, China. He is the author of *China's Diplomacy* and *U.S. Arms Sales Policy towards Taiwan: A Decision-Making Perspective*.

Introduction
Studying China and strategic priorities

Jonathan H. Ping

Consider the magnitude of the People's Republic of China (PRC or China) in the context of our global age – the world's most populous state, holding approximately 20 per cent of the population. Not surprisingly, thus, it is the world's largest consumer of energy as well as a wide range of food products, vehicles, apparel and manifold consumable goods. Its leaders have lifted the greatest number of people from poverty since the Second World War, and it is positioned to be the first billion-plus population state ever to industrialise.[1]

Its size relative to states that have already developed through the industrial age reify its own rapid progress. The enterprises of states and economies that seemed normal and controllable have been dwarfed by the PRC, making the implications for the global system as a whole appear to be anomalous, overwhelming and beyond human agency. This is the situation for the PRC itself, as it is for other states observing – those that in addition are experiencing diminishing authority and power. How do we respond to this actuality? Perhaps this rephrased Chinese aphorism encapsulates a foundational mind-set:

> We must all feel for the stones in order to find our way across the turbulent unknown river.[2]

This book identifies the most significant *new* issues and problems that have arisen as a result of the momentous development of the PRC. It addresses the question: What must the PRC accomplish or resolve that it presently is unaware, unable or unwilling to address? In other words: What are its *strategic priorities*? This book thus uniquely discusses the contemporary international relations of China by identifying China's domestic and international strategic priorities that have systemic and structural consequences if left unattended. Accordingly, relative to the rephrased Chinese aphorism, this book points out the *turbulent eddies in the river's flow*, which we must negotiate together to make a successful crossing.

China's Strategic Priorities aims to create a debate by drawing attention to critical issues in China's relations with the international system. The book aspires to facilitate such debate by placing these matters on the scholarly agenda as well as that of the practitioner. It provides factual evidence, progressive findings, justification and a rationale for action, expert analysis and the resulting policy prescriptions. It ominously – but importantly and commensurately – also points out the liable costs of failing to address China's strategic priorities. It is thus a foundational work that begins tasks to be completed over the coming years.

This book does not seek to catalogue every event, concern, or point of fear or delight. Its task is constrained and clear. *China's Strategic Priorities* offers an original thesis which has resulted from international collaboration, field research in China and interdisciplinary scholarship. The primary vehicles for this have been the East Asia Security Centre (EASC) and the East Asia Security Symposium and Conference (EASSC) held annually at the China Foreign Affairs University, Beijing.[3]

This book alerts academia and contemporary global society to the global importance of China's management of its own politics and economics. This is a new area of research in that it enquires into the critical issues which must be addressed by China in order to maintain the stability and prosperity of all nation-states. The PRC is increasingly shaping international relations as a result of its population size, economic development and political character. These have been magnified by the economic and political failures of the developed Western world (which began in 2008 and are continuing). Due to the implications of the PRC's actions as a global power, all nation-states have a vested interest – and to varying degrees are liable – for the consequences of Chinese actions.

Why a multi-authored, co-edited book? The trend toward gigantism in the PRC could be captured by a large number of individually authored books on specialised subjects from the members of the EASSC, and indeed this is occurring. However, this takes a considerable amount of time and does not adequately account for the other reality of modern China – the rapid pace of change. In order to respond to the reality in a timely and useful manner, a co-authored book allows for a specific and unique thesis to be pursued, whilst being advanced by the collective specialised knowledge of the authors. Second, a multi-authored book stores canonical knowledge in a single tome that – via commercial publication – provides the information to all parts of the world, including those without access to journals or the Internet. Third, a co-authored book enables the PRC perspective to be evidenced, as Chinese scholars benefit from the assistance of the editors in gaining a publishing contact and meeting the protocols of publishing.

Finally, the legal publishing structure of an edited book allows the editors and publisher to translate the book meaningfully in parts, or eventually as a whole, into Mandarin. Many books have, as a secondary process, been translated from English to Mandarin, starting waves of theoretical discourse in China. For example, from 1895 Yen Fu began translating Charles Darwin's *On the Origin of Species* (as well as many other scientific works).[4] This system has continued across the last century, with a good contemporary example being the translation of Alexander Wendt's *Social Theory of International Politics* by the former Vice President of the China Foreign Affairs University, Qin Yaqing. In both cases, as a result of the time taken to translate, Chinese scholars engaged in a time-lagged, independent and isolated debate about the ideas subsequent to the debate in the English-speaking world. Independent, disassociated knowledge resulted.

Consequently, this edited book format allows our scholarship to continue a long tradition of translation from English to Mandarin and provides access to knowledge for the non-English-speaking majority in the PRC. However, it is distinctively different in the speed, accessibility and functionality that our edited book process allows. *Chinese Engagements*[5] and all publications of the EASC are progressively being made available in Mandarin by design. The design provides low-cost distribution, verified translation and quick transfer of knowledge across language and other barriers.

With the great assistance of the China Foreign Affairs University, our translation process correctly employs the norms and technical language being employed by scholars in the PRC.[6] As editors, we can ensure that a range of specialised knowledge is bundled into a book and then conveyed in a clear, standardised and purposeful manner into Mandarin. Through the EASC, *Peer Reviewed Publishing Site* at Bond University, conference papers, book chapters and books by Chinese and Western scholars are available in both English and Mandarin.[7] Routledge places the same information before students, scholars and thinkers globally. To contextualise this: what a politician in London is reading is being read by a student in Beijing.

This co-edited book is thus part of a larger publishing process designed purposefully to expand common knowledge produced through the EASC and the EASSC so that *we may all feel for the stones together in order to find our way across the turbulent, unknown river*. Through study of China, scholarship and common knowledge, we find that our world is not anomalous, overwhelming and beyond human agency.

This book presents the scholarly work of twelve academics who are employed by prestigious universities (or colleges or institutes of technology) and governments in the PRC, the United States of America (US), the Commonwealth of Australia, the United Mexican States and the Czech Republic. They have all conducted years of field research in Beijing and elsewhere in China (two having been Fulbright scholars in the 1980s), and are specialists in strategic studies, international relations, global political economy and history. The findings of individually authored chapters form a monograph about China's greatest challenges. Brett McCormick and I introduce and conclude the work, and have developed a unifying thesis in corroboration with all of the authors.

The importance of this work derives from its unique source: the interaction between senior Chinese military, government and academic individuals and Western academics. The exclusive access granted to this book's authors as participants in the EASSC was initiated in 2006, when the participants in the EASSC of that year were the first group of foreign academics to be invited to visit the Ministry of Foreign Affairs of the PRC (the Ministry). In 2011, the Ministry – which funds the China Foreign Affairs University – granted the non-Chinese academics private and direct access to the Ministry and its spokesperson.[8] This level of access makes the book conceivable and functional; without such support, the strategic priorities addressed in the book would not be valid or acknowledged by China.

The experience that Brett and I, and many of the authors of the book, have had in visiting Beijing annually for almost 10 years, being given unique access to the

4 Jonathan H. Ping

minds and thoughts of key participants in the development of policy in the PRC, has greatly affected this book's findings. The remarkable change in the PRC over the last decade has brought the long-term view to the fore. Seemingly intractable issues such as Taiwan (agreed at the EASSC as essentially resolved around 2008) have been overcome, and unique policy has been canvased. Ideas such as public goods, concepts of hegemony and global intergovernmental organisations (IGOs) have been discussed openly and with purpose. In 2012 the EASSC discussed the formation of a Beijing-based IGO, and in 2015 the Asian Infrastructure Investment Bank was formed. In minor ways it is hoped that the work of the EASC and the annual EASSC has made a contribution to the national interests of the Commonwealth of Australia, the PRC and the US, as well as all states. The EASC generates and disseminates knowledge, and maintains personal, professional and institutional linkages to support international relations, and this book forms part of this ongoing work.

Quintessentially, *China's Strategic Priorities* is an interdisciplinary, co-edited text that identifies the most pressing issues that China must address for universal benefit. The thesis of this book is that China – as a global, pivotal and essential actor in international relations – must pursue these issues urgently in order to avoid systemic and structural catastrophes.

This book thus identifies priorities. The complexity of doing so is difficult and controversial because of the dichotomous and unprecedented nature of contemporary China. For example, the PRC has limited resources as a developing state, and yet it has great power capacity. It is managing the largest industrial revolution in history, and being gigantic within the society of states may face resource, market or environmental constraints. It is a new state – only decades old – but one founded upon a far older civilisation. It has built a unique and extremely successful development model, but one which is challenging to manage within its domestic political structures. It sits securely at the eastern end of the legendary Eurasian continent, but is tasked to become a maritime and global power. In such a complex position, the largest strategic matter is to isolate the priority: What to do first? Why? For whom, and how?

Of great use is the discipline of strategic studies. This is essentially about planning – with the use of existing knowledge and analytical skill, within ongoing events – to achieve a specific desired outcome. Traditional definitions will emphasise military power and its use, whilst contemporary understandings would also include other forms of power, such as economics, and issues and actors beyond states competing politically within a military balance of power.[9] The common theme of *strategic* within this book does not prescribe to a standardised definition, but rather accepts it as the lodestar from which priority may be awarded.

Awarding priority, it is argued, will assist the PRC to focus on specific issues which may be achieved. The purpose is to encourage the PRC to develop its capacity to conduct international relations so it may pursue and match the intention of its grand narratives with practical outcomes. Visions and concepts such as Panchsheel, New Security Concept, Harmonious World, aspirations of Peaceful Rise, Neighbouring Diplomacy – or, most recently, the Belt and Road initiative –

are all useful and welcomed, but complicated by contrasting events such as the Nine-Dash Line–related sand-dredging operations in the South China Sea, or immolating Buddhist monks in Tibet.[10]

This book also wishes to identify strategic priorities that China may create, or specific strategic opportunities it may use as a great power dominant within its immediate region – but within, and with our global society. It thus identifies specific strategic priorities selected in relation to PRC interests and capacity; those which are most possible within the present system, with the resources available, and to avoid conflict with other states.

This introduction has discussed the study of China and established the thesis, and will now explain the structure and aims of the book. This book has two sections. The first section focuses on Chinese domestic issues, representing strategic priorities which impact on international relations. The second section identifies and discusses Chinese international issues, which are strategic priorities that impact on international relations as a whole. Chapter 1 has strategic culture as its strategic priority. This chapter exposes five myths of Chinese strategic culture and presents, from a historical analysis, five alternative points that have been central to the Chinese military experience.

Chapter 2 addresses the geographic imbalance of China's development. Whilst the coastal provinces are developing and looking outward, those of central and western China are underdeveloped and inwardly focused. This disparity is a Chinese domestic strategic priority that, if unaddressed, threatens to destabilise China and the international system. The chapter nevertheless argues that China is historically a western rivers civilisation that is capable of surmounting – and indeed compelled to overcome – the imbalance. The chapter employs unique Chinese methods and concepts of international relations, history and culture to depict a quintessentially Chinese – rather than Western – strategic approach.

Chapter 3 identifies the changed domestic context of the construction of Chinese foreign policy. The use of professional staff unhindered by communist ideology – and the attention of the public – is increasingly constraining and guiding Chinese international relations. For example, when nationalist Chinese[11] call for action against the Japanese arrest of Chinese fishermen, how can the Chinese Communist Party justify inaction? The role of leaders is identified as an emerging area of study.

Chapter 4 considers a related issue, which is the management of crises. Without established and functional mechanisms, insignificant events can unexpectedly and rapidly create global predicaments. An important strategic priority for China is thus the ability to create mechanisms that will prevent degeneration of international relations, and potentially enable a resolution of historically unsolvable problems.

The second section of the book identifies China's international strategic priorities. Chapter 5 focuses on the Diaoyu/Senkaku islands. The involvement of the US in the China-Japan territorial dispute complicates the matter, as China recognises that its most important strategic relationship is with the US. China's priority is thus to maintain high-level dialogues with the US on a broad range of issues, as well as the territorial disputes, in order to deemphasise the dispute with Japan. The chapter explains why the US is involved and posits future scenarios.

Chapter 6 employs the discipline of global political economy and critical theory to consider relations between China and India. The border dispute is identified as a strategic priority, not only for the two great powers, but also for the system as a whole. The chapter finds that that the ongoing border negotiations may be furthered by the addition of critical theory to the presently utilised problem-solving theory so as to progress the decade's old, stalled process. Chapter 7 studies the menacing nexus of nuclear weapons, nuclear proliferation and terrorism, which arguably constitute the basis of relations between Pakistan, China and the US. In the wake of Osama bin Laden's killing, China has the opportunity to exert a significant and increasing influence in Pakistan, India and South Asia, and upon the 'War on Terror'. This strategic priority, however, also embodies a potential source of increased cooperation between the US, China and India. Chapter 8 questions the effectiveness, utility and character of Chinese regionalism in Central Asia. The Shanghai Cooperation Organisation, once heralded as a policy success, is being undermined by problematic outcomes in relations with Russia. China's strategic priority thus is to counter, reform or abandon its use of regionalism. The conclusion draws together and summarises the findings, linking these to the thesis and broader field of study, and identifies areas for future enquiry.

Chinese strategic priority issues are addressed in the book through the disciplines of strategic studies, international relations, global political economy, history and a Chinese international relations perspective. These will all, it is hoped, be advanced as disciplines by their use within this book. Analysis and application of these disciplines is furthered by a thoughtful understanding of the current events in the Asia-Pacific, Northeast Asia and South Asia regions, and the selection of specific events is thus added to the canonical scholarly record. Concepts such as strategy, structural power, or civilisation are explored in the context of the broad scholarly community and given further substance. The immediate outcome of this book is to focus Chinese great power statecraft to create and seize strategic opportunities for the success of the PRC, and to create a stable and developing international system. On a grander scale, the result aimed for is the furtherance of human knowledge, cross-cultural insight and the betterment of future scholars.

Notes

1 These measures are available from many sources. For information and comment about Chinese gigantism, see for example Population Reference Bureau, <www.prb.org/> (accessed 14 June 2015); 'China Tops U.S. in Energy Use Asian Giant Emerges as No. 1 Consumer of Power, Reshaping Oil Markets, Diplomacy', *Wall Street Journal*, 18 July 2010, <www.wsj.com/articles/SB10001424052748703720504575376712353150310> (accessed 14 June 2015); 'China Emerges as Global Consumer', *BBC News*, 17 February 2005, <http://news.bbc.co.uk/2/hi/asia-pacific/4272577.stm> (accessed 14 June 2015); A. Payne and N. Phillips, *Development*, Cambridge: Polity, 2010; J.H. Ping, *The Chinese Development Model*, 2011, <http://works.bepress.com/jonathan_ping/25/> (accessed 14 June 2015) or 中国发展模式: 国际发展与霸权, <http://works.bepress.com/jonathan_ping/27/> (accessed 14 June 2015).

2 The author's rephrased Chinese aphorism (这条未知的大河水流湍急，我们所有人必须要摸着河里的石头过河。) from one originally employed in the 1980s (他们努力尝试摸着石头过河。) to explain that the Chinese Communist Party had to blaze a new trail in developing the PRC primarily through the Open Door policies: *they are trying to feel for the stones in order to cross the river.*
3 The EASC is a global collaborative enterprise between Bond University, China Foreign Affairs University and the University of New Haven. It is a platform for research, scholarship and exchange. The EASC maintains and builds upon the more than a decade-long success of the East Asia Security Symposium and Conference. The EASSC is an annual event that has been held at the China Foreign Affairs University in Beijing for over a decade. See <http://epublications.bond.edu.au/eas_centre/> and <http://epublications.bond.edu.au/eass_conference/> (accessed 1 April 2015).
4 See J.R. Pusey, *China and Charles Darwin*, Cambridge, MA: Harvard University Press, 1983.
5 See <http://epublications.bond.edu.au/eass_conference/> (accessed 14 June 2015) and B. McCormick and J.H. Ping (eds), *Chinese Engagements: Regional Issues with Global Implications*, Robina, Queensland: Bond University Press, 2011.
6 For example, a translation of East Asia Security Symposium and Conference by a Mandarin-speaking Australian results in 'security' being translated as 'security' (保安), whereas a Mandarin speaker in Beijing, who is also a scholar of international relations, will translated it as 'safety' (安全). In the PRC, the 'East Asia Security Symposium and Conference' is translated correctly into the language of the international relations discipline as the 'East Asia Safety Symposium and Conference'.
7 <http://epublications.bond.edu.au/eass_conference/> (accessed 14 June 2015).
8 For more information about the relationship between the Ministry and the China Foreign Affairs University, please see <http://epublications.bond.edu.au/eass_conference/attendee_info.html> (accessed 14 June 2015).
9 E. Luttwak, *Strategy: The Logic of War and Peace* (Rev. ed.), Cambridge, MA: Belknap Press of Harvard University Press, 2001; and P. Paret, G.A. Craig and F. Gilbert, *Makers of Modern Strategy: From Machiavelli to the Nuclear Age*, Princeton, NJ: Princeton University Press, 1986; M.E. Howard, M. Eliot, C. Von Clausewitz, P. Paret and EBL Ebook Library, *On War*, Princeton, NJ: Princeton University Press, 2008; D. Goldstein, *Andrew Wilson – The Art of War – interview, Goldstein on Gelt*, May 2013, <www.youtube.com/watch?v=OXQ1WV9ux_A> (accessed 14 June 2015).
10 These concepts are noted within chapters throughout this book, and see: J.H. Ping, 'China's Relations with India's Neighbours: From Threat Avoidance to Alternative Development Opportunity', *Asian Journal of Political Science*, vol. 21, no. 1, 2013, p. 23; Associated Press, 'US Navy: Beijing Creating a Great "Wall of Sand" in South China Sea', *Guardian*, 1 April 2015, <www.theguardian.com/world/2015/mar/31/china-great-wall-sand-spratlys-us-navy> (accessed 14 June 2014); and Y. Choesang, 'Buddhist Monk Dies in Self-Immolation Protest in Eastern Tibet', *Tibet Post International*, 23 December 2014, <www.thetibetpost.com/en/news/tibet/4360-buddhist-monk-dies-in-self-immolation-protest-in-eastern-tibet> (accessed 14 June 2015).
11 The Chinese Ministry of Foreign Affairs is regularly mailed Viagra and calcium by nationalist citizens enraged by the lack of vigour in the policies being pursued.

1 Myth-busting
Challenging the conventional wisdom on Chinese strategic culture

Andrew R. Wilson[1]

Introduction

As China becomes more militarily capable and politically assertive, especially in its relations with its immediate neighbors such as Japan, the Philippines, Taiwan, and Vietnam, we who are interested in China are well advised to familiarize ourselves with the historical and cultural antecedents of China's military and strategic behavior. In other words, we should try to understand what (if anything) constitutes Chinese strategic culture and the Chinese way of war. Fortunately, one does not have to look far for pithy and appealing distillations of the core elements of China's strategic culture. In this chapter I refer to these as the five myths: the Great Wall myth, the *Sunzi* myth, the Good Iron myth, the Zheng He myth, and the myth of *shi*. Of these five, the first three predate the contemporary emergence of China and were proposed as early as the nineteenth century to explain the apparent contrast between China's military passivity and Europe's martial vigor. The last two are of a more recent vintage, but have quickly joined the mythic pantheon of the Chinese strategic culture discourse. Unfortunately, however, these myths enjoy little historical basis and even less explanatory power for understanding contemporary Chinese strategy. At best they are reductionist and misleading. And yet these five myths in their various forms and combinations continue to dominate today's discussions of Chinese strategic behavior. This is the case among outside China watchers and even among the Chinese national security elite. This presents a double challenge: to historians of China the challenge is to try to discern more accurate patterns of Chinese strategic behavior. To those concerned with the future of security and stability in East Asia the challenge is to disabuse the Chinese elite and their foreign interlocutors of dangerously simplistic explanations of Chinese strategic intent and strategic behavior. This chapter offers a tentative step toward meeting both of these challenges as they affect China's strategic priorities.

The Great Wall myth: China's defensive strategic culture

Chinese statesmen and soldiers, and not a few foreign experts, frequently assert that China possesses a wholly defensive strategic culture and that every war ever fought by a Chinese state has been either the suppression of an internal rebellion or a defense of Chinese territorial integrity. China's 1998 Defense White Paper was particularly poetic on this point:

> The defensive nature of China's national defense policy also springs from the country's historical and cultural traditions. China is a country with 5,000 years of civilization, and a peace-loving tradition. . . . During the course of several thousand years, loving peace, stressing defense, seeking unification, promoting national unity, and jointly resisting foreign aggression have always been the main ideas of China's defense concept. The defense policy of New China has carried forward and developed such excellent Chinese historical and cultural traditions.[2]

China's strategic culture is therefore the antithesis of the Western tradition: a tradition grounded in the cult of the offense and a thirst for imperial expansion. The mundane version of this conventional wisdom typically points to the Great Wall as the embodiment of the Middle Kingdom's cult of the defense, while more sophisticated explanations cite the texts of China's classical period, 770–256 BCE. This assertion draws on both the Confucian tradition, with its apparent disdain for the martial, and the military classics, *Sunzi bingfa* (*Sun Tzu's Art of War*) paramount among them. The foundations of Chinese strategic culture, or perhaps more accurately the tradition of strategic debate in China, are, however, vastly more complex and interesting than contemporary caricatures of the classical discourse, and the treatment of the Great Wall as symbolic of China's eternal defensive posture is almost entirely ahistorical.

Many Chinese wars were defensive, but they were also fought to defend territory previously seized from neighbors. In addition, the wars of the classical age were primarily campaigns of conquest, not merely beyond the Chinese cultural sphere, but also within the Sinic zone. Most of China's iconic philosophers and strategic theorists accepted that the future of Chinese civilization would be determined not by the geographically limited states along the Yellow River, but rather by the kingdoms on the periphery that enjoyed the fruits of expansion. Only the large, populous, and thoroughly militarized states like Qi in the north, Qin in the west, and Chu in the south could hope to harness the manpower and material necessary to play the role of unifier of China's Warring States. In short, an 'harmonious order' may have been an ideal in the core of the Sinic zone, but expansion of the frontiers was the enabler of the imperial consolidation that was achieved by the state of Qin in 221 BCE Rather than eschewing war and expansion, the Chinese classics offer abundant rationales for and rationalizations of offensive military action.

Understandably, the justifications for expansion at the expense of non-Chinese peoples were more common, explicit and far less problematic, as seen in Nicola Di Cosmo's *Ancient China and Its Enemies*.[3] The histories commonly linked to the early Confucians, the *Spring and Autumn Annals* and the *Zuo zhuan*, deal extensively with warfare, and the Han era historical chronicle, *Shiji*, notes some 483 wars in the period covered by these earlier histories. Viewed through the Confucian tradition these wars can be seen as cautionary tales against naked aggression and royal hubris, but they are also the source of many of the critical rationales for expansion and the subjugation of non-Chinese peoples. Confucianism thus presents inherently mixed messages to the military leaders and rulers of the classical and Imperial China. That world insists that the Son of Heaven be a moral exemplar, but is nonetheless obligated to march against anyone who does not acknowledge his authority.

Within the Sinic zone the moralist Confucians and naturalist Daoists ultimately resigned themselves to wars of conquest and annexation. The latter-day disciples of Confucius never abandoned the position that moral excellence was the necessary precondition for political supremacy, but historical realities forced them to concede that morality was not a sufficient precondition. The new forms of political and military organization that emerged during the Warring States era (403–221 BCE) were so efficient at consolidating and concentrating the resources of the state that even Confucius' most important disciple, the moral idealist Mencius, was forced to admit that a ruler might be as virtuous as the sage-kings of antiquity, but if he did not govern a state of '10,000 chariots' he could never become the Son of Heaven.[4] The Huang Lao School of Daoism and the Legalists of the state of Qin, who took inspiration from it, were even more direct:

> Thus when the sage attacks and annexes another's state he tears down their walls, burns their bells and drums, disperses their stores, scatters their sons and daughters, divides their territory in enfeoffing the able, this is known as 'Heaven's achievement'.[5]

In other words expansion, subjugation and annexation were core tenets in Chinese classical thought long before the Qin consolidation in 221 BCE.

During the Imperial era (221 BCE–1911 CE), the whole question of defense versus expansion shifted from the contest for internal hegemony to debates about the correct nature and application of Chinese imperial power. At this point the argument revolved around the relationship between the state and commerce. Some saw commerce as a legitimate arm of state power and wanted to see the government partner with the merchants to expand government revenues that could then be devoted to improving the state's commercial and strategic infrastructure. This created an incentive for imperial adventures in places like Turkestan, Korea, and Vietnam in a quest to open and control new trade routes. On the other side were those who, for ideological reasons, wanted to see the state's finances drawn entirely from agricultural taxes. Within a certain school of Confucian orthodoxy (most clearly laid out in the Salt and Iron Debates of the Western Han), tying the state's finances to commerce and territorial expansion was always aberrant. Both commerce and imperial adventurism are driven by greed. Instead, these Confucians argued, the state should always ally itself with the better part of human nature and what was in the public good.[6] Debates on this subject continued into the Ming (1368–1644 CE) and the Qing Dynasties (1644–1911 CE), proving that despite the establishment of imperial 'orthodoxy' as far back as the second century BCE, disputes over expansion and defense remained robust.

If the philosophical foundations of this myth about China's innate defensiveness are disputed, its physical manifestation, The Great Wall, is also deeply problematic. The 'long walls' of the Spring and Autumn periods and Warring States era, from which the first Great Wall was strung together by the First Emperor of China, were as much about defining and holding conquered territory as they were about defending traditional borders.[7] Long walls, like extensive Qin and Han highways, also served as convenient logistical channels along which supplies and manpower could be moved and massed in anticipation of further campaigns of conquest and expansion. From the Han in the second century BCE to the Northern Song in the eleventh century CE, every major Chinese dynasty undertook significant military action to the north and west of the original line of Qin's long walls. To impute the defensive purpose of later grand fortifications to those earlier walls is therefore ahistorical and ignores the restless expansionism that has characterized many Chinese states. Even the iconic Great Wall of the Ming era, which *was* designed as a defensive bastion against the Mongol menace, represented the culminating point of early Ming expansion rather than some natural dividing line between civilization and barbarity.[8] Even today, to see the Great Wall from the north is to be struck by the immense power and energy that once lay behind it. Hadrian's Wall could never be construed as representing the modest or defensive inclinations of Imperial Rome.

Moreover, there was no equivalent of a Great Wall marking China's southern frontier. Even if they were holding in the north, Chinese states have progressively absorbed vast swathes of the modern China coast, the southwest regions of Yunnan, and the foothills of Tibet, and have occasional attempted to annex portions of what are now Vietnam and Myanmar.

The impetus to expand has historically been rooted in security and prosperity. Chinese polities have expanded territorially to support ever-larger populations and have built buffer zones around the cultivated core. In this sense, China was little different from many ancient agrarian empires. The continued control over and even expansion of imperial territory was also bound up in the legitimacy of the ruling dynasty. The inability to control or expand territory hinted at a decline in the power and influence of the emperor and has historically been viewed as emblematic of inexorable dynastic decline. The Chinese Communist Party and the people of the People's Republic of China (PRC) have inherited this mania for territorial integrity and for stark interpretations of sovereignty. That they continue to do so in a world that is generally becoming less obsessed with sovereignty is particularly dangerous (see Chapter 6). When China's growing power and military confidence, its nationalist obsession with territory, and its crushing insecurity regarding sovereignty combine, the results can be explosive (the balance between these is discussed in Chapter 3). Fortunately the countervailing tradition of opposition to imperial adventurism codified by the Neo-Confucians of the later imperial period and China's own rich history of imperial overstretch may induce more caution on the Chinese leadership when setting priorities.

The *Sunzi* myth: the acme of skill is to win without fighting

One of the most quoted passages from the *Sunzi* is loosely translated 'the acme of skill is to win without fighting.' To someone contemplating the costs of blood and treasure suffered in combat this is a particularly appealing concept. It seems very much in line with the *Sunzi*'s other admonition that the superior use of the military is to attack the enemy's strategies and alliance; the inferior use of the military is to attack his armies or his cities.[9] However, to understand the author's meaning requires historical context. The *Sunzi* first appeared in China's Warring States era (403–221 BCE), in the context of the rise of states that were large and lethal enough to vie for mastery over all of Ancient China. As war became more lethal it also became more expensive. This made the military both the guarantor of the wealth and power of the state and the biggest drain on the state's resources. Thus winning without resort to costly battle insists that the ultimate purpose of the military is to enhance the wealth and power of the state.

This passage is also directed at anachronistic notions about the purpose of war and the nature of military leadership. Although new technologies and new forms of organization were being deployed on the field of battle, the warrior aristocracy of the earlier Bronze Age still held considerable political power, and old aristocratic values still prevailed. For the aristocrat two qualities were paramount: their noble status in peace and their valorous conduct in war. Rejecting battle precluded a display of martial virtue and social status and completely subverted the aristocrat's reason for going to war. The *Sunzi*'s twofold argument forces the reader to look at battle not as an end in itself, but as a means to an end. It is an ideal type and meant to shock the Warring States' aristocracy out of their antiquated mind-set.

In addition, if winning without fighting was the dominant prescription of the text, we would likely see much more on how this feat might be accomplished. There is a lot in the *Sunzi* about deception, maneuver, and overawing opponents, but there is even more on what is involved in actually winning the battle itself. War in the *Sunzi* is a good deal more violent and purposeful than this one passage would imply. The *Sunzi* does not eschew battle, but seeks to guarantee that those who command armies – 'the greatest affair of the state' – were selected for the right reasons. Only the ruler who employed the *Sunzian* general stood a reasonable chance of success in the zero-sum Warring States contest. The army he commanded was premised on two tasks: maintaining the credible threat of destruction and actually destroying things. Even Sun Wu, the putative author of the *Sunzi*, was famous for winning battles.[10] Subjugating the enemy without resort to battle is best seen as an ideal type rather than practical advice.[11]

Even though the practicality of winning without fighting does not hold up to much scrutiny, the myth endures that it is a core tenet of the Chinese way of war. The oft-cited examples of winning without fighting are the Chinese propensity to use soft power over hard power: to buy off would-be invaders with gifts of gold and girls, to practice deft diplomacy and/or to use 'barbarians to control barbarians'. In cases of actual invasion, the answer was to overcome foreign invaders, like the Manchus, through sinicization. One overturns foreign conquest by culturally conquering the invader.[12] True, there are abundant examples of these types of stratagems, but so too are there abundant examples of the successful use of force by Chinese states. Arthur Waldron's chapter in *The Making of Strategy* and Iain Johnston's *Cultural Realism* have gone the furthest in demolishing the myth that the Chinese have a traditionally dismissive attitude toward the utility of force.[13] Nowhere is this more the case than with Mao Zedong, whom Samuel Griffith treats as the *Sunzi*'s most important disciple.[14] For Mao a revolution was an act of violence by which one class overthrew another. A revolutionary war therefore required a sustained campaign of organized violence to unseat the entrenched power of the dominant class, a class that holds immense material and military advantages and will certainly not give up without a fight. For Mao, winning without fighting was inconceivable.[15]

If at best winning without fighting is an ideal type, we can nonetheless admire that very early in the formation of the Chinese strategic canon the *Sunzi* enshrined the concept that battle was only a means to an end, not an end in itself. It also enshrined the necessity to think holistically and strategically about the use of force. While contemporaries in the ancient West were certainly pondering the same topics, it was not until at least the Renaissance that a similar canon of strategic thought coalesced in Europe.[16] China, therefore, had a significant lead in strategic analysis and critical thinking, one that may be aspired to by contemporary planners.

The Good Iron myth: the preeminence of the civil over the martial

China's abject humiliations in the nineteenth and twentieth centuries convinced many in China (and in the West) that the Chinese lacked a traditional martial ethos. The old adage that 'good men are not used for soldiers, good iron is not used for nails' [好男不当兵，好铁不打钉] undergirded this cultural explanation of China's military weakness.[17] Keeping the best men – the good iron – for *wen* (civil) tasks, such as staffing the imperial bureaucracy, meant that China tended to be well governed internally, but the lack of good men tasked for *wu* (martial) tasks rendered China vulnerable to foreign aggression by more martial civilizations. The disparaging tone of the good iron adage also speaks to a perception that the martial has historically been disdained by the civilian elites. Historically, the early bureaucratization of Chinese states also seemed to imply that from a very early point there was very little need for a hereditary Chinese warrior class. As with our other myths, the veracity of the good iron concept does not hold up to much scrutiny.

First, from the Bronze Age to at least the tenth century CE China had a warrior class that competed and collaborated with the civilian bureaucracy. As Ralph Sawyer so skillfully argued, rather than a stark dichotomy between *wen* and *wu*, *wendao* and *wudao* (the civil way and the martial way) are subsets of the larger *wangdao* (kingly way).[18] For example, we have already seen that the *Sunzi* is as much an assault on preachy Confucian moralists as it is an argument against the pretensions and privilege of the warrior aristocracy of the Warring States era. The *Sunzi* is trying to strike a balance between the two extremes. David Graff's *Medieval Chinese Warfare, 300–900* carries this dynamic forward by chronicling the centrality of the martial throughout the Tang, considered the most quintessentially Chinese of China's imperial dynasties.[19]

One might concede that this is all true, but once Confucianism, and especially the decidedly antimartial Neo-Confucianism became imperial orthodoxy in the Song Dynasty that *wen* won out, but that was not the case. For example, during the eleventh century CE the Song waged two wars against the Tangut Xi Xia Kingdom of the Ordos region. The first Sino-Tangut War of 1038–44 saw 1.25 million Chinese troops mustered against 826,000 Tanguts. A second war in the 1080s had close to a million Song soldiers driving deep into Tangut territory before their elaborate logistical train was severed by Tangut cavalry, and the Song forces retreated after suffering 600,000 casualties.[20] The martial continued in symbiosis with the civil.[21]

As to the civilian officials' disdain for military men, there are certainly abundant examples of this, especially in the late Ming when the Neo-Confucian bureaucracy rebelled against the military adventurism and promilitary inclinations of the Wanli emperor, but these were more policy battles than deeply ingrained cultural inclinations.[22]

Someone still enamored of the Good Iron myth might concede all of this, but argue that *wu* matters most in the founding of dynasties, the time when you need more good men to be soldiers, but gradually the balance shifts to the *wen*. Dynasties endured because they allowed the civil to gain ascendance, or as put to me once by a Chinese friend, 'China may have been conquered on horseback, but it has never been ruled from horseback.' And yet, we see examples of martial vigor well into both the Ming and Qing Dynasties. In the 1592–98 Korean campaign, professionally led Ming armies were equipped with standardized firearms, supported by artillery, cavalry, and naval forces. Their operations were enabled by immense and complicated logistics.[23] In the nineteenth century, during the Taiping Rebellion and Moslem Rebellions, we have civilian officials like Zeng Guofan and Li Hongzhang, exam graduates steeped in the civil orthodoxy of Neo-Confucianism, rising admirably to the tasks of organizing and leading armies against the rebels.[24]

With the Good Iron myth thoroughly tarnished, what glint of the true Chinese way of war might we discern? For one, even early Chinese states followed a model more similar to the *strategoi* of Athens than to the warrior kings of Sparta. This may have given rulers and officials greater flexibility in moving back and forth between civil and military roles. That the Chinese Communist Party and the People's Liberation Army (PLA) are still so closely entwined might be viewed as a continuation of this tradition as much as it is a holdover from Lenin and Mao. The subordination of both the *wendao* and the *wudao* to the *wangdao* further means that the Chinese were better intellectually prepared for transitions from war to peace to war. Finally, the fact that Chinese states have traditionally valued bureaucratic skill at least as highly as military skill explains China's early and impressive military history. Chinese states have historically been far larger in area and population and far more bureaucratic than Western states, and they have been able to fight wars on a scale that was inconceivable in the West until the modern era. As a result, China had a much longer experience with many of the strategic, operational, and logistical issues that have been the obsession of Western statesmen and commanders since the eighteenth century. In prioritizing, of note is the reality that without *wen*, *wu* would have been very short-lived.

The Zheng He myth: China has no history of overseas colonialism or gunboat diplomacy

Recently at the East Asia Security Symposium and Conference in Beijing,[25] an official of China's Ministry of Foreign Affairs patiently explained to a group of foreign academics that the Chinese 'have no expansion in their DNA', and that one need only look at the remarkable voyages of the Ming Dynasty admiral Zheng He for proof of this blanket assertion. Over the past decade, the Zheng He narrative has been invoked as a popular metaphor for China's peaceful rise.[26] It has been pointed out that in the fifteenth century China built the biggest ships on the planet – the medieval equivalent of aircraft carriers – but China did not use them for gunboat diplomacy or to seize overseas colonies. Thus, as China continues to evolve as a maritime power in the twenty-first century it will follow the tradition of Zheng He, not the example of foreign colonial powers or Western and Japanese navies. This is an attractive storyline, but it bears little resemblance to the actual voyages of Zheng He.[27]

Zheng, a eunuch retainer of the Yongle emperor, rose to prominence as a military commander and as head of the Directorate of Palace Servants. Zheng's unique role as both senior palace eunuch and comrade-in-arms made him an obvious choice to lead some of the Yongle's most ambitious projects: the voyages to the Western Ocean.

The seven voyages that Zheng He commanded are divided into three groups. The first group includes the first (1405–7), second (1407–9), and third (1409–11) voyages targeted at reopening the Straits of Malacca and reinitiating contacts in the Indian Ocean.[28] The second group includes the fourth (1412–14/15), fifth (1417–19), and sixth (1421–22) voyages that expanded Ming trade and diplomatic contacts to the Middle East and East Africa. A seventh voyage (1431–33) retraced earlier voyages as far as Hormuz and sent out smaller contingents to East Africa. In addition to the huge distances covered on these voyages, the scale and the likely expense of the enterprise is truly astounding. One voyage might involve 250 ships or more and 27,000 personnel. Among the ships, between forty and sixty were 'treasure ships', the largest of which may have displaced more than 20,000 tons. While impressive in scale and technological sophisticated, Zheng He's fleet was relatively slow. Nor were these vessels warships: the fleet was not designed to fight other navies at sea, but rather to overawe potential adversaries, or barring that, to disembark large numbers of soldiers.

These were not voyages of exploration to discover new worlds or new markets in the European vein, as they travelled along well-established trade routes, but they did serve diplomatic, informational, military, and economic purposes. Of these four, the diplomatic and informational were foremost. The military aspects, however, cannot be denied. Both Yongle and Zheng He were soldiers, and the voyages were organized and manned as a military operation. Nor was Zheng He averse to using force, as he did against the Chinese pirate Chen Zuyi at Palembang during the first voyage and against the king of Ceylon on the third voyage. In addition, every voyage stopped at the main Champan port – Champa being Yongle's ally in his war against the northern Vietnamese kingdom of Annam. The strategic and military components of the voyages are therefore readily apparent. Neither Yongle nor Zheng He saw a distinction between the civil and the martial; rather, they saw all instruments of Ming power as of one piece.[29]

On the issue of colonies, unlike Europeans who went out looking for trade and for the control of key trading hubs, the gravitational pull of the Chinese market brought the trade to it. Zheng He's primary purpose was to advertise the glories of the Ming Dynasty and to expand the axes along which Ming China's gravitational pull could be felt. The Ming were not out to colonize maritime Southeast Asia or the Indian Ocean, but they were in the business of recruiting client states that would 'recognize the unique and superior status of the Chinese emperor'.[30] Moreover, many of the ports visited were already Chinese 'colonies' in an economic sense, and at least one of them, Palembang, was ruled by ethnic Chinese. Finally, while Zheng He was not a colonizer, Yongle was at the time attempting to conquer and annex Annam.

In conception and execution the Zheng He voyages were almost the polar opposite of the Zheng He myth as still perpetuated by elites in Beijing, but even if we dismiss the voyages as an aberration in Chinese maritime history, the myth of no overseas colonies and no gunboat diplomacy still does not hold water. After a century of relative neglect, the Ming returned to the sea with a vengeance in the mid-sixteenth century. In response to piracy and smuggling along the China coast, Ming civilian and military officials, notably Hu Zongxian and Qi Jiguang, adopted tactical, operational, and technological innovations to counter pirate landing parties. Success against pirates on land quickly morphed into operations against offshore bases and to intercept raiding parties at sea. By the late 1560s the Ming were deploying large numbers of naval vessels, almost all armed with cannon, to meet the piracy threat. Nor were the Ming averse to pursuing pirates very far afield. In the 1570s the Ming navy chased Lin Feng as far as Luzon and even cooperated with the Spanish to oust the Chinese corsair from his base at Lingayen. During the Imjin War of the 1590s, Ming naval proficiency bought the Chinese and their Korean ally precious time to build up the ground forces needed to push the Japanese off the peninsula. In addition, Ming maritime power meant that Hideyoshi could not seize Taiwan, attack Chinese ports, or harass Chinese trade. During and after the war, the Ming were also not averse to threatening retaliation against neighbors who might side with the Japanese or otherwise act against Chinese interests. Finally, in the 1660s, Zheng Chenggong, the Ming proxy known to history as Koxinga, would forcibly oust the Dutch from Taiwan and threaten the Spanish enclave in Manila. In other words, the Chinese have been more than willing to use gunboats in both war and peace.[31]

Returning to the issue of colonies, the arrival of European traders in East Asian waters sparked a surge in Chinese emigration. By the beginning of the seventeenth century there were large Chinese enclaves in southern Japan, Taiwan, Luzon, Batavia, and Malacca. These entrepôt represented a species of hybrid colony, with a small number of Europeans in charge; 20,000–30,000 Chinese traders and craftsmen making the place economically viable; and a larger but generally unskilled indigenous population. Formal overseas colonization by the Chinese state was therefore unnecessary. The principal exception was Taiwan, but its annexation was by no means a certainty. For the first three decades of the Qing, there was little that the new dynasty could do to oust the Ming-loyalist Zheng family from Taiwan. In the 1680s, Shi Lang, a former Zheng lieutenant employed a mix of bribes, amnesties, and military operations to force the capitulation of the Zheng remnants in 1683. He also successfully lobbied for the formal annexation of Taiwan into the Qing polity, a step that the Ming had never attempted, but was now viewed as critical to Qing coastal security. Ultimately, that annexation was facilitated by the fact that because of the earlier Dutch presence, Taiwan already had a large ethnic Chinese population.[32]

While far from the European mold, China nonetheless has a modest history of gunboat diplomacy and overseas colonization. What then can we discern from this history about the Chinese way of naval warfare? First, nontraditional naval missions, such as coastal defense, counter-piracy and near-seas sea lane security, have been part of the Chinese tradition since at least the fourteenth century. Second, and despite the ambitions of the Zheng He voyages, far seas operations have never been a practical mission for Chinese naval forces. China's security and prosperity were better served when foreign navies fulfilled those missions, although the People's Liberation Army – Navy's modest deployments to the Gulf of Aden and to the expatriate evacuation from Libya show that symbolic far seas deployments have value. Finally, even within the first island chain, formal colonization is rare except where core security interests are at stake and/or where local governance is weak.

The myth of *shi*: the traditional reliance on the 'propensity of things'

Of the five myths about the Chinese way of war, the importance of *shi* is the least historically problematic. The term *shi*, variously translated as strategic advantage, strategic configuration of power, propensity, and momentum (to name just a few), is in fact a core concept in the military classics of China's Warring States era from whence it migrated into other works on topics such as politics, logic, statecraft and even painting. In the *Sunzi*, *shi* makes its first appearance midway through the first chapter:

> Assess relative advantage by heeding the answers to these questions, use this to achieve *shi* in order that you might use it beyond your borders.[33]

In this context, *shi* derives from manipulating the scales (the balance between the five factors of *dao*, weather, terrain, command, and doctrine) to maximize your relative strategic advantages against your likely opponent. Elsewhere in the *Sunzi*, *shi* is compared to a drawn crossbow or a mass of water released from a great height. Obviously it is a relative and contingent gauge of battlefield conditions based on tangible factors (terrain, numbers, weaponry) as well as intangible factors (morale, surprise, deception, etc.). At first glance then, *shi* looks like a fairly straightforward military concept that would be as understandable to Julius Caesar as it would be to the emperor of China. Some, however, have pointed to *shi* as a point of fundamental difference between East and West and between the Chinese and Western ways of war. Francois Jullien's sweeping *The Propensity of Things: Toward a History of Efficacy in China* elevates *shi* to a central place in Chinese epistemology. Jullien defines *shi* as a nonteleological explanation of outcomes based on relative configurations at a unique time and place, and the intrinsic tendency of a situation to evolve along a particular course. In the realm of the military this equates into a uniquely Chinese way of war that is utterly alien to Western conceptions of cause and effect and theory and practice.[34] Roger Ames's brilliant translation of the *Sunzi* adopts a similar take on *shi* to argue that the 'immanental' epistemology of Ancient China conditioned Chinese strategists to wait to gauge the relative *shi* of an engagement rather than to try, in the Western mold, to control it in advance through elaborate planning or the consideration of different strategic theories.[35]

Ames and Jullien have produced thought-provoking and important works, and there is much to be said for seriously interrogating whether *shi* is a true dividing line between East and West. I hesitate to embrace this interpretation of the meaning and importance of *shi* because it inclines students of Chinese military thought and practice to default to the most abstract or mystical explanations of events. When you start to unpack *shi*, especially in the *Sunzi* (which means unpacking the five factors of *dao*, weather, terrain, command and doctrine) things get much less abstract very quickly and very much less alien. I am willing to accept that *shi* evolved over the course of Chinese history into a very abstract concept, but when it comes to the *Sunzi* and the other military classics, *shi* sounds a lot like what a Caesar or a Clausewitz would talk about when considering why discipline, morale, terrain, timing, chance, and genius can combine in surprising ways on the battlefield. It is also premature to assert, as do Mott and Kim in *The Philosophy of Chinese Military Culture*, that 'Chinese strategists have used force through *Shih*-strategy throughout the twentieth century.'[36] These authors further claim that Mao's use of the military in the Chinese Civil War, in Korea, and in the PRC's subsequent border disputes are inexplicable in Clausewitzian terms.

Mott and Kim's embrace of the explanatory power of *shi* is intriguing, but it is also deeply flawed. First it assumes that Chinese strategic culture and Chinese culture writ large are monolithic and hegemonic, a notion that others have already demolished. Second, it ignores the impact that non-Chinese ways of war, notably German and Soviet, have had on China's modern strategists. Mao may have been a product of a traditional Chinese background and steeped in Chinese popular culture, but he was also a devout Leninist. This had a profound impact on his strategic insights. Moreover, Mao was directly and indirectly influenced by Clausewitz. Mao read *On War* in the late 1930s, and many of his lieutenants had studied Clausewitz in China and abroad. Lenin also lifted extensively from Clausewitz. Thus while Mott and Kim fail to see Clausewitz in China's modern wars, Mao had no trouble explaining his strategies in Clausewitzian terms. Finally, Mott and Kim's historical claims, for example, that the Communists largely achieved victory in the Civil War 'without fighting', have been thoroughly disproven in the scholarship of the last two decades.[37]

If *shi* can tell us anything about a Chinese way of war, it is the propensity of Chinese strategic theorists and military historians to see god in the details. At numerous points in the *Sunzi*, the general is equated to a god and his soldiers to mindless automatons. The *Sunzi*'s ideal general has godlike abilities, distancing him from mere 'mortals' in the uniqueness of the skillsets involved and the extent of the specialized knowledge required to command. Rather than trying to plumb the divine though omens, the *Sunzian* general becomes divine and imposes order on the infinite complexity of war. Over the course of China's military history, this context-specific invocation of godlike powers has evolved into a general notion that in war the general is the puppet master, able to plumb and manipulate the complexities of the engagement. Or as we see in David Lai's 'Learning from the Stones: A *Go* Approach to Mastering China's Strategic Concept, *Shi*', both Chinese strategy and grand strategy are explicable in terms of the board game *wei-qi* (*Go* in Japanese).[38] This tends to overly simplify war into just the mental contest between opposing generals who move armies to create strategic advantage in the same way that *wei-qi* players move featureless black and white stones. That war is ultimately a contest of wills goes without saying, but to ignore Clausewitzian fog, friction and chance may lead to a dangerous and misguided confidence by some Chinese that their strategic culture and even their traditional board games give them an inherent advantage. In my estimation, neither can give a Chinese belligerent the upper hand in controlling an engagement or in controlling the escalation of a crisis. Especially when it comes to territorial disputes, China's leaders need to be disabused of the notion that since they have read the *Sunzi*, or played *wei-qi*, or have thought about *shi* that they truly know the enemy, know themselves, know the weather, and know the terrain.

Conclusion

Having reconstructed these five cardinal myths in more historically accurate forms, the question remains of the extent to which any aspect of China's military tradition still informs contemporary Chinese strategy. Do they influence China's strategic priorities? One thing is certain: there is no one 'Chinese' way of war. We must take history and culture seriously when considering any state's strategic inclinations, and as the scholarship of the past two decades on Chinese military history and culture clearly shows, China's military traditions are rich and diverse. But a Chinese strategist today who believes that the future trajectory of Chinese geo-strategy is determined by an intrinsic Chinese way of war is no more correct in his estimation of China's historical legacy than an ancient Confucian who predicted that the empire could only be united by a sage king. Now, as then, Chinese political and military leaders are free to choose between different models of military action in forming policy, and though culture is one resource upon which they may draw, it does not confine their actions to a readily predictable range. The problem is that while interest in the classics is on the rise in China, as is interest in the great campaigns and captains of Chinese history, the move back to tradition is tentative and superficial. Most of what appears in China's popular media relies on the tropes demolished earlier in this chapter, and with a few exceptions the scholarly output from the mainland is unimpressive. Many in China's security studies community obsess over the concept of strategic culture. They remain convinced that there is a Western way of war and therefore feel compelled to articulate a Chinese antithesis. This effort parallels others among the Chinese elite to connect Chinese contemporary rise with China's past greatness. That is difficult to do given China's tumultuous modern history. There may have been a Chinese way of war in the past, but that and other elements of the Chinese tradition have been under such intense assault for most of the last century, and the worldview of China's leadership is so conditioned by foreign ideologies and military doctrines that it is hard to find much continuity with that past. China's strategic priorities may thus, when set free of a desire for a unique Chinese way, be parallel to if not complementary to the globalizing twenty-first century.

There *are* aspects of contemporary Chinese strategy that do resonate with the past, but they may just be coincidental. A deeper understanding of how statecraft has been practiced in peace and war in China is needed, but in the near term we should not be surprised to see a continuation of the self-Orientalizing reductionism that has characterized the debate to this point. That said, if I were forced to summarize what has historically been central to the Chinese military experience, I can imagine five counters to the five myths that this chapter began with:

1 Territory matters: Chinese states have waged countless wars of territorial expansion and defense. Since control of territory, both continental and maritime, is intimately tied to a regime's political legitimacy, Chinese states have tended to overemphasize the value of territorial objectives.
2 Size matters: Given the size of the Chinese population, the relative prosperity of China's economy and the historical sophistication of its bureaucracy, Chinese states have tended toward gigantism in their military actions. From massive continent-spanning fortifications, to treasure fleets, to the PRC's Herculean efforts in the Korean War (1950–53), even new Chinese governments have been able to quickly translate immense military potential into immense military capability.
3 Strategy matters: Quantity may have a quality all its own, but for all of the gigantism of Chinese states past and present, China has produced some of the world's most important works of strategic theory, among them the *Sunzi bingfa* and the military writings of Mao Zedong. Perhaps it is due to the scale of warfare possible in China that thinking systematically about the linkages

between military operations and their larger political context has enjoyed a rich tradition in China.

4 The 'Near Seas' matter: China has historically been a continental power, but since at least the tenth century CE the Chinese have been going to sea. China's Near Seas, often referred to as the 'First Island Chain', have therefore been crucial to Chinese security and prosperity (see Chapter 4). For most of Chinese history, this area has been characterized by uncertain and overlapping sovereignties. That has generally worked to the advantage of Chinese states, because as long as no hostile power dominated the Near Seas then China could enjoy the fruits of maritime trade without the expense of a big navy. Contemporary Chinese views are, however, conditioned by China's century of humiliation. If they have the military capability, Chinese states will go to war at sea.

5 Culture matters: Here I am referring not to what constitutes Chinese strategic culture, but rather the assumptions that Chinese states have made about themselves and about the strategic cultures of their adversaries. The yin-yang dialectics of traditional Chinese philosophy and the dialecticism of Marxism-Leninism may condition Chinese strategists to see the strategic inclinations of their adversaries as the polar opposite of their own. The Chinese are not alone in this pathology, but we should nonetheless be concerned about an insecure state of the size and military potential of China that presently thinks about war and strategy in such simplistic and reductionist ways.

Notes

1 The views expressed in this chapter are those of the author and do not reflect the opinions of the United States Naval War College or the United States Department of Defense.
2 Information Office of the State Council of the People's Republic of China (1998), *China's National Defense*, Beijing, <www.nti.org/media/pdfs/6a_5.pdf?_=1317155142> (accessed 29 March 2012).
3 N. Di Cosmo, *Ancient China and Its Enemies: The Rise of Nomadic Power in East Asian History*, New York: Cambridge University Press, 2002.
4 *Mencius*, trans. D.C. Lau, New York: Penguin, 1970, pp. 75–76.
5 M.L. Li, 'Mawangdui Hanmu boshu zhengli xiaozu 馬王堆漢墓帛書整理小組', *Mawangdui Hanmu boshu* 馬王堆漢墓帛書, Beijing: Wenwu, 1980, p. 45.
6 S. Nishijima, 'The Economic and Social History of Former Han', in D. Twitchett and J.K. Fairbank (eds.), *The Ch'in and Han Empires, 221 B.C.–A.D. 220*, Cambridge History of China, vol. 1, Cambridge: Cambridge University Press, 1986, pp. 545–607.
7 Di Cosmo, *Ancient China and Its Enemies*, pp. 127–58.
8 See in particular A. Waldron, *The Great Wall of China: From History to Myth*, Cambridge: Cambridge University Press, 1990, pp. 104–12.
9 Sun Tzu, *The Art of War*, trans. S.B. Griffith, New York: Oxford University Press, 1971, p. 77.
10 A. Meyer and A.R. Wilson, '*Sunzi Bingfa* as History and Theory', in B.A. Lee and K. Walling (eds.), *Strategic Logic and Political Rationality: Essays in Honor of Michael I. Handel*, London: Frank Cass, 2003, pp. 99–118.

11 There are some, among them the French sinologist Francois Jullien, who would argue that the ideal/real or theory/practice dichotomy is a Western conceit not shared by the ancient Chinese. F. Jullien, *A Treatise on Efficacy: Between Western and Chinese Thinking*, Honolulu: University of Hawaii Press, 2004, p. 15.
12 For a review of the arguments for and against the Sinicization thesis, see P. Ho, 'In Defense of Sinicization: A Rebuttal of Evelyn Rawski's "Reenvisioning the Qing"', *Journal of Asian Studies*, 1998, vol. 57, no. 1, pp. 123–55.
13 A. Waldron, 'Chinese Strategy from the Fourteenth to the Seventeenth Centuries', in W. Murray, A. Bernstein and M. Knox (eds.), *The Making of Strategy: Rulers, States, and War*, Cambridge: Cambridge University Press, 1996, pp. 85–114; A.I. Johnston, *Cultural Realism: Strategic Culture and Grand Strategy in Chinese History*, Princeton, NJ: Princeton University Press, 1998, p. 109.
14 Sun Tzu, *The Art of War*, trans. S.B. Griffith, pp. 45–56.
15 Mao T.-t., 'On Protracted War', in *Selected Military Writings of Mao Tse-tung*, Peking: Foreign Languages Press, 1967, vol. II, pp. 143–44.
16 See in particular B. Heuser, *The Evolution of Strategy: Thinking War from Antiquity to the Present*, Cambridge: Cambridge University Press, 2010.
17 See M.H. Fried, 'Military Status in Chinese Society', *American Journal of Sociology* 1952, vol. 57, no. 4, pp. 347–57.
18 R.D. Sawyer, 'Martial Prognostication', in N. Di Cosmo (ed.), *Military Culture in Imperial China*, Cambridge, MA: Harvard University Press, 2009, pp. 45–64.
19 D. Graff, *Medieval Chinese Warfare, 300–900*, New York: Routledge, 2001, pp. 160–251.
20 P.C. Forage, 'The Sino-Tangut War of 1081–1085', *Journal of Asian History* 1991, vol. 25, pp. 1–28.
21 See in particular K. Ryor, 'Wen and Wu in Elite Cultural Practices during the Late Ming', in Di Cosmo (ed.), *Military Culture in Imperial China*, pp. 219–41.
22 H.S. Miller, *State Versus Society in Late Imperial China, 1572–1644*, unpublished doctoral dissertation, Columbia University, 2001.
23 K.M. Swope, *A Dragon's Head and a Serpent's Tail: Ming China and the First Great East Asian War, 1592–1598*, Norman: University of Oklahoma Press, 2009, pp. 230–31, 298–99.
24 M. Yu, 'The Taiping Rebellion: A Military Assessment of Revolution and Counterrevolution', in D.A. Graff and R. Higham (eds.), *A Military History of China*, Boulder, CO: Westview Press, 2002, pp. 135–51.
25 East Asia Security Symposium and Conference, Beijing, <http://epublications.bond.edu.au/eass_conference/> (accessed 2 June 2012).
26 The series in China's official navy newspaper to commemorate the 600th anniversary of Zheng He's voyages offers a recent example of this. See, for example, 徐起 [Xu Qi], '敦睦友邻——郑和下西洋对中国和平崛起得启示' ['A Friendly Neighbor Promoting Friendly Relations: The Inspiration of Zheng He's Voyages to the West in China's Peaceful Rise'] 人民海军 [*People's Navy*] (12 July 2005), p. 3.
27 The single best English-language treatment of the Zheng He voyages is E.L. Dreyer, *Zheng He: China and the Oceans in the Early Ming Dynasty, 1405–1433*, New York: Longman, 2007, pp. 238–85.
28 For a discussion of Malacca's interaction with China, see J.H. Ping, *Middle Power Statecraft: Indonesia, Malaysia and the Asia-Pacific*, Aldershot: Ashgate, 2005.
29 A.R. Wilson, 'The Maritime Transformations of Ming China, 1360–1683', in A.S. Erickson, L.J. Goldstein and C. Lord (eds.), *China Goes to Sea: Maritime Transformation in Comparative Historical Perspective*, Annapolis: United States Naval Institute, 2009, pp. 238–85.
30 G. Wang, 'Sojourning: The Chinese Experience in Southeast Asia', in A. Reid (ed.), *Sojourners and Settlers: Histories of Southeast Asia and the Chinese*, Asian Studies Association of Australia, Southeast Asia Publications Series, Sydney: Allen and Unwin, 1996, pp. 1–14.

31 A.R. Wilson, 'Zheng He or Zheng Chenggong?', in B. McCormick and J.H. Ping (eds.), *Chinese Engagements: Regional Issues with Global Implications*, Robina, Queensland: Bond University Press, pp. 69–88.
32 T. Andrade, 'Pirates, Pelts, and Promises: The Sino-Dutch Colony of Seventeenth-Century Taiwan and the Aboriginal Village of Favorolang', *Journal of Asian Studies*, 2005, vol. 64, no. 2, pp. 295–320 and *How Taiwan Became Chinese: Dutch, Spanish, and Han Colonization in the Seventeenth Century*, New York: Columbia University Press, 2006.
33 This author's translation.
34 F. Jullien, *The Propensity of Things: Toward a History of Efficacy in China*, New York: Zone, 1999, p. 32.
35 Sun-Tzu, *The Art of Warfare*, trans. R.T. Ames, New York: Ballantine Books, 1993, pp. 39–63.
36 W.H. Mott IV and J.C. Kim, *The Philosophy of Chinese Military Culture*, New York: Palgrave MacMillan, 2006, p. 13.
37 Ibid., pp. 1–44. For the 'war' side of the Chinese Civil War, see O.A. Westad, *Decisive Encounters: The Chinese Civil War, 1946–1950*, Stanford: Stanford University Press, 2003.
38 D. Lai, 2004, *Learning from the Stones: A Go Approach to Mastering China's Strategic Concept, Shi*, Carlisle, PA: U.S. Army Strategic Studies Institute, <www.fas.org/man/eprint/lai.pdf> (accessed 6 June 2012).

2 Western river civilization and the logic of China's strategic behavior

Su Hao and Cui Yue

Introduction

It's a bold view that natural conditions determine the course of history, but it also enables an unconventional and often insightful perspective. Studies conducted by Professor Zhang Ping[1] from Lanzhou University and German scholar Jeralt Haug, for example, show there is a correlation between the decline of the Tang Dynasty and the diminishing monsoons.[2] More broadly, American scholar Jared Diamond notes in his masterpiece, *Guns, Germs, and Steel*, the histories of different nations follow different paths, not because of differing human capacity, but because of differences in their respective environments.[3] Underneath these seemingly whimsical studies thus lays a profound truth: geography is a powerful underpinning of human behavior. The location and geographical conditions of a country or a nation thus often determine its course of historical development, as well as its status and influence in the world. That is to say, the geopolitical factor acts as an invisible hand, playing a significant role in the modernization process of a nation's civilization. This chapter contends that the Chinese nation and the modernization of its civilization are no exception to this process.

The geopolitical environment has also been employed to analyze and predict China's strategic behavior. George Friedman, founder of Stratfor,[4] in his book *The Next 100 Years* theorized that China does not have an expansionist tendency due to its continental location and the constraints of its surrounding geography. Friedman pointed out that China is akin to a geopolitically isolated island, cut off by sparsely populated Siberia to the north, the Gobi Desert in the west, the Qinghai-Tibet Plateau and Hengduan Mountains in the south, and the vast Pacific Ocean to the east. Thus not having a powerful navy and fenced in by stark geographical barriers on land, China never contemplated an expansionist ambition given the insurmountable and yet secure circumstances.[5]

Thus we ask in a similar manner, what sort of logic can be found behind China's strategic priorities? This chapter's inquiry therefore is through an understanding of the relationship between politics and geography instead of through the more commonplace narratives of historical development or national integration, or through the employment of pure history, politics, or diplomatic studies. Arguably, we find stronger and thus more convincing explanations by combining these within *geopolitics* to address questions such as: How and why has China formed the territorial domain it has today? Does its territory determine or require specific strategic priorities? How has China maintained such a large multi-ethnic empire for such a long time? Is the notion of 'Grand Unification',[6] so deeply rooted in the hearts of Chinese people, a prerequisite arising from geography? Most broadly, has the link between lands and people shaped Chinese civilization, and how does this guide the present? Both in China and abroad scholars have addressed similar questions, and yet here we contemplate from a geopolitical perspective so as to determine China's strategic priorities.

China's geopolitical center of gravity

Generally speaking, geopolitics, for Chinese scholars, takes a nation as a political unit, to analyze the influence of its government and the decisions made by that government based on the entire humanity and geography within its territory.[7] Therefore, geopolitics is a discipline that objectively investigates the relationship between people and the land on which they live. Thus by examining the influence of geographical factors on political, economic, military, and cultural aspects of human societies, geopolitics attempts to be an effective research tool to find conclusions about subjects such as a nation's historical evolution or the structure of its political economy. The geopolitics of a nation may also thus be extended to strategic studies and international relations. The geopolitical relations a nation develops from its unique geographic environment may project direct or indirect influence on its national political traditions and thus shape its conduct towards other nations.[8] Finally it should also be noted that China is a good subject for the employment of geopolitics as a discipline of inquiry due to its long history and large complex society. This chapter's utility in determining China's strategic priorities is thus in part an analysis of the usefulness of geopolitics to the study China.

Geopolitical center of gravity and Sanjiangyuan

"Geopolitical center of gravity" borrows the concept of the center of gravity from physics to explain political phenomenon. The so-called center of gravity is the point at which the resultant forces caused by gravity concentrate; it is the point that decisively affects the stabilization of an object. If we could find the center of gravity on a piece of board and suspend the board at that point, we would be able to keep the board balanced and stable. Correspondingly, in the field of politics, based on the development process of human civilization and the geographic layout of current international politics, international society consists of a few relatively independent yet also interrelated geopolitical plates. Thus within these geopolitical plates, as analogous to physics, is there a center of gravity? Being an abstract center of gravity, a geopolitical center of gravity would refer to the geographical core location in a specific region, whose geographical features determine the survival as well as the development path of the region. It is both physical and psychological, weighing heavily with the society constructed by people, affecting their strategic behavior and priorities. More importantly, it may be viewed as vital to the stability of that particular society.

We may argue that such geopolitical centers of gravity exist in almost every geographic plate in the world. Countries at the geopolitical plates' center of gravity could be termed as countries having geopolitical gravity. These countries are often seen to play decisive roles in the peace and development of the region. For example, France and Germany together are the geopolitical center of gravity in Western Europe; China plays the geopolitical gravity country role in East Asia; Russia serves this purpose on the Eastern Europe and Northern Asia (the Commonwealth of Independent States) plate; on the South Asian subcontinent is India; the United States of America is undoubtedly the one for North America, or even the entire Americas; and Australia can be regarded as the geopolitical center of gravity in Oceania.[9]

Consequently, we may ask whether there are geopolitical centers within these geopolitical gravity countries. Are there geopolitical centers of gravity within their territories? We argue that there is one such location in China that works as its geopolitical center of gravity and that has had an intangible yet real influence on China's historical development, political formation, economic model, and strategic priorities.[10] This is the Sanjiangyuan area in Qinghai Province (which may be translated as 'the three rivers' water head).[11] With average elevation of 4,000 to 6,000 meters above sea level, Sanjiangyuan is a world of ice and snow, lofty mountains, and high ranges. Known as the Restricted Zone of Life, the area hosts barren land and very few people. However, it is right at the hinterland of the Qinghai-Tibet Plateau that props up the backbone of China, and it is also the origin of the three 'Mother Rivers' for the Chinese people: the Yellow River, the Yangtze River, and the Lancang River. Pouring down from the Sanjiangyuan, the Yellow River scours the yellow land that cradled Chinese civilization. The winding torrents of the Yangtze River irrigate the fertile farmlands that feed hundreds of millions of people. The Lancang River runs all the way to the South, bringing the blood of Chinese civilization into the Yunnan-Guizhou Plateau.

Sanjiangyuan is reputed to be the 'Third Pole' on the earth, the snowcapped Kunlun Mountains, the Bayan Har Mountains, the Tanggula Mountains, the Gangdise Mountains, and the Himalayas being its skeleton. The Qinghai-Tibet Plateau, where Sanjiangyuan is located, is not only China's 'water tower' but also the largest glacial area other than the South and North Poles. It contains one-sixth of the world's total freshwater volume and more than 35,000 glaciers.[12] The thousand-year-old ice and snow gradually melt during warmer months. The ancient water droplets converge and give birth to the three Mother Rivers. Ultimately, approximately 25 percent of the water in the Yangtze River, 49 percent of the Yellow River, and 15 percent of the Lancang River (called the Mekong outside China) comes from Sanjiangyuan.

China's geopolitical center area

Expanding from China's geopolitical center of gravity – Sanjiangyuan – the three Northwest provinces of Qinghai, Gansu and Shaanxi (from west to east along the

Yellow River) are the geopolitical center area for China. Even though this area is far from the current political center (i.e., North China) and the economic center (i.e., the Yangtze River Delta), it has controlled and is still a controlling lifeline of Chinese civilization. This area has been the impetus to China's historical evolution, and is a key element in the stability of Chinese society, and is hence arguably the geopolitical center area of the whole country.

The Western region diffused from Sanjiangyuan is strategic for the security of China. To the southwest of the Sanjiangyuan are the Himalayas. Stretching for more than 3,000 kilometers, they consist of more than one hundred mountains higher than 7,000 meters, with thirteen higher than 8,000 meters.[13] Being the highest mountains in the world, the Himalayas have been a natural Great Wall protecting China's hinterland. As a result of this geography – the Himalayas and the Qinghai-Tibet Plateau – historically invaders have arrived instead across the Northern grasslands. Such was the rationale for building the Great Wall in North China. On the northwest side of Sanjiangyuan the Gobi Desert is a natural barrier defending the Central Plain[14] against foreign invaders. With these natural and constructed barriers, China's hinterland is relatively easy to defend and relatively secure. Thus, the unique geographic location and condition of Sanjiangyuan set the contour and structure of China's development geography.

For densely populated East China, water from Sanjiangyuan is a crucial resource. The availability of freshwater from Sanjiangyuan affects drinking water supplies for hundreds of millions of people, determines agricultural production and food supplies, and constrains the expanding demand for water for the industrial manufacturing that is principal to the recent development of the country.

However, since ancient times, the importance of water conservancy has always been a significant issue to the Chinese nation and society. For example, as early as 256 BC, Li Bing, a governor of Shu in the Qin state, built the Dujiangyan irrigation system, a water diversion without a dam. Dujiangyan still stands intact as a legacy from a long-gone era, and surprisingly is a factor in the local water use and management of the grand water conservancy project.[15] In today's modern world, Dujiangyan best represents the unique oriental philosophy that "Tao models itself after nature."

Thus the development of water conservancy is a long-held and ongoing strategic priority as the development of the society is conditioned by Sanjiangyuan. Water conservancy leaped forward in North China during the Han Dynasty, and extended to the Yangtze River region in the Tang Dynasty. In the twenty-first century, water remains one of the greatest challenges facing China. The exhaustion of water resources is having far-reaching consequences on the Chinese people and the sustainability of China's economic prosperity.

At the same time, the ever-growing water crisis brings constant and increasing domestic pressure and international attention.[16] Realizing the seriousness of the situation, the Chinese government has attached unprecedented strategic importance to the water conservancy work. Thus the importance of Sanjiangyuan has increased in this century as it serves as a key area for China's water conservancy enterprise. Historically, and presently, it is a geographic location that gives rise to the politics of security and development, and thus continues as a lifeblood for Chinese civilization.

The theory of Sanjiangyuan as China's geopolitical center of gravity described here is mainly employed by Chinese scholars to illustrate the strategic importance of Northwest China, where Qinghai, Gansu, and Shaanxi are located, as well as its core position in China's geopolitical map. This chapter extends the thesis to encompass Chinese strategic priorities within the modern globalizing world. Sanjiangyuan is a foundation of Chinese civilization. Chinese civilization is an ancient and powerful influence on the strategic thinking of the People's Republic of China.

Western rivers and the Chinese civilization

The western rivers that originate from Sanjiangyuan sculpt the fundamental forms and features of Chinese civilization. These three rivers flowing across China from west to east introduce the water element to Chinese culture, which determines the basic form of Chinese civilization. As a result – and this is not often acknowledged in the West – Chinese civilization is a river civilization. This is unsurprising, as the three rivers supply water that irrigates more than 80 percent of Chinese land and supports more than 80 percent of the Chinese population.

In *Tao Te Ching*,[17] Lao Zi[18] chose water to be the external form of Tao. The *Classic of Mountains and Seas*[19] located and recorded the great mountains and rivers all over ancient China. The *Commentary on the Waterways Classic*[20] marked 1,252 rivers. Many great poets and writers eulogized the Yellow River and the Yangtze River. All of these weave a western rivers geopolitical gene into contemporary Chinese civilization.

Big rivers, terrains, and the origin of Chinese civilization

During the agrarian age, human beings depended on rivers and irrigation for farming. Ancient Chinese people settled and migrated along the western rivers. The construction of grand water irrigation projects resulted in the faster development of farming culture. The efforts in flood control and drought relief as well as water diversion and irrigation turned into a national organization system. The famous Chinese archaeologist Su Bingqi argues that the farming-based division of labor led to social differentiation and acted as the starting point of Chinese civilization. Thus in China, ancient people carried out farming activities along the western rivers, during which division of labor appeared and complex social organization resulted. Su Bingqi reasons that 6,000 years ago the Chinese clan societies started to constitute states. He contends that over thousands of years, the origin and development of a state progressed through three phases – the advent of agriculture, the invention of new tools constituting the premises for labor division, and labor division – thus forming the first steps of Chinese civilization.[21]

Thus the origin of the Chinese culture and civilization was on the geopolitical center of gravity of China. The Loess Plateau (in Shaanxi Province today) witnessed the historical evolution of Chinese social development where human beings on this land moved from barbarism to civilization. As analyzed by Guo Yugang:

> The dawn of Chinese civilization emerged from the Loess Plateau, because ages ago it was easier to develop agriculture here. It did not have the most fertile soil, but it was not threatened by floods from the Yellow River either for its high elevation. Because the Loess Plateau was easy to exploit, it did not require a high level of organizing capability or advanced tools. As such it was chosen by the ancient Chinese to develop their civilization and society. Back then, because of the periodic floods from the Yellow River, the downstream plains of the Yellow River were rich soil, but a fair amount of labor was needed to manage the floods and to utilize the water before people could possibly develop agriculture. That was out of the reach of the ancient Chinese people . . . It seems that Chinese ancestors started with areas that were easy to exploit, developed their skills and technologies, and then marched into the more challenging areas.[22]

The overarching geographical features of China are the highlands in the West and the lowlands in the East. The ancient Chinese realized the relationship between this feature and rivers, geography, and society. The *Huaianzi*,[23] a classic from the early Han period, vividly described this feature and its relationship with agriculture and water control: "Given this geographical pattern, the rivers run towards the east; people needed to work on managing the water before they could utilize it to irrigate farmlands; then the crops could grow."[24] Sima Qian, the great Chinese historian, also commented on the geographical pattern of China: "Mountains and rivers in Central China extend towards the Northeast, starting from Long and Shu, and end at Bohai Sea and Jieshi Mountain."[25] Zhang Shoujie in the Tang Dynasty interpreted this statement in his well-respected work *Notes on Historical Records*:[26] the great mountains and rivers on the Central Plain mostly follow a northeast line; mountains in the south start from Congling of the Kunlun Mountain, stretching towards the northeast and connecting with the Long Mountain, the South Mountain and the Hua Mountain; after crossing the Yellow River, the mountain range stops at Jieshi Mountain and merges into the Bohai Sea. The topography of high West and low East is bound to cause the main rivers in China to flow from west to the east, thus one can recognize Chinese civilization as a river civilization nurtured by the western rivers.

Some Chinese philosophers put forward the Kunlun-Center Theory, taking Kunlun (i.e., the current Gansu) as the primary land in traditional Chinese geography. Bao Gan, an ancient Chinese scholar, explicitly stated that "Kunlun is the primary land of China and the lower capital of Emperor Shi-Wei, surrounded by deep rivers and mountains."[27] And in Buddhism, Kunlun Mountain is believed to be the geographical center of the world.[28] The foundation of Kunlun-Center Theory is that the Yellow River originated from Kunlun, which indicates the iconic status that the Yellow River holds in China's civilization. From another perspective, it also confirms that the northwest area has always been the geopolitical center of gravity for China.

The civilization history of Northwest China – the geopolitical center of China

Sima Qian, the distinguished Chinese historian raised a noted conclusion that in China, "the initiators always rise from the Southeast, while the gains are always garnered in the Northwest."[29] Five examples were given to support this argument: Dayu thrived from west Qiang; Tang rose from the capital Bo (West Bo); the king of the Zhou Dynasty dispatched troops from Fengjing and Gaojing to fight Yin; Emperor Qin-Shihuang prospered by utilizing Yongzhou; and it was from the Kingdom Shu-Han that the Han Dynasty developed.[30] Sima Qian added that it is in the east where things start to grow, and it is in the west where things mature.[31] Is this merely a historical coincidence? Or is it a consequence of something more fundamental? In an analysis of power struggles during the Warring States period, Sima Qian commented on the rise of Qin:

> In terms of righteousness, Qin cannot even match that of the vicious Lu and Wei; in terms of military strength, it cannot match that of Sanjin. However, it is Qin who eventually united China. It may not necessarily be attributed to the natural advantage Qin can leverage to harbor itself, but looks like it was the will of the heaven.[32]

In today's view, what Sima Qian described as "the will of the heaven" should be the geopolitical logic discussed here.

The Northwestern gravitational area indeed possessed invisible political power in ancient Chinese legends. Dating back to the legendary prehistoric times, the Three Wise Kings and Five August Emperors were associated with this area. Fuxi, the leader of the kings and emperors, was probably born in today's Tianshui in Gansu Province. He invented the Chinese symbols of the Eight Diagrams to explain the changes in nature and the ethical order of human society, and thus is considered the founder of Chinese society and Chinese culture. His sister, Nuwa, patched the sky using five-color stones, caused by the war between the fire deity Zhurong and the water deity Gonggong. By doing so, Nuwa restored peace and order to the land. The Yellow Emperor Xuanyuan, born in the Central Plains, defeated the Yan Emperor from the Southeast and the leader of the nine tribes, Chiyou, unified the North and the South, and laid a foundation for what we call the Chinese people today.[33] After his death, he continued to watch over the Central Plains from Qiaoshan, Shaanxi Province, where he was buried. These Chinese ancient legends subtly reflect how the Northwestern region cultivates and advances Chinese civilization.

In the following five millennia, the Northwestern region continued to be an integral part of the historical logic that shaped the Chinese civilization. The Yellow Emperor Xuanyuan started Chinese farming activities along the upper and middle reaches of the Yellow River. Yao and Shun's well-known abdications were relished by people in the history. Yu was successful in managing the floods of the Yellow River and went on to demarcate nine provinces, forming the earliest form of states for China. King Wu's defeat of Shang-Zhou resulted in the feudal system in the Western Zhou Dynasty. Emperor Qin leveraged the geographical stronghold of the West to rise to supremacy and rule the whole country. The first emperor of the Han Dynasty occupied the inner lands and crushed Xiangyu with a humiliating defeat. As the capital, Chang An[34] witnessed the prosperity of both the Han Dynasty and the Tang Dynasty.

Genghis Khan and his sons initiated their epic conquest by conquering West Liao and West Xia in the west. The founding emperor of the Ming Dynasty relocated his capital to Beijing so that he could control the Northwest and thus stabilize the whole country. Li Zicheng also regathered his forces at Mount Shangluo in Shaanxi before placing his banner at the Hall of Supreme Harmony in Beijing. The Chinese dynasties succeeded one another, supporting Sima Qian's statement, "the initiators always rise from the Southeast, while the gains are always garnered in the Northwest." This gave rise to a Chinese proverb, "the wits are from Jiangnan;[35] the generals are from Shandong; the Emperors were buried by the soil in Shaanxi."

Qishan County in Shaanxi Province is the birth place of the ancient Zhou culture, representative of the early Chinese civilization. The Zhou culture is not only the ancestral culture of the Chinese civilization, but also a symbol of Chinese civilization that shines with infinite vitality, mystery, and vigor.[36]

In the modern era, the ancient mystical power of the Northwestern region seems to continue to act its mythical role. Zuo Zongtang advocated for combining coastal defense with border defense, and took a leading position in putting down the revolts in the West, contributing to the Grand Unification of China. The 'Xi'an Incident' forecasted the eventual fall of the Kuomintang administration, and it was also for this reason that until his death Chiang Kai-shek denied Zhang Xueliang's freedom. The Japanese imperial ambition of commanding East Asia fell apart for not being able to place the Western region under their control, although the Japanese army had conquered the wealthy coastal cities. On the contrary, the Chinese Communist Party established their base in Northern Shaanxi following the Long March, which set the stage for the overwhelming victory over the Kuomintang and the birth of new China. Coincidentally, Professor Chen Yinque[37] emphasized in his research that the Northwestern region played a much more significant role than the Southeastern in Chinese history.[38]

Co-residence of ethnic groups and the concept of Grand Unification

The Chinese usually regard themselves as descendants of the Yan and Huang Emperors. According to archeological research, the Huang Emperor was born somewhere near Qinyang and Tianshui in today's Gansu Province, and the Yan Emperor was born on the Loess Plateau, around today's east Gansu and Shaanxi Provinces. These all fall in the Northwestern region. At the same time, the Chinese people originated from the Northwest and moved to the Southeast, Northeast and Southwest along the major rivers. Residential areas were formed along the three rivers with the Han as the majority. Afterwards the Northeast became Chinese through the Northeastern minorities moving inland and the Han venturing out, and Inner Mongolia became so through southern flows of the Huns and Mongolians as well as the Han moving westward.

During this process, the Han as the major ethnic group continuously merged with the surrounding minorities and even neighboring foreign races, and after extensive integration formed the modern Han. In fact some minorities were originated from the Loess Plateau too. According to *Historical Records*, the Huns were descendants of Chunwei, a Miao who lived in the post-Xia period. They are also known as Shanrong, Xianyun, and Xunzhou,[39] living in the North and being nomadic.[40]

Genealogical research via ancient records has found that Xia-Yu's father was named Gun. The Zhuanxu Emperor had a son named Gun. The Zhuanxu Emperor was the son of Changyi, and Changyi was the son of the Yellow Emperor. Therefore, Xia-Yu was the great grandson of the Zhuanxu Emperor and a descendant of the Yellow Emperor.[41] If Xia-Yu was a descendant of the Yellow Emperor, and if the Huns were proved to be descendants of Xia-Yu, they would also be descendants of the Yellow Emperor, and thus be shown to be the related to the Han, who had yet pursued an agrarian lifestyle.

Genealogy and ancient records are inconclusive; nevertheless we may find that the integration process was so long and exhaustive that we are no longer able to locate any purebred Han today.[42] Paradoxically, thousands of years of evolution within the Chinese hinterland resulted in the populations residing in various geographical regions evolving into diverse ethnic groups, each possessing their own customs and traditions. This eventually resulted in an overall cohabitation of different ethnic groups on the vast land of China, with the existence of smaller areas where some ethnic minorities gathered and live uniquely.[43] Thus the unified multi-ethnic Chinese empire did not exist right from the beginning, but was formed gradually in the long course of history. This lengthy and complicated evolution witnessed the change from dispersion to localized unity, from localized unity to the grand unity.

The reliance on the river networks determined the coordination and labor division among the people inhabiting this land. The concept of Grand Unification is deeply rooted in the minds of Chinese people. Thus the three rivers from the same source are like vessels branching out from the same heart, binding the diverse ethnic groups firmly within the Chinese family and to Sanjiangyuan.

These prominent characteristics of China's river civilization led Karl Marx to raise the notion of an Asiatic Mode of Production in his analysis of social patterns.[44] Taking the perspective of river civilization to rationalize the stability of Chinese Grand Unification tradition also seems to support the main argument of Wittfogel's "Oriental Despotism".

Thus within the gravitational pull of Sanjiangyuan and under the Grand Unification tradition, the Han constitute the majority (more than 90 percent) of Chinese people, and yet the land inhabited by the minorities accounts for more than half of the Chinese territory. Hence, the construction of Chinese civilization cannot be a mere extension of Han chauvinism, but has been a coordination and interaction between the Han and minorities. In fact, the Eastern region inhabited mostly by the Han and the Western region inhabited mostly by the minorities are interdependent of and indispensable to each other.

Therefore, after the establishment of Republic of China by Sun Yat-Sen, there was an apparent philosophical shift from the initial Republic of Five Ethnicities to a nationalistic Han Centralism. During his presidential inauguration speech, Sun emphasized the equality among the Han, Manchus, Mongolians, Huis and Tibetans in building the republic, but he soon came to realize that this would put the minorities in a favorable position striving for independence and building new states, undermining the integrity of China. Hence, in his speech in 1921, he began to amend the notion of the Republic of Five Ethnicities, arguing the inability of these four minority ethnic groups to defend themselves against the colonial invasions of the Western powers and the help they would need from the Han in defending and developing themselves. This brought about the idea of building the Chinese nation centering around the Han while assimilating other ethnic groups.[45]

Ancient China was an empire comprised of Han ethnic regions and minority ethnic regions. Modern China as a traditional empire was integrated directly into a single modern Westphalian state as a complete entity, and its internal regions did not transform into nation states. Modern China built its modern state framework on the strategy it learned from the Qing Dynasty on governing different ethnic groups. This kept the various ethnic groups within China from establishing their primacy through nation building, and also reinforced their cultural identity of being part of China's Grand Unification.[46] Thus the geopolitical center of gravity of China gives rise to the geopolitical logic of Chinese civilization and entails geographical integrity as a strategic priority. The diverse ethnic groups inhabiting this land are thus an integral part of the Chinese empire within a Grand Unification grounded and sustained by an ancient and inviolable geography.

The geopolitical logic behind Chinese strategic behavior

Is there a geopolitical logic that shaped China's strategic priorities in ancient time and continued into the present? If we use a visual graphical code to describe China's geopolitical logic, '103' will be the magical number.[47] The Western barrier is '1' – the Tarim Desert / Tianshan Mountains / Junggar Basin, the Qinghai-Tibet Plateau and the Himalayas. Xinjiang and Tibet constitute this Western barrier. Xinjiang hosts what is called the 'three mountains and two basins'. The Altai Mountains lie on the North, the Tianshan Mountains in the central area, and the Kunlun Mountains at the southern boundary. Between Altai and Tianshan lies the Junggar Basin, and between Tianshan and Kunlun there is the Tarim Basin. Entering the southern side of the Tibetan Plateau, there are the Karakoram Mountains, followed by Tanggula, then the Himalayas, and finally the Hengduan Mountains. Xinjiang and Tibet together form the western block of the Chinese geopolitical plate, with the Himalayas as its core. This big vertical '1' shows that China's Western frontier serves as a barrier, guarding the inner Grand Zero Region – China's geopolitical center of gravity. The '1' is a strategic priority, as China's rise needs a secured Western frontier; losing it will lead to the disintegration of a unified China.[48]

The Northwestern region, where Sanjiangyuan lies, is '0'. This is the Grand Zero of China's geopolitical landscape. The three lifeline rivers originating from Sanjiangyuan are '3' – the Yellow River, Yangtze River and Lancang River – as well as the Eastern regions through which they flow. Sanjiangyuan connects the human activities along these three rivers, functioning like a special bond to the Chinese nation. Ancient Chinese sought survival and development along rivers, and rivers required that people acquire irrigation skills so that they could farm the land and produce agricultural products. These efforts led to a national organization system and agricultural production manifest as key elements in the birth of a civilization. Hence, Sanjiangyuan not only shaped Chinese people's life, production, and governance, but also gave birth to the Chinese civilization.

Thus '103' represents China as a land country, or in another term, a land power. In order to develop, China needs first and foremost to successfully manage its land issues. The primary component of China's Grand Strategy is to prioritize the West. Only if the hinterland is stable can China truly realize and maintain its stability; only if the hinterland has developed can China truly become prosperous. This is recognized in the new administration led by Xi Jinping and Li Keqiang. Only twenty-four of the sixty-seven officials above the ministerial level have work experience in the coastal provinces (including Xi and Li themselves). The remaining forty-three officials only have experience with inland provinces.[49]

However, being a land power does not mean that China should ignore the seas. China's land integrity was not compromised during the Qing Dynasty, nor did China suffer from disunity. However, China was easily defeated in naval warfare, invaded by maritime Western colonial powers, and quickly turned into a weak, poor, and divided state in the nineteenth century. Thus China's recent history demonstrates that in the modern world a country needs to have naval power to be secure. Therefore, to include a maritime element in China's geopolitical code we may add a colon to the number '103'. The top dot of the colon represents Taiwan and its surrounding water, meaning that China needs to safeguard Taiwan and maintain China's integrity to manage the potential challenge coming from the Pacific Ocean. The bottom dot of the colon represents Hainan Island and its surrounding water, meaning that China needs to develop a naval force to safeguard its southern tip while at the same time wisely manage the island disputes in the South China Sea. The geopolitical landscape thus determines strategic priorities as represented by '103:' that are characterized in China as being 'diversity in unity'.[50]

Following such geopolitical logic, what has been China's strategic behavior and what do we see as future priorities? First of all, the geopolitical code requires that China must have a centralized government system. The great thinker Gu Yanwu in the late Ming and early Qing Dynasties, when discussing the issue of governing China in relation to its geopolitical environment, noted that the disadvantage of an 'enfeoffment system' is that the local authorities are overpowered, and the disadvantage of a 'county system' is that the imperial power is overconcentrated. His conclusion was that in spite of the drawbacks of a county system it would not work to go back to an enfeoffment system.[51] To him, to manage its vast land and the challenge of diversity in unity, China needs to have centralized management and control, specifically an effective bureaucracy for management and power control.

Professor Xiong Wenzhao also believes that diversity in unity requires a strong form of macro-control in China. He advocates for "a strong central government, weak provinces and empowered cities and counties."[52] National revenue should be allocated by the 4:2:4 ratio among the three levels. In this way, central government and local governments can be better coordinated, and a more effective system of government achieved.[53] Diversity in unity also strategically requires the integrality of China as a nation. Different ethnic groups in China are living in a big community, not only sharing a life together, but also sharing the same fate when facing the rest of the world.

This is quite different from the recent European colonial empires or even the empire structure of the former Soviet Union.[54] China, however, has experienced a paradox of size, national management, and control in the cycles of Chinese history for thousands of years: conservatism and radicalism cycles; the country often losing its vigor when unified, but experiencing turmoil when power is decentralized.

In order to break this cycle, and to avoid the tragedy caused by great schisms, China strategically may need to absorb potentially useful elements from Western civilization, such as democracy, so as to overcome the requirement for centralized national management and the paradox of conservatism which leads to radicalism and decentralization and turmoil. However, democracy is created by human society itself. To this day there is not yet an ultimate model of democracy nor a universal form of democracy that suits every country. For China, a country dominated by patriarchal tradition and a culture built over thousands of years, it has been and will continue to be challenging to incorporate this foreign element into its current system. Although the concept of democracy has become fashionable, it often remains rhetorical. A real and effective democracy will not be easy to achieve.[55] China needs to build a democratic management and control system of Chinese style in acknowledgement of '103:' and diversity in unity.

Second, '103:' makes the economic development of the West a strategic priority for China. Since the late 1970s, the Chinese economy has made great progress under the opening and reform policies. With easy access to the sea lines, the Eastern coastal areas benefited from the open door policy, exports and trade. Problematically, the Western areas have been left far behind the East in terms of economic development. This imbalance is causing tension and pressure not only between the East and the West, but also on the whole of Chinese society. The Chinese government thus adopted the Great Development of the West strategy to address the issue. This has been demanded by the geopolitical '103:'. Indeed the renowned military strategist Liu Yazhou declared: "The Western region of China is the heart of Asia . . . China should set its great strategy as going westward over the next 10 years."[56] Thus for both economic development and as advocated by military strategists, China's strategic center is prioritized to move westward.

The barrier for national security

The Western region hosts a few of the biggest provinces and autonomous regions in China: Xinjiang, Tibet, and Qinghai. With the total area of a little less than 1.7 million square kilometers, Xinjiang constitutes one-sixth of China's land mass, being the largest among all the provinces and autonomous regions. With the land area of 1.2 million square kilometers, Tibet constitutes one-eighth of China's land mass, ranking third. The land area of Qinghai is about 0.7 million kilometers. The total area of these three provinces constitute one-third of China's total land mass.[57]

More importantly, Xinjiang and Tibet are the key element in protecting the unification and security of China. Without the '1' in the geopolitical code, China will transform from '103' to '3', with the possibility of even losing the '3'. In all states there are critical strategic areas that pertain to the security of the whole country; Xinjiang and Tibet are this area for China. Under the protection of the Himalayas, the core part of the Western barrier, Tibet is indispensable to the survival of the Chinese nation. Therefore, the stability and development of Tibet is an important issue to the survival and development of China. China needs Tibet; Tibet also needs China for the support to develop itself. Tibet is an important part of Chinese territory; Tibetan people are also an important part of the Chinese family. A Western scholar, Khanna, compared China and the United States as the following: "Without them [Tibet and Xinjiang], the country [China] would be like America without all territory west of the Rockies: denied its continental majesty and status."[58] Different parts of China are interconnected and interdependent. If one is moved, there will be a domino effect. The loss of Tibet would entail the loss of China's geopolitical center of gravity; without Xinjiang, China would lose the ability to safeguard its geopolitical center of gravity. Similarly, if Taiwan became independent from China, all other parts would be affected.

Located on the high-elevated Qinghai and Tibetan Plateau, Qinghai and Tibet have been historically isolated and thus politically and economically dislocated from the country. Transportation has been the major obstacle blocking them for the outside world and thus their development. The opening of the Qinghai-Tibet Railway in 2006 changed this reality. People now enjoy much easier access to and from these two regions; more importantly, Qinghai and Tibet may use these transportation lines to further develop themselves. Chinese scholars have put forward the idea of a Big West Line, arguing to build a new grand canal system to restructure China.[59] Although it is not a practical or realistic policy, it is an aspirational concept that highlights the desire to connect the Qinghai-Tibet Plateau with the future development of China.

Since the beginning of the opening-up reforms in 1978, the central government has adopted the fiscal transfer payment policy to the Western provinces. Taking Xinjiang as an example, a survey taken by the Chinese Academy of Social Sciences in 1998 showed that the total fiscal revenue of Xinjiang during the 1996–97 financial year amounted to US$16 billion: half local tax and half national tax. The central government did not take the US$8 billion away; instead, it subsidized Xinjiang by providing US$2 billion. The transfer payment thus amounted to US$10 billion in that year. It has been estimated that the total transfer payments to Xinjiang have been more than US$50 billion.[60] This is a wealth transfer from East to West in the form of government grants, industry development, labor mobility, and income distribution. Direct investment is especially encouraged, showing that the East and the West are both integral parts of China. Whether the Chinese economy can really take off in the twenty-first century is tightly associated with the rise of the West. Only by engaging the West in further economic and social development can Eastern China sustain its growth and embed the 1978 reforms.

Strategic resources

Western China is a region rich in energy resources. Of the total resources in China, it is estimated that Xinjiang has 30 percent of the oil, 34 percent of the natural gas, and 40 percent of the coal. Coal is presently the main source of energy in China and is unevenly distributed; 76 percent of the coal resources are located in the North and the Northwest, whereas more than 70 percent of the demand for coal is in the East. Thus enormous amounts of coal are transported from the West to the East. However, the cost of coal transportation by train is extremely high. The current trend is therefore to generate electricity first and move it through an expanded power grid so as to reduce the cost of energy and also the pressure on the rail network. A national shift from coal to oil or gas would still link the energy rich Xinjiang to the Eastern consumers.

The Western provinces are also rich in precious mineral resources. The reserves of chromium and copper in Tibet rank as the highest in China, with a great potential for more copper discoveries. The geological structure in Gansu is more complex, therefore it has twelve minerals ranking the first nationally. Qinghai has coal in the north; nonferrous metals in the south; salt, oil and gas in the west; nonferrous metals and noble metals in the middle; and nonmetallic minerals in the East.[61] Shaanxi overlaps both the Yellow River and the Yangtze River, and is thus especially rich in the critical resource of water.

For China, Xinjiang is an increasingly important strategic transportation corridor to Central Asia. In recent history, due to the dominance of maritime trade routes, Central Asia has not been treated as a geopolitically important area. However, with the discovery of proven reserves of oil, natural gas, and other energy resources, Central Asia will become a supplier region for global energy demands. In the context of China's rapid economic development through industrialization, Central Asia is thus of increasing strategic importance. Guided by the 'surrounding-countries-are-of-primary-importance' policy, the Chinese government, together with Russia, has built close ties to neighboring Central Asian countries through the Shanghai Cooperation Organization. Thus, as well as being rich in energy resources, Xinjiang will increasingly serve strategically as a transportation corridor for oil and natural gas delivery from Central Asia to China.

Water was a crucial element in governing China, and this is still true today. In the Chinese language, there are two characters with the same pronunciation that have the meaning of managing or governing. One is '治', with its left radical meaning water; and the other one is '制', with its right radical meaning knife. During the 15th National Congress of the Chinese Communist Party, there were discussions on which character should be used to express the meaning 'ruling the country by law'. The final report, accepted on September 12, 1997, adopted the character with the water radical. This example vividly illustrated the importance of water in Chinese society. Only by managing water well will it be possible to manage the country well.

The first document issued by the Central Committee of the Chinese Communist Party in 2011, 'Decision on Accelerating Reform and Development of Water Conservancy by the Central Committee of the Chinese Communist Party and State Council', stated:

> Water is the source of life, as it is the necessary condition for modern agriculture; water is the key to production, as it provides the irreplaceable support for economic and social development; and water is the basis for ecology, as it is an indispensable part in improving the ecological environment.[62]

This reveals that accelerating reform and development of water conservancy relates not only to the development of agriculture and rural areas in China, but also to overall social development, food security, and even national security. For the first time, water conservancy was elevated to the strategic height of economic, ecological and national security. On July 8, 2011, of the same year, the Central Water Conservancy Work Conference opened in Beijing. It was the first conference of this kind at the highest level.

On January 1, 2013, the State Council of China officially approved plans for the building of hydropower stations at the middle and lower reaches of the Lancangjiang River, Yalong River, Dadu River, upper reaches of the Yellow River, and middle reaches of the Yaluzangbu River. Three hydropower stations were planned to be built around Zangmu in Tibet on the Yaluzangbu River: one with an installed capacity of 640 megawatts at Dagu, eighteen kilometers upstream from Zangmu; one with an installed capacity of 320 megawatts at Jiacha downstream of Zangmu; and one at Jiexu, eleven kilometers upstream from Zangmu.[63]

Many Asian rivers originate from China. The Himalayas in Tibet are the main source of fresh water for Southeast Asia. The biggest rivers in Pakistan and Myanmar – the Indus River and the Irrawaddy River, respectively – both get water from the Tibetan region. China also shares a few cross-border rivers with neighboring countries in the south and in the west. When Premier Wen Jiabao visited India in 2010, he gave a talk at the World Affairs Committee of India on the topic: the cross-border river is the source of the life for people residing along the river. His main argument was that it is our common responsibility to make good use of it and manage it well. He also promised that China would exploit the shared river in consideration of its neighboring country, striving for a balance in the benefits between the upstream region and the downstream region.

Streams from Sanjiangyuan converge into surging rivers, which have fostered the Chinese people and irrigated Chinese land for thousands of years. Although this mountainous area is sparsely populated, it balances Eastern and Western China by its weight, and protects the foundation of national unity by its height. If the success China has achieved thus far can be attributed to the strategy of developing the East first, then the future prosperity of China rests upon the strategy of successfully developing the West.

Conclusion

The history of Chinese civilization displays that China is an inherent land power. Recently, however, the Chinese nation and society has been modernized, via an export-oriented, maritime trade, economic model, and this has formed and become an integral component of Chinese social development. However, as a land power, China's future success must incorporate the land as a strategic priority, as this is where the vast bulk of Chinese people live. For the Chinese government, the stability of the East and the West should both be taken into consideration. The security of the East and the West are closely connected, and a rebalance between the East and the West needs to be reached.

The affluence and prosperity of China has been dependent on the development of the East, but for this to be sustainable and stable more emphasis must increasingly be placed on the rise of the West. For example, as a result of the rapid development of the East by exports to sea, it has been a common theme of Chinese society that the stability and security of China cannot be maintained without the inclusion of Taiwan, a focus of islands in seas and sea lines of communication – and yet this argument is even more pertinent and relevant to Tibet and Xinjiang. This is best explained and understood through the geographic and civilizational region called the Northwest in China, more specifically and powerfully known as Sanjiangyuan.

We may reach the conclusion here that Sanjiangyuan is the origin of life, civilization, and history in China. It is the mother of the Mother River, the Yellow River. Sanjiangyuan is China's geopolitical center of gravity that has contributed imperceptibly to create the brilliant Chinese civilization over the *long* history. The great Northwest region of China, where Sanjiangyuan is located, with its long-lasting hidden force, still affects the peace and security of China. How this geopolitical center of gravity, and its region, may play a positive role during the modernization process of Chinese civilization should thus be carefully considered, reawakened, and made a strategic priority. As affluence is the basis for power, so power is the result of affluence. As Sanjiangyuan is the basis of China, so China is the result of Sanjiangyuan.

Notes

1 The Chinese authors' names used in this article are surname first and then given name.
2 '唐朝灭亡与气候有关？学者：是压倒骆驼的"稻草"', 央视网, 2009年1月23日, <http://news.cctv.com/china/20090123/102248.shtml> (accessed 4 March 2015).

3 J.M. Diamond, *Guns, Germs, and Steel: The Fates of Human Societies*, New York: W.W. Norton, 1999.
4 G. Friedman, *The Next 100 Years*, <https://www.stratfor.com/> (accessed 4 January 2015).
5 （美）乔治·弗里德曼:《未来100年大预言》, 魏宗雷、杰宁娜译, 海天出版社, 2009年版.
6 Original Chinese as '大一统'.
7 （英）杰弗里·帕克:《地缘政治学: 过去、现在和未来》[*Geopolitics: Past, Present and Future*], 刘丛德译, 新华出版社, 2003年版, 第12页.
8 高金钿等:《国际战略学概论》[*Introduction to International Strategy*], 国防大学出版社1995年版, 第130页; 王恩涌、沈伟烈等编者:《政治地理学: 时空中的政治格局》 [*Political Geography: The Political Landscape in Time and Space Dimensions*], 高等教育出版社, 1998年版, 第4–5页.
9 苏浩'地缘重心与世界政治的支点' [*Geopolitical Center of Gravity and Pivot Point of World Politics*],《现代国际关系》2004年第4期.
10 苏浩'中国的地缘重心: 一个认识中国政治地理的假说' ['China's Geopolitical Center of Gravity: A Hypothesis to Understand China's Political Geography'], 个人博客。, <http://blog.voc.com.cn/blog_showone_type_blog_id_13678_p_1.html> (accessed 11 October 2013).
11 Map of Qinghai, China, <https://www.google.com.au/maps/place/Qinghai,+China/@35.4035034,96.2376978,5z/data=!4m2!3m1!1s0x370087977b620bed:0x28edcba67db79dbf> (accessed 5 March 2015).
12 BBC. *Wild China: Tibet*. BBC television program, co-produced by the BBC Natural History Unit and China Central Television (CCTV), May to June 2008.
13 Ibid.
14 The Central Plains refer to the middle and lower reaches of the Yellow River.
15 邓仁:'都江堰与水利工程伦理' [*Dujiangyan and the Ethics of Water Conservancy*],《华北水利水电学院学报(社科版)》2010年第4期.
16 MarketWatch, 'China Faces Its Worst Economic Crisis: Water', *The Tell* (The Markets News and Analysis Blog), <http://blogs.marketwatch.com/thetell/2013/07/31/china-faces-its-worst-economic-crisis-water/> (accessed 11 October 2013).
17 '《道德经》' in Chinese characters.
18 Also known as Lao-tzu, '老子' in Chinese characters.
19 Romanized as Shanhaijing or formally as Shan-hai Ching, '山海经' in Chinese characters.
20 Romanized as Shuijingzhu, '水经注' in Chinese characters.
21 苏秉琦'文明发端玉龙故乡——谈查海遗址' [*Origin of the Civilization and Hometown of Ade Dragon-on Chahai Site*], '关于重建中国史前史的思考' [*Thoughts on Reconstruction of China's Prehistory*], 1991年。'国家起源与民族文化传统(提纲)' [*Origin of the State and the Traditional National Culture (Outline)*], 1994年1月写作.
22 郭玉刚:'先秦民族源流研究' [*The Study of Pre-Qin Ethnic Origins*], 2007年11月6日, 天涯博客。, <http://blog.tianya.cn/blogger/view_blog.asp?BlogName=yegal> (accessed 11 October 2013).
23 '淮南子' in Chinese characters.
24 《淮南子·修务训》[*Huainanzi*], p. 27. Original Chinese text as '夫地势, 水东流, 人必事焉, 然后水潦得谷行; 禾稼春生, 人必加工焉, 故五谷得遂长。听其自流, 得之其自生, 则鲧、禹之功不立, 而后稷之智不用也'.
25 司马迁:《史记·卷二十七·天官书》[*Historical Records*], 中华书局, 1982年版, 第1347页. Original Chinese text as '中国山川东北流, 其维, 首在陇、蜀, 尾没于渤、碣'.
26 Romanized as Shjizhengyi, '史记正义' in Chinese.
27 （晋）干宝:《搜神记》[records searching for deities], 卷一三, 明、清重编印, p. 88. Original Chinese text as '昆仑之墟, 地首也, 石惟帝之下都, 故其绝以弱水之深, 又环以炎火之山'.

28 尚永琪：'3～6世纪僧人的流动与地理视阈的拓展——论对华夷观念变迁与'昆仑中心论'产生的地理学考察' [*The Migration of Monks between the Third and the Sixth Century in Relation to the Expansion of Geographical Perspective*], 陈尚胜主编《儒家文明与中国传统对外关系》, 山东大学出版社, 2008年版, 第78–79页.
29 Q. Sima and B. Watson. *Records of the Grand Historian: Han Dynasty*. Hong Kong u.a.: Columbia University Press, 1993, p. 206.
30 《史记·卷十五·六国年表》 [*Historical Records*], 中华书局, 1982年版, 第685~686页. Original text as '夫作事者必于东南, 收功实者常于西北', '禹兴于西羌, 汤起于亳（西亳）, 周之王也以丰镐伐殷, 秦之帝用雍州兴, 汉之兴自蜀汉'.
31 Ibid. Original text as '东方物所始生, 西方物之成孰'.
32 Ibid. Original text as '论秦之德义不如鲁卫之暴戾者, 量秦之兵不如三晋之彊也, 然卒并天下, 非必险固便形埶利也, 盖若天所助焉'.
33 In Chinese language, Chinese people are also expressed with the term 'descendants of the Yan and Huang Emperor', as in '炎黄子孙'.
34 Xi'an's old name, in today's Shaanxi Province.
35 South of Yangtze River.
36 '陕西岐山周公庙考古首次破译周文王父亲名字' ['Archaeological Studies at Zhougong Temple First Time Decoded the Name of Zhou-Wen King's Father'], 新浪网, 2009年4月9日。<http://news.sina.com.cn/o/2009-04-09/223715442011s.shtml> (accessed 11 October 2013).
37 Also named Chen Yinke, '陈寅恪' in Chinese characters.
38 陈寅恪：《唐代政治史述论稿》 ['A manuscript for the political history of the Tang Dynasty'], 北京：三联书店, 2001年版.
39 Original Chinese as '山戎、猃狁、荤粥'.
40 《史记·卷一百十·匈奴列传》 [*Historical Records*], 中华书局, 1982年版. Original text as '匈奴, 其先祖夏后氏之苗裔也, 曰淳维. 唐虞以上有山戎、猃狁、荤粥, 居于北蛮, 随畜牧而转移'.
41 《史记·卷二·夏本纪》 [*Historical Records*], 中华书局, 1982年版. Original text as '夏禹, 名曰文命. 禹之父曰鲧, 鲧之父曰帝颛顼, 颛顼之父曰昌意, 昌意之父曰黄帝. 禹者, 黄帝之玄孙而帝颛顼之孙也'.
42 '中国纯种汉族人如今无存, 曾生活在中原地区' [*Purebred Han Chinese Extinct Today: Used to Inhabit the Central Plains*], 《重庆晚报》, 2010年2月7日.
43 Termed in Chinese '大杂居小聚居'.
44 赵家祥、丰子义：《马克思东方社会理论的历史考察和当代意义》 [*The Historical Evaluation and Contemporary Significance of Karl Marx's Oriental Society Theory*], 北京：高等教育出版社, 2002年版.
45 杨念群'何谓'东亚'？——近代以来中日韩对'亚洲'想象的差异及其后果' [*What is East Asia? Differences in Perception of Asia among Contemporary Chinese, Japanese and Koreans and Their Consequences*], 《清华大学学报(哲社版)》, 2012年第1期.
46 Ibid.
47 '专家解读中国地缘密码——"1-0-3"' [*Expert decodes Chinese geopolitical code – "1-0-3"*], 中国社会科学在线, 2013年01月29日, <www.csstoday.net/Item.aspx?id=46484> (accessed 2 October 2013).
48 徐亮：《帝国兴衰与帝国边疆的崩塌》 [*Vicissitude of Empires and the Collapse of Their Borderland*], 法律出版社, 2011年版.
49 '中国政要新阵容' [new cast of Chinese politicians], 新浪网。<http://news.sina.com.cn/pc/2013-03-14/326/3025.html> (accessed 2 October 2013).
50 Original Chinese as '多元一体'.
51 （清）顾炎武：《天下郡国利病书》 [*Merits and Maladies of Ming Prefectures and Counties*], 昆山顾炎武研究会编, 上海科学技术文献出版社, 2002年版.
52 W. Xiong, 'Seminar on Promotion of Law-Based Administration and Construction of Government Ruled by Law'. Renmin Law School, Renmin University, Beijing, 2014.
53 凤凰卫视：'世纪大讲坛'的演讲, 2013年1月7日.

54 见尤里·普罗科菲耶夫'苏联解体：谁之罪？怎么办？' [*The Dissolution of the Soviet Union: Who's to Be Blamed and What's to Be Done?*]，《红旗文稿》，2012年第14期。（转引自《新华月报》，2012年第8期，第60页。）
55 华生、周志兴：'改革符合执政党的长远利益' [*Reform Gears to the Long-Term Interest of the Governing Party*]，《同舟共进》2012年第6期。
56 刘亚洲：'大国策' [*Policy of a Great Power*]，爱思想，2004年4月15日，<www.aisixiang.com/data/2884.html> (accessed 2 October 2013).
57 See information of various provinces at Chinese central government website, <www.gov.cn/test/2005–08/11/content_27116.htm> (accessed 2 October 2013).
58 P. Khanna, 'Just Like America, China Is Building a Multi-ethnic Empire in the West', *Guardian*, 25 March 2008.
59 邓英淘等:《再造中国》 [*Remaking China*]，上海：文汇出版社，1999年版；李伶:《西藏之水救中国》 [*The Water of Tibet Saves China*]，北京：中国长安出版社，2005年版。
60 '专家称新疆打砸抢烧事件不会影响民族团结大局' [*Experts: The Xinjiang Accident Will Not Affect the National Unity*]，新浪网，2009年7月28日，<http://news.sina.com.cn/c/sd/2009–07–28/101618313014.shtml> (accessed 2 October 2013).
61 See information of various provinces at Chinese central government website, <www.gov.cn/test/2005–08/11/content_27116.htm> (accessed 2 October 2013).
62 王仁贵、张楠：'辛卯大治水战略玄机' [*Great Strategy on Water Management in 2011*]，《瞭望》新闻周刊，2011年第28期，<www.lwgcw.com/NewsShow.aspx?newsId=21911> (accessed 4 October 2013).
63 中国人民共和国国务院:《能源发展'十二五'规划》 [*The Twelfth Five-Year Plan for Energy Development*]，2013年1月1日。

3 Analyzing China's foreign policy
Domestic politics, public opinion and leaders

Eric Hyer, Zhang Qingmin and Jordan Hamzawi

Introduction

The study of Chinese foreign policy is not a new field, but the systematic and scientific study of Chinese foreign policy, especially by Chinese scholars, is a relatively new endeavor. Recent developments in China, such as more access to practitioners, a more engaged scholarly community, and a relatively more open press, have made this possible. Competing paradigms guide the study of Chinese foreign policy by the newer generation of scholars. Each of these paradigms is based upon a particular theoretical analysis and offers competing explanations of China's foreign policy. Scholars of international relations have focused their attention on the international system as the primary unit of analysis. Scholars of foreign policy analysis have focused their attention on state and individual levels of analysis.[1] The state-level focus on domestic politics includes domestic political institutions, civil society, and public opinion. Analysis of individual leaders draws primarily upon political psychology. However, both neoclassical realism and constructivism intersect with decision-making theories and offer new insights on the individual-level of analysis.[2]

Arising from the expanding study of Chinese foreign policy, this chapter is thus tasked to consider how China's strategic priorities are formed. It considers who has an influence on what they are, the changing nature of the way they are formed, and how new inputs are affecting these strategic priorities. However, before considering the impact of domestic politics, leadership, and public opinion on Chinese foreign policy and strategic priorities, a brief summary of the systemic level of analysis is in order. This systemic analysis can be divided into a neorealist or structural conflict model, and neoliberal or neoliberal institutionalist model.

Neorealism

The neorealist or structural conflict model is based upon theories of political realism.[3] A basic assumption of this model is that the world is an international system of independent states existing in a situation of anarchy. Because no world government exists to force states to cooperate, all states naturally seek their own national interests. This does not mean that states are constantly at war with each other, but simply that the possibility of war is ever present and so all states must always be prepared for war. In the first decade of the twenty-first century, a new constellation of powers emerged in the international system. China's large size – geographically, economically, and militarily – makes China a great power. Great powers, by nature, are usually in conflict with each other as they seek to assert some form of hegemony over other states and seek allies to counterbalance the growing power of other nations.

As China becomes more powerful both economically and militarily, asserting its leadership and seeking hegemony is normal for such a rising power. With China assuming a major role in East Asia, if not the world, some degree of conflict with the United States of America (U.S.) seems inevitable. China will certainly seek to enhance its dominating role in Asia and perceives the U.S. as an adversary in achieving that goal.[4] As China's capabilities have increased it has projected its naval power away from land defense to include anti-access and area-denial capabilities for 'active defense' against an invasion from the sea and to defend territorial sovereignty claims, and protect maritime rights in order to secure its strategic interests and challenge the U.S. naval dominance in the western Pacific Ocean. China has protested the U.S.-South Korean exercises in the Yellow Sea and challenged U.S. Navy activities in the South China Sea. During negotiations in August 2009 on maritime safety, China 'called on the U.S. to phase out its military surveillance missions' close to China's coast and asserted that China 'will not tolerate American dominance indefinitely in an area it views as its strategic sphere of influence'.[5] This position has not been modified but rather strengthened over time.

Developments in Taiwan, the East China Sea, or the South China Sea, where Beijing has asserted it has 'core interests', could trigger armed conflict.[6] As early as 1996 China's missile tests near Taiwan underlined the realists' pessimistic conclusions of China's perceptions of the U.S., arguing that as China grows stronger economically and militarily, it is more likely to challenge the U.S. position in the region. Suspicion and mistrust are increasing, and threat perception is magnified under the circumstances.[7]

However, Chinese leaders are aware that the perceptions of the U.S. and other states in the region can result in pessimistic inferences of China's behavior that exacerbate the security dilemma. This awareness can make the theorized outcome unlikely because Chinese leaders realize that efforts at 'strategic reassurance' can defuse tensions and improve relations, thereby averting the outcome neorealism predicts.[8]

Neoliberalism

Similar to the neorealist model, the neoliberal or liberal institutionalist model adopts a rationalist assumption, but it is rooted in political liberalism rather than political realism.[9] Liberals assume that economic development and international trade reinforce the potential for interstate cooperation motivated by mutual benefit. According to this model, the economic transformation of China has dramatically changed Chinese strategic perceptions, and China now shares with other major powers a common stake in global economic development, military security, and political stability. The dependence of China on international markets and the complex web of bilateral relationships in other areas mean that China cannot afford a breakdown in its international relationships. If political friction drove a wedge between China and others in the international community, China would suffer potentially enormous economic costs. China is export dependent, and any disruption in foreign trade would be very costly in economic terms of lower profits for export-oriented companies and lost jobs for workers. Therefore, Beijing will strategically attempt to tamp down crises that could disrupt trade relations.

According to the neoliberal institutionalist model, as countries' mutual interests grow, the likelihood of serious conflict will diminish. Despite the accidental American bombing of China's Belgrade embassy in May 1999, which caused the death of three Chinese embassy staff, and the April 2001 U.S. reconnaissance plane incident, which resulted in the death of a Chinese fighter pilot, the impact was short-lived. Chinese leaders, despite widespread public protests demanding strong actions, exerted maximum effort to ensure that economic and diplomatic relations were not seriously disrupted. And in terms of regional security issues, cooperation is critical, with Beijing taking a leading role in attempts to prevent nuclear proliferation in North Korea and pressuring Pyongyang to stop provoking tensions in the region. The Six-Party Talks framework to deal with the North Korean nuclear issue is the clearest example of how China's leadership is critical to cooperation when facing regional security challenges.

The neoliberal institutionalist model concludes that as globalization becomes more complex, the central foreign policy organs of the state lose total control and epistemic communities begin to play a more important role. This assumption looks beyond government when analyzing China's foreign relations by adopting the perspective that nongovernmental organizations play an important role in international relationships.[10] Scientific developments are tying the world together in ways that governments cannot easily control. Social media makes spontaneous communications across borders possible. This means that Chinese can now establish international relationships that are not mediated by the government. Chinese scholars maintain communication and collaborate with their epistemic communities around the world. A vast network of business relationships and cultural exchange is developing as well. These are examples of how difficult it has become for China to control the nongovernmental transactions across its borders.

Cultural exchanges, scholarly exchanges, and scientific exchanges all contribute to a growing network of relationships that transcend governments and are influential in shaping China's foreign relations and strategic priorities. Various interest groups in China often share common concerns with their foreign counterparts and seek to influence government policy. Environmental groups, human rights organizations, and the business community in China often lobby the government for policy changes. For example, in the 1990s, China's budding entrepreneurial class pushed for China's admission to the World Trade Organization (WTO), and in 2015 the nexus of environmental concerns about smog were vented via the documentary *Qiongding zhi xia* [*Under the Dome*], which included a broad network of domestic actors and international comparisons.[11] The implications of such developments are very significant politically. As these nongovernmental networks expand, they exert a growing influence on China's foreign policy processes. People who accept the assumption of the institutionalist perspective are optimistic about international relations as these networks gain a greater influence in China's policy-making circles.

However, this optimism should be dampened somewhat by the fact that China's rapid economic growth has outpaced the acceptance of China's new role as a major world power, and Chinese resent the continued resistance to China playing a larger role in the global financial system, global economic policy deliberations, and other international institutions. Many Chinese scholars argue that the time has come for China to take a more assertive or confrontational approach in its foreign policy.[12] While many Chinese scholars and officials accept the neoliberal institutionalist perspective and believe China's development benefits from 'playing by the rules', others Chinese argue that Beijing should 'exert more leverage . . . and mold its engagement with the rest of the world'.[13] This perspective envisions a more powerful China being able to effectively press its national interests.[14] It is clear that as China becomes more powerful, Beijing wants other great powers to reciprocate and also reassure China that China's 'core interests' will be respected.[15]

In recent years Beijing has increased pressure on other countries to ban visits by the Dalai Lama or the Uyghur activist Rebiya Kadeer, or prevent Chinese dissidents from participating in international events. Former foreign minister Yang Jiechi made Beijing's perspective explicit in March 2009 when he stated that satisfying Beijing's demands on these issues is 'not a matter of doing a favor to China, but rather an obligation under the basic principles of international relations . . . [and] other countries should respect the principals of international relations'.[16] According to Wu Guoguang, the 'message was that those who want to benefit from China's economic prosperity must carefully observe Beijing's political criteria and follow them when Beijing demands, even if China's criteria conflict with domestic public opinion and democratic procedures'.[17] Susan Shirk, a former deputy assistant secretary for Asian and Pacific affairs in the State Department, concluded that the 'era when China made all the compromises in the relationship has passed'.[18] But China's more assertive attitude does not necessarily mean that China is seeking to change basic international norms and principles. China is a 'limited-aims revisionist power' and shares with other great powers a mutual interest in nonproliferation, climate changes, global health, and other concerns that engage China and the other great powers together as world leaders. But just as the U.S. did in the post–World War II era, China may strategically press for a reorientation of international norms and institutions so that they reflect China's core values and hierarchical prestige.

Domestic politics

The domestic politics model assumes that a state's domestic politics largely determine its foreign policy.[19] China's foreign policy has gone through a process of institutionalization and pluralization, becoming more complex due to the increase in the number of domestic players and crosscutting bureaucratic interests.[20] China's maturing state bureaucracy has resulted in a less centralized foreign policy decision-making structure that has complicated China's foreign policy bureaucratically. All ministries and agencies of the central government have departments of foreign affairs or international cooperation, and along the east coast all provinces, municipalities, and autonomous regions have foreign affairs offices. Even the counties and townships in peripheral areas have such offices. The number of personnel in these offices has increased significantly and their roles in their respective organizations or localities have become more and more important. A relatively new development is the increasing public persona of the People's Liberation Army (PLA) and outspoken officers advocating policy, and an important question that we turn to in this chapter is the role of the PLA in determining foreign policy. Former Chinese Foreign Minister Qian Qichen recognized the changes in the foreign policy process in China when he proclaimed in 1990 that 'foreign policy is the extension of China's domestic politics.'[21]

The old stewards of China's foreign policy have passed away. Chairman Mao Zedong, Zhou Enlai, and Deng Xiaoping enjoyed a status that allowed them to make controversial decisions and take bold steps. Bold moves, like Mao's initiative for rapprochement with the U.S. or Deng Xiaoping's proclamation of the 'one country, two systems' formula to deal with Hong Kong and Taiwan, are now more difficult given the new complexities of the foreign affairs bureaucracy and a more collective leadership. Mao understood the strategic imperative of containing the Soviet Union and took the bold steps necessary to initiate diplomatic relations with the U.S. in the late 1960s. In 1978, Deng Xiaoping made the bold decisions necessary to finally normalize Sino-American diplomatic relations, even though the U.S. continued to sell arms to Taiwan.

China's new fifth generation of leadership faces significant challenges at home due to slowing economic development and important related structural and policy challenges. The new leadership is untested and does not have the same stature as the revolutionary generation. Their ability to make the bold policy changes necessary is yet unknown. China's new leadership is consumed with domestic concerns and unable or unwilling to take domestic political risks that many believe are imperative for China's diplomacy. Even if these leaders were inclined to, domestic political considerations make it difficult for them to undertake any new initiatives to deal with nationalistically sensitive issues like the Diaoyu/Senkaku Islands dispute with Japan or controversies over the South China Sea. The present top leaders in China have no solid base of support and are always looking over their shoulders for the approval of the previous generation of leaders. With China's growing economic and military power, these younger leaders are extremely sensitive to any perceived condescension or reluctance to recognize China's status as an emerging great power and the popular blowback that can occur if they do not vigorously respond to such slights or challenges to China's sovereignty.

Public opinion

Within the context of the domestic determinants of China's foreign policy we can drill down to even more specific issues such as public opinion, a newly emerging, if less clearly understood, influence on China's foreign policy process. Feelings of nationalism are heightened as communist doctrine no longer provides legitimacy to the Chinese Communist Party's (CCP) rule and 'patriotic education' replaces Marxism-Leninism-Mao Zedong thought. China's discourse of a 'century of humiliation' still casts a shadow over Chinese, but China's rapid rise as a world power make Chinese more confidently arrogant and assertive, and China's new leadership feels compelled to follow the prompt of public opinion. An example of the difficulty of balancing domestic politics with diplomacy is, in the face of increasing pressure from the public and within the Party and military, taking a more assertive position on territorial disputes with Japan, the Philippines, and Vietnam. At a July 2013 Politburo meeting, Xi Jinping reiterated Deng Xiaoping's position of 'shelving' disputes but balanced this by declaring that China would 'never give up its legitimate rights and interests'.[22]

Among analysts of foreign policy the default assumption has been that public opinion was not a factor in the foreign policy processes of nondemocratic nations. However, while China is still governed by a single-party dictatorship, China is increasingly a pluralistic nation in which media is no longer completely under the control of the CCP and the various state bureaucracies. Beginning in the 1980s there has been a proliferation of newspapers, journals, publishing houses, television stations and cable TV outlets. Along with the availability of social and commercialized media, China's information borders have expanded by providing more avenues for the expression of opinion on foreign policy not mediated by the government-controlled press. Public intellectuals that pontificate on television and radio talk shows, scholars that openly debate foreign policy in journals and newspapers, and opinions expressed by the world's largest online community opens a new frontier in the analysis of China's foreign policy. Peter Hays Gries argues that the 'Internet clearly is altering the natures of politics in the People's Republic of China'.[23] The important question this more open debate over China's foreign relations raises is how this affects leaders' decisions on foreign policy. The role of outspoken PLA officers' influence on public opinion also is an important but complicated question. Do more public attention and debate limit the autonomy and flexibility of decision makers? Does it encourage more inflammatory rhetoric by leaders and increase the propensity to escalate?

Alastair Iain Johnston offered a 'first cut' at understanding if, and how, publically expressed opinion impacted China's foreign policy in *New Directions in the Study of China's Foreign Policy*. He concluded that it is still unclear what, if any, influence popular opinion has on decision makers, and it is hard to tell if popular attitudes have any political effect on the policy process. However, to the degree policy makers view public opinion as a 'political force' it will influence internal policy debates. Johnston's takeaway message is that in China, 'state socialization' to 'inculcate uniform attitudes toward major public policies – especially foreign

Analyzing China's foreign policy

policy' has broken down and this will have some impact on China's foreign policy.[24] James Reilly concludes that recent scholarship shows that public opinion does influence Chinese foreign policy.[25] By implication, China's diplomacy is a 'two-level game' in which foreign policy is influenced by domestic politics and public opinion – although we do not have a good grasp of to what degree this is so.[26] One reality is that the Ministry of Foreign Affairs, like its Western counterparts, now spends a good deal of time and energy managing domestic public opinion on foreign policy issues. In an attempt to channel nationalistic sentiment in the desired direction, the Foreign Ministry communicates directly with the public to explain China's foreign policy. It has established a Division of Public Diplomacy and regularly invites representatives of the general public to engage with ministry officials, even the foreign minister himself, on foreign policy topics. In addition, the Foreign Ministry participates in dialogue via the Internet regarding foreign affairs.[27] Moreover, when China engages in international negotiations, coordination among the many ministries and agencies is necessary to gain support for certain positions or making necessary concessions. Sometimes the core foreign policy leaders must become involved in settling the differences among the various ministers and departments.[28]

Starting in the 1990s, the CCP and the state have relied more on promoting a nationalist discourse to sustain its legitimacy, and this has had an important influence on the dynamics of public opinion on China's foreign policy. As one scholar observed, in cases where the government has taken a clear position to defend specific Chinese interests, such as territorial sovereignty, 'domestic sentiment is a formidable driver of policy. In other words, the domestic audience is not only part of the decision-making process but also has the power to hold the leadership accountable for failing to defend these assurances.'[29] Senior Foreign Ministry presenters attending the annual East Asia Security Symposium and Conference regularly express their awareness, and the increasingly shrill complaints, of public opinion by recounting the anecdote that the Foreign Ministry is regularly shipped the impotence drug Viagra as well as traditional Chinese medicines for the same affliction.

As China's public opinion becomes a more significant influence in Beijing's foreign policy, and given the heightened sense of nationalism among Chinese and the increased social space within which they can express their views and even discontent with the Party's leadership, leaders may feel pushed to take a hard-line to satisfy 'compelling domestic expectations' even when they would rather seek conciliation.[30] A Chinese leader's ability to make concessions and seek a compromise resolution is more difficult given the constraints of public opinion. Pressure on Chinese leaders to take uncompromising positions could be triggered by a combination of negative international factors and domestic political pressures. Leaders cannot risk being accused of being 'soft' or not vigilantly protecting China's national interests and sovereignty. This compels Chinese leaders to take extreme foreign policy positions out of a fear of not satisfying the patriotic expectations of a population that is much more politically savvy and interconnected by modern communications technology.

The attentive public is now more engaged in debates over Chinese foreign policy and has become more active in attempting to influence China's foreign policy through online chat rooms, microblogs, and public demonstrations. Feelings of nationalism are widespread, as demonstrated when the traditional Olympic torch relay leading up to the 2008 Beijing Olympics became a rallying point for anti-China demonstrations in other countries. The popular response among Chinese was intense anger toward those who used the Olympic torch as an anti-China rallying point. In their minds China was being robbed of its deserved moment to shine before the world and these anti-China demonstrations were sullying China's 'debut' as a world power with the Olympics as a celebration of China's new stature in world politics. The global recession had a big impact on Chinese perceptions of China's place in the world. A BBC World Service poll found that 92 percent of Chinese believe that China has a positive global influence and another survey found that 54.4 percent believe China has the 'power to lead the world'. Pew Research found that 59 percent of Chinese believe that China will eventually replace the U.S. as the leading global superpower (8 percent believe China already has replaced the U.S.).[31] Chinese harbor more negative views of Japan, especially since 2010 when tensions over the Diaoyu/Senkaku Islands issue began to spike. Chinese harbor a very negative view of Japan – 92.8 percent of Chinese have unfavorable views of Japan – and this has risen dramatically by 28 percent in the past year. The Diaoyu/Senkaku Islands issue is the major driver of this these negative views – 77.6 percent of Chinese identified this dispute as the primary reason for their anti-Japanese views – while historical grievances were cited by 63.8 percent of respondents. Over 50 percent of Chinese feel that China and Japan will go to war sometime in the future.[32] This type of public opinion is bound to have an impact on Beijing's foreign policy, especially regarding the territorial disputes with Japan.

A recent book, *China Is Unhappy* (*Zhongguo bugaoxing*) tapped this nationalistic nerve and the phenomenon that as China becomes more connected internationally, many Chinese are in fact becoming more hostile toward international criticism of China on issues such as trade, human rights, Taiwan, and Tibet.[33] Even the complexities of currency exchange rates are the topic of a bestselling book – *Currency Wars* (*Huobi zhanzheng*) – written by an American-educated Chinese writer who argues that the U.S. Federal Reserve will support a global currency in order to saddle China with the consequences of the declining U.S. dollar as an international currency reserve.[34] The book appeals to the popular feelings in China of pessimism about U.S.-China relations and resentment toward the U.S. domination of the world's economy.[35] These books tap into a fundamental nationalistic dissatisfaction over the disrespect Chinese perceive China is subjected to by other countries.[36]

The influence of public opinion on foreign policy is exemplified by China's response to President Obama's decision to impose tariffs on Chinese tire imports in September 2009. According to one policy expert, 'all kinds of policymaking [in China], not just trade policy, is increasingly reactive to Internet opinion.' Following on the heels of a 'crescendo of nationalistic vitriol' on social media, Beijing responded by accusing Obama of 'bowing before domestic protectionist forces', condemned the decision to impose a tariff as a 'grave act of trade protectionism', and threatened retaliation. China's 'more combative stance' in this relatively minor trade dispute was driven by Chinese public opinion.[37]

In the past the government adopted a dual approach: working at the official level to improve relations with foreign countries while manipulating public opinion and taking advantage of popular nationalism to enhance regime legitimacy. However, the increased availability of social media and microblogs has grown into a powerful influence on public opinion that has undermined the government's ability to manipulate popular opinion, and it has increased the difficulty of managing this dual approach. In the past, mass demonstrations were orchestrated by the government, and the few that were not, such as at Tiananmen Square in 1976 and 1989, were met by decisive crackdowns. However, more recently, public opinion has exerted increasingly higher levels of influence on China's foreign policy, even restricting the government's ability to carry out its preferred policies.[38] These seemingly diametrically opposed policies make sense within the framework of an authoritarian regime attempting to increase its standing abroad while keeping its citizens supportive of the government at home.

This dual policy allowed China to engage in pragmatic diplomacy while moving beyond the past; the anger, frustration, and passion rooted in historical conflicts was neatly tucked away in the domestic politics side. The government could secure support for the regime through nationalism, yet engage in pragmatic foreign relations. For example, in the 1970s and 1980s, visits to the Yasukuni shrine by Japanese officials and history textbooks that euphemized many of Japan's war atrocities were resented by Chinese officials, but the scale of official protest remained relatively calm.[39]

The important question is whether or not the public any longer accepts rhetoric provided by the government and follows its attempts to orchestrate popular opinion or remains quiescent when the government does increase the harshness of its public rhetoric and adopts strong policies in protest. During the Mao and Deng eras, public opinion stayed mostly in line with government rhetoric, particularly on foreign policy issues.[40] However, where the government was once immune to criticism of its foreign policy, in recent years there has been an explosion of antiforeign demonstrations and it now faces mounting difficulty reigning in public opinion. The recent flare up in popular passions over the Diaoyu/Senkaku Islands dispute illustrates the challenge faced by the government. Reilly points out how the government's

> efforts at moderation were undermined by Beijing's legacy of using historical disputes for diplomatic leverage and domestic legitimacy. . . . It was as if they believed they could continue the approach of the Mao and Zhou era: telling the Chinese public one thing while foreign policy moved in the opposite direction.[41]

With this increase in popular attention to foreign policy and growing use of social media by the public, the government's efforts to dampen antiforeign demonstrations is met with contempt as citizens challenge the government's claim of defending China's national integrity. The government has redoubled its efforts to stop the growing number of protests but has been forced to capitulate to the public sentiment somewhat and adopt much more assertive rhetoric on sensitive foreign policy issues. The contradictions of China's dual approach frustrated the governments domestic and foreign policy goals rather than enhanced them. What initially was a tactic used to increase loyalty to the regime resulted in necessary backpedaling to contain protests that were undoing foreign polices the government had tirelessly worked to establish. Beijing now continually feels pressure from an assertive public to use uncompromising rhetoric and adopt assertive policies. Simultaneously, foreign policy leaders are keenly aware of the need to moderate relations with other countries vital to China's security and economic interests. The government is caught in a pincer: nationalist sentiment that the government encouraged to enhance regime legitimacy now prevents Beijing from adopting pragmatic and strategically formed policies. Reilly describes the impact of this on Sino-Japanese relations:

> The contradictions between these two approaches – a willingness to deemphasize the wartime past for strategic and economic reasons and the temptation to use history for diplomatic leverage and domestic legitimacy – have repeatedly provided an opening for public pressure to emerge and influence China's relations with Japan.[42]

Starting in the 1990s, it became more difficult for the government to control the domestic side of its dual approach to fuel nationalism for domestic regime legitimacy and public outcry over foreign policy issues increased, especially targeting Japan. For example, in the spring of 2005 as Japan was seeking a permanent seat on the United Nations Security Council, anti-Japanese demonstration in China, instigated by activists using the Internet and text messages focusing on Japanese textbooks and Yasukuni Shrine visits by government officials, provided an excuse for the Chinese government to take a harder line toward Japan. As the demonstrations came to a climax, Premier Wen Jiabao announced publicly that China would oppose Japan's bid to become a permanent member of the United Nations Security Council. Since 2010, the Diaoyu/Senkaku Islands dispute has become the primary focus of anti-Japanese demonstrations. The government is stuck both between supporting and suppressing protesters and between the imperatives of a pragmatic foreign policy and its claim to be the defender of Chinese sovereignty. The ability to control public opinion's influence on foreign affairs has weakened, and the government must respond to popular outcries or risk becoming the target of public anger for not vigorously defending China's sovereignty and responding to China's legacy of national humiliation and suffering from imperialism.[43] It is now clear that as international disputes develop, it has become difficult for the government to continue a dual policy without severe backlash from the Chinese public, pushing the government to adopt a more unyielding and assertive foreign policy.

The People's Liberation Army

A layer of domestic politics that complicates the analysis of foreign policy is the role of the PLA. Recent research on the PLA's role in determining foreign policy concludes that over the past fifteen years its influence has attenuated as the PLA has become more professional. This was the result of a 'deliberate decision to remove the military from elite politics and the most powerful decision-making councils'.[44] While many press reports identify an 'ominous creep of PLA influence over Chinese politics', Chinese politics is a 'top-down system' dominated by the Politburo Standing Committee, and 'people who challenge that system rarely prosper,' as the recent Bo Xilai case has shown. The PLA knows its place within this system and has been uninvolved in the major foreign policy decisions of recent years.[45] However, while the PLA is now a modern and professional force controlled by the Party, one important question is to what extent do civilian leaders 'truly understand the capabilities and limitations of the PLA and the options it puts forward – and how that understanding affects decisions of war and peace'. Moreover, there is some concern that 'China's civilian leaders [do not] have the intellectual experience or the ability to draw on military expertise independent of the PLA to manage the PLA's increasing competence and influence.'[46] There are questions about the PLA's willingness to be completely transparent with the Party leadership, and this has influenced the resolution of several well-known diplomatic crises such as the 2001 U.S. EP-3 spy plane incident and the 2007 antisatellite weapons test.[47]

While it is true that the Party exercises tight control over the PLA, the Party now abides more public expressions of opinion by PLA officers, something that was not the case a decade ago. Increasingly PLA officers now speak more freely to the press, especially the press that caters to popular opinion, such as the *Global Times*. This can inflame nationalistic sentiments among the public, but the impact of this relatively new phenomenon on foreign policy is hotly debated among Chinese scholars and Western scholars of Chinese foreign policy as well. Many scholars conclude that while these publically expressed PLA perspectives on foreign policy may now be more common in the 'commercial' press, the official Party-controlled media, like the *People's Daily*, carefully represents the central leadership's measured views on foreign policy.[48] Nevertheless, the impact of such statements cannot be gainsaid. Wang Jisi, a leading Chinese international relations scholar and advisor to top Party officials, voiced concern that this results in 'reckless statements, made with no official authorization', and Chinese diplomats have warned that this is something that is not helpful to China's diplomacy.[49]

The questions this raises are why these PLA personnel are outspoken and what impact does it have on policy. Three general arguments have been put forward. First, these outspoken officers have no impact because they are either retired or not operational commanders. Second, they are simply giving voice to more hawkish members of the PLA, and this reveals policy debates within the military or more hawkish members of the PLA trying to push the Party leadership to adopt more aggressive policies. Third, these officers are simply promoting institutional policy preferences of the PLA. And in this case, these outspoken PLA personnel may be authorized by the PLA General Political Department to function as 'external propaganda experts' and according to one officer, this 'propaganda is subject to discipline'.[50] Based on the research and analysis on the military's influence on Chinese foreign policy, we can conclude that a distinction should be made between publically expressed 'propaganda' and debates within the PLA over foreign policy and attempts to influence the policy process. The 'pundits with military rank' reflect domestic propaganda imperatives, like promoting national unity and protecting the regime from 'public dissatisfaction with the policy status quo', more than government policy or internal policy debates.[51]

A great deal of the hawkish rhetoric is for 'external consumption' and an effort to influence foreign governments rather than internally directed to influence China's foreign policy. In a classic 'two-level game', Chinese diplomats leverage public pressure (stoked by PLA propaganda workers) when engaged in negotiations over sensitive international issues, especially issues related to China's 'core interests' and territorial sovereignty. The goal of such propaganda is not to provoke military conflict, but rather, leverage to some extent the public's involvement in foreign affairs to gain bargaining influence for Chinese diplomats as they seek a resolution favorable to China and avoid military conflict. But balancing reassuring a domestic audience of China's military prowess, bolstering domestic popular support for (or constraint upon) diplomats, and alarming an international audience concerned about China's more assertive policies is difficult. This tactic does 'perpetuate the narrative that a hawkish faction exists in the military' and raises concerns about its influence on foreign policy, but it also supports regime legitimacy in an era when nationalism is a form of political capital that the CCP wants to generate.[52]

Based on recent scholarly research, it is clear that today the government is more responsive than ever to domestic politics, and to some degree China's foreign policy is influenced by public opinion.[53] This increasing influence of public opinion on foreign policy complicates Chinese diplomacy. David Shambaugh concludes that China still suffers from a 'century of shame and humiliation' encouraged by the government, and as a result

> contemporary Chinese nationalism is not really self-confident . . . [because] many present-day challenges to Chinese policy are filtered through this historical prism. One might have expected China's growing power to help overcome this insecurity and defensiveness, but in fact it seems to have fueled it.[54]

Thus a 'defensive China' will be 'reluctant and difficult to engage in the years to come'.[55]

Leadership

Not enough attention has been paid to the role of Chinese leaders in the analysis of China's foreign policy despite the fact that paramount leaders have played an important role historically but more than they do today. Nevertheless, the profile of 'core leaders' has grown as the more recent generations of leaders have simultaneously held the position of general secretary of the CCP, chairman of the Central Military Commission, and president of the country. This is reflected in an important change in Chinese foreign policy since the end of the Cold War, namely the very public role of the 'diplomat-in-chief' of China.[56] Despite the collective leadership style of the present regime, individual leaders do make a difference, but this is determined more by the prestige and personal power of the individual. Therefore, the integration of the study of personality and Chinese foreign policy is one more level of analysis that helps to better explain and understand China's foreign policy. This requires bridging the subdiscipline of political psychology and Chinese foreign policy to explain how leadership personality has shaped Chinese foreign policy historically, especially during the eras of Mao and Deng, and brings leadership personality back into focus as an important component when analyzing Chinese foreign policy and understanding its strategic priorities.[57]

Relying only on neorealist or neoliberal models of foreign policy analysis fails to explain some significant and seemingly contradictory changes that took place in Chinese foreign policy during the Cold War. For example, if the international balance of power is the primary determinant of China's foreign policy, why did China switch from 'leaning to one side' (pro-Soviet) to a 'dual adversary' policy (anti-Soviet and anti-U.S.) during the 1960s despite the fact that there were no major changes in the balance of power? Moreover, the collapse of the Eastern Bloc and the end of the Cold War was the biggest power shift since World War II, but resulted in no profound changes in China's strategic orientation. To more fully understand Chinese foreign policy requires alternative explanations that focus more on leadership.

The contrast in China's foreign policy between the Maoist era and Deng's leadership is very significant, including China's overall international orientation, its relations with major powers, and its regional policies. This disjuncture divides the diplomatic history of the People's Republic of China into two contrasting periods: the Maoist period from 1949 to 1978 and the Deng period after 1978 until his death in 1997. While Mao sought to position China between the two superpowers by tacking back and forth between the two, Deng sought good relations with both superpowers. The importance of leadership is illustrated by how these individual leaders played such a dominant role in determining China's foreign policy. Contrasting Mao's handpicked successor Hua Guofeng's weak leadership with Deng's dynamic and visionary leadership underscores the importance of leadership. Mao and Deng's personalities played a very important role in the dramatic differences when we compare the two periods in China's foreign policy. But a more nuanced and theoretical analysis of leadership in the study of China's foreign policy is not very well developed in the comparative analysis of China's foreign policy and decision-making processes, and has not taken advantage of the theoretical models developed by scholars of foreign policy analysis.[58]

The impact of a particular leader on a state's foreign policy is determined primarily by that leader's belief system. But the leader's interest in foreign policy, training, and sensitivity to the policy-making environment are intervening variables that condition the extent of the leader's influence over foreign policy. Leaders interested in foreign affairs are more likely to be consulted and kept informed about foreign policy and usually participate in the foreign policy decision-making process. Leaders with more training and more experiences in foreign affairs have a wider repertoire for policy tools than those with little or no training and experience. Leaders with little or no training and experience fall back on their individual problem-solving predispositions. The most important variable is sensitivity to the policy-making environment. More sensitive leaders accommodate themselves to new information, respect constraints, and are open to new information.[59] Leaders' personalities are therefore likely to influence their countries' foreign policies.

Mao and Deng were very powerful leaders and according to Hermann, such leaders have the 'ability to stifle all opposition and dissent as well as the power to make a decision alone if necessary'.[60] Both had the final say on foreign policy while the policy was later refined and implemented, usually by a close circle of foreign policy experts. Neither Mao nor Deng had any formal training in foreign relations, or any long-term diplomatic experience, but both were deeply interested in foreign affairs and made the major foreign policy decisions while in power. The continuities in Chinese foreign policy through the end of the Cold War can be explained to some degree by the similar aspects of their personalities. Both emphasized Marxist internationalism as one of the guiding principles for Chinese foreign policy and both insisted on the principle of independence in handling foreign affairs, believed that sovereignty was supreme and insisted on noninterference in China's internal affairs.

However, focusing on the differences between Mao and Deng's personalities helps to explain the dramatic changes in China's foreign policy that are not well explained by the neorealist and neoliberal models. Mao's ideological rigidity made him generally closed to new information and he was inclined to interpret incoming information in a way consistent with his belief system. However, Deng differed from Mao in his openness to new information and the way he processed information, and in the way he worked within the policy-making environment. Deng's famous statement that 'we cannot afford to lock our doors, refuse to use our brains and remain forever backward' set the stage for the opening and reform policies initiated in 1978.[61] Specifically addressing foreign policy concerns, Deng said that in the post-Mao period

> we have made two important changes in our assessment of the international situation and in our foreign policy. . . . The first change is in our understanding of the question of war and peace. We used to believe that war was inevitable and imminent and many of our policy decisions were based on this belief . . . [but] after a careful analysis of the situation, we have . . . conclude[d] that it is possible that there will be no large-scale war for a fairly long time to come and that there is hope of maintaining world peace. . . . [T]he second change is in our foreign policy. In view of the threat of Soviet hegemonism, over the years we formed a strategic line of defense. . . . Now we have altered our strategy and this represents a major change.[62]

Mao and Deng had different personalities: Mao was closed to information, inclined to challenge constraints, and made foreign policy through a top-down process, and his motivation was achievement focused. By contrast, Deng differed from Mao in almost every respect and was an 'opportunistic', 'pragmatic', and 'accommodative' leader. Mao focused on ideological issues and imperialism while Deng saw fundamental changes in the international system and changed policies accordingly. Mao pushed for his ideologically driven goals forcefully with 'armed struggle' and 'people's war', two of his major tactics for a revolutionary foreign policy. Deng rejected letting differences in ideology or political systems impact Chinese foreign relations. Moreover, Deng adopted pragmatic policies, and in doing so China began to open to the outside world and gradually integrate itself into the international system rather than struggle to change that system.

The foregoing analysis has illustrated, however briefly, the necessity and benefits of integrating the study of personality types with Chinese foreign policy analysis. A more systemic analysis of Chinese foreign policy is needed that takes advantage of theories on personality types and puts decision makers at the center while considering other domestic variables as well as international structural constraints. This will provide an important framework for analyzing Chinese foreign policy and understanding its strategic priorities. This not only provides a model for analyzing the personalities of Chinese leaders, but gives analysts operationalized tools to make comparisons. Empirically, the extent to which leadership personality impacts foreign policy depends on whether the leader's power is firmly consolidated or whether the leader is predominant enough. Given the consensus-driven leadership of the Standing Committee of the Politburo and the Foreign Affairs Leading Small Group in contemporary China, leadership personality certainly plays a role, but to what extent is an important new frontier in the study of China's foreign policy. China's leaders no longer enjoy the same political capital and charisma as their predecessors. But as long as the Chinese hierarchical decision-making structure remains along with its authoritarian political system, the role of the core leader will continue to be central to understanding major features of Chinese foreign policy.

Conclusion

This chapter has outlined three models in an attempt to explain China's foreign policy and strategic priorities. Multiple international and diverse domestic factors are competing to shape China's foreign policy acting to both create and prioritize. The external factors such as globalization's influences on China are unprecedented. So are changes in China's domestic politics. As China has become more integrated into the global political and economic system, more government agencies have become involved in foreign affairs. As Marxist ideology loses ground in China, the Chinese have turned toward traditional culture and history for an ideological foundation, and rising nationalism is gaining strength in Chinese politics and influence on China's foreign policy. New developments in social media and public opinion and constraints imposed on the government by bureaucratic politics are driving China's foreign policy more than in the past. But caution is in order. In fact, these are only models for the analysis of foreign policy, and reality may prove otherwise, because China's foreign policy is contingent and subject to unfathomable factors. Unanticipated events can have significant consequences for China's domestic politics and foreign policy. But it is clear that a more nuanced and integrated model is needed that takes account of domestic politics, including public opinion and leadership personality, while also taking into consideration external factors. China's foreign policy is influenced by any combination of these models, but may follow a pattern not envisioned by any of them.

From a general perspective, it is safe to say that the changes taking place in China's national power are causing domestic and international structural changes that will affect China's foreign policy. Mutual interests tie China and the other great powers together, but friction will occur over issues of trade, arms exports, Taiwan, human rights, intervention in crisis situations, and other issues. These issues will influence China's foreign policy but are not completely under the control of the Chinese governments, either.

China's desire for economic prosperity and political stability are strategic priorities that motivate its foreign policy. The debate within China now focuses on how an economically and militarily powerful China should assume global leadership. While larger structural forces buffet China it is increasingly necessary to pay careful attention to domestic politics, public opinion, and leadership in order to fully grasp China's foreign policy and be able to offer a more penetrating analysis of China's foreign policy process.

Notes

1 For a detailed analysis, see V.M. Hudson, *Foreign Policy Analysis: Classic and Contemporary Theory* (2nd ed.), Lanham, MD: Rowman & Littlefield, 2013.
2 C. Alden and A. Aran, *Foreign Policy Analysis: New Approaches*, New York: Routledge, 2012.
3 R.O. Keohane (ed.), *Neorealism and Its Critics*, New York: Columbia University Press, 1986; J.J. Mearsheimer, *The Tragedy of Great Power Politics*, New York: W.W. Norton, 2001. For an application to U.S.-China relations, see A.L. Friedberg, 'The Future of U.S.-China Relations: Is Conflict Inevitable?', *International Security*, vol. 30, no. 2, Fall 2005, pp. 16–24.
4 Mearsheimer, *The Tragedy of Great Power Politics*, p. 4. See also R. Terrill, *The New Chinese Empire and What It Means for the United States*, New York: Basic Books, 2003, p. 255.
5 K. Hill, 'China Urges US to End Coast Surveillance', *Financial Times*, 27 August 2009, <www.ft.com/cms/s/0/13335cca-9329-11de-b146-00144feabdc0.html?nclick_check=1> (accessed 12 November 2014).
6 China has not defined either the South China Sea or the East China Sea as a 'core interest', but some have hinted that these areas are 'part of China's core interests'. See M.D. Swaine, 'China's Assertive Behavior Part One: On "Core Interests"', *China Leadership Monitor*, no. 34, Winter 2011, pp. 8–10, <http://news.xinhuanet.com/english2010/indepth/2011-08/31/c_131086932.htm> (accessed 10 August 2014).
7 K.G. Lieberthal and J. Wang, 'Addressing U.S.-China Strategic Distrust', John L. Thornton China Center Monograph Series, no. 4, Washington, DC: Brookings Institution, March 2012.

8 R. Jervis, 'Thinking Systemically about China', *International Security*, vol. 31, no. 2, Fall 2006, pp. 206–8.
9 R.O. Keohane and J.S. Nye, *Power and Interdependence*, New York: Longman, 2001; D.A. Baldwin (ed.), *Neorealism and Neoliberalism: The Contemporary Debate*, New York: Columbia University Press, 1993. For an application to U.S.-China relations, see Friedberg, 'The Future of U.S.-China Relations', pp. 12–16.
10 S. Khagram, J.V. Riker, and K. Sikkink (eds.), *Restructuring World Politics: Transnational Social Movements, Networks, and Norms*, Minneapolis: University of Minnesota Press, 2002; M.E. Keck and K. Sikkink, *Activists Beyond Borders: Advocacy Networks in International Politics*, Ithaca, NY: Cornell University Press, 1998.
11 J. Chai, *Under the Dome*, <https://www.youtube.com/watch?v=T6X2uwlQGQM> (accessed 13 March 2015).
12 G. Xiao, 'Superficial, Arrogant Nationalism', *China Security*, vol. 5, no. 3, 2009, p. 55.
13 G. Dyer, 'The Dragon Stirs', *Financial Times*, 24 September 2009.
14 Ibid.
15 S. Yi, 'Consensus Based on Mutual Respect and Equality: The Cornerstone of "Strategic Reassurance"', *PacNet Newsletter*, no. 73A, Pacific Forum Center for Strategic and International Studies, 12 November 2009.
16 NPC, CPPCC Annual Sessions 2009, <http://news.xinhuanet.com/english/2009-03/07/content_10961657.htm> (accessed 8 December 2014).
17 G. Wu, 'A Shadow over Western Democracies: China's Political Use of Economic Power', *China Perspectives*, no. 2, 2009, p. 82.
18 S. Shirk, 'A Mountain to Climb: Don't Expect any Earth-Shattering Agreements during Barack Obama's First Summit in China', *South China Morning Post*, 28 October 2009.
19 R.D. Putnam, 'Diplomacy and Domestic Politics: The Logic of Two-Level Games', *International Organization*, vol. 43, Summer 1988, pp. 427–60.
20 Q. Zhang, 'Continuities and Changes in China's Negotiating Behavior', in P. Kerr, S. Harris, and Y. Qin (eds.), *China's "New" Diplomacy: Tactical or Fundamental Change?* New York: Palgrave Macmillan, 2009, pp. 156–58.
21 Q. Qian, 'Qian Qichen on the World Situation', *Beijing Review*, vol. 33, no. 3, 1990, pp. 16–18.
22 M.T. Fravel, 'Xi Jinping's Overlooked Revelation on China's Maritime Disputes', *Diplomat*, <http://thediplomat.com/2013/08/15/xi-jinpings-overlooked-revelation-on-chinas-maritime-disputes/> (accessed 15 August 2014).
23 P.H. Gries, 'Chinese Nationalism: Challenging the State', *Current History*, vol. 104, September 2005, p. 252.
24 A.I. Johnston, 'The Correlates of Beijing Public Opinion toward the United States, 1998–2004', in A.I. Johnston and R.S. Ross (eds.), *New Directions in the Study of China's Foreign Policy*, Stanford, CA: Stanford University Press, 2006, pp. 340–77.
25 J. Reilly, *Strong Society, Smart State: The Rise of Public Opinion in China's Japan Policy*, New York: Columbia University Press, 2012, p. 17.
26 Putnam, 'Diplomacy and Domestic Politics', pp. 427–60; Q. Zhang, 'Continuities and Changes in China's Negotiating Behavior', in Kerr, Harris, and Qin (eds.), *China's "New" Diplomacy*, p. 154.
27 Q. Zhang, '*lun zhongguo waijiao de sanwei fazhan*' ('On the Three-Dimensional Development of China's New Foreign Policy'), *Journal of Foreign Affairs College*, no. 3, 2004, p. 14.
28 D.M. Lampton (ed.), *The Making of Chinese Foreign and Security Policy in the Era of Reform, 1978–2000*, Stanford, CA: Stanford University Press, 2001, pp. 17–18.
29 J.M. Norton, 'China's "Warfare" Strategies and Tactics', *Diplomat*, <http://thediplomat.com/2013/08/18/chinas-warfare-strategies-and-tactics/> (accessed 18 August 2014).
30 D. Roy, 'China's Democratized Foreign Policy', *Survival*, vol. 51, no. 2, April–May 2009, pp. 28–30.

31 Public opinion data (unless otherwise noted) come from Committee of 100, *Hope and Fear: Full Report of C-100s Survey on American and Chinese Attitudes toward Each Other*, New York, 2008; Chicago Council on Global Affairs, *Global Views 2008*, Chicago, 2008; Pew Research Center, *Global Attitudes Project 2009*, Washington, DC, 2009; F. Hanson and A. Shearer, *China and the World: Public Opinion and Foreign Policy*, The Lowy Institute China Poll, Sydney, Australia, 2009; B.S. Glaser and L. Morris, 'Chinese Perceptions of U.S. Decline and Power', *China Brief*, vol. 9, no. 14, 9 July 2009, <www.jamestown.org/programs/chinabrief/single/?tx_ttnews%5Btt_news%5D=35241&cHash=db..#.Vfjd7BGqpBc>

32 'The 9th Japan-China Public Opinion Poll Analysis Report on the Comparative Data', Tokyo: The Genron NPO, 12 August 2013.

33 X. Song, X. Wang et al., *Zhongguo bugaoxing* [*China Is Unhappy*], Nanjing: Jiangsu Renmin Chubanshe, 2009; T. Branigan and D. Chung, 'David or Goliath? China's Battle to Win the War of Perceptions', *Guardian*, 21 May 2009, <www.guardian.co.uk/world/2009/may/21/china-identity-foreign-relations> (accessed 4 February 2015). For a review of anti-American books, see H. Li, 'China Talks Back: Anti-Americanism or Nationalism? A Review of Recent "Anti-American" Book in China', *Journal of Contemporary China*, vol. 6, no. 14, 1997, pp. 153–60.

34 H. Song, 'Huo bi zhan zheng' ['Currency Wars'], *Song Hongbing bian zhu Zhong xin chu ban she*, Beijing: Shi, 2007.

35 C. Buckley, 'China Bestseller Sees Plots and Profit in Financial Crisis', *Reuters*, 21 September 2009.

36 G. Xiao, 'Superficial, Arrogant Nationalism', *China Security*, vol. 5, no. 3, 2009, p. 52.

37 I. Johnson, 'China Strikes Back on Trade', *Wall Street Journal*, 14 September 2009; K. Bradsher, 'China Weighs Tariffs on Some U.S. Exports as Tensions Rise', *New York Times*, 14 September 2009.

38 Reilly, *Strong Society, Smart State*, p. 83.

39 Ibid., p. 58.

40 A.S. Whiting and J. Xin, 'Sino-Japanese Relations: Pragmatism and Passion', *World Policy Journal*, vol. 8, no. 1, Winter 1990–91, pp. 108–12.

41 Reilly, *Strong Society, Smart State*, p. 97.

42 Ibid., p. 56.

43 Z. Wang, *Never Forget National Humiliation: Historical Memory in Chinese Politics and Foreign Relations*, New York: Columbia University Press, 2012.

44 M.D. Swaine, 'China's Assertive Behavior Part Three: The Role of the Military in Foreign Policy', *China Leadership Monitor*, no. 36, Winter 2012, pp. 4–5.

45 T. Moss, 'PLA Influence over Chinese Politics: Fact or Fiction?', *Diplomat*, <http://thediplomat.com/flashpoints-blog/2012/08/10/pla-influence-over-chinese-politics-fact-of-fiction/> (accessed 10 August 2014).

46 P. Mattis, 'How Much Power Does China's People's Army Have?', *Diplomat*, <http://thediplomat.com/china-power/how-much-power-does-chinas-peoples-army-have/> (accessed 13 July 2014).

47 L. Jakobson and D. Knox, 'New Foreign Policy Actors in China', *SIPRI Policy Paper*, no. 26, September 2010, pp. 15–16.

48 A. Miller, 'Dilemmas of Globalization and Governance', in R. MacFarquhar (ed.), *The Politics of China: Sixty Years of the People's Republic of China* (3rd ed.), Oxford: Cambridge University Press, 2011, pp. 528–599.

49 Quoted in W. Lam, 'China's Hawks in Command', *Wall Street Journal*, <http://online.wsj.com/article/SB10001424052702304211804577500521756902802.html> (accessed 1 July 2014).

50 A. Chubb, 'Propaganda, Not Policy: Explaining the PLA's Hawkish Faction (Part One)', *China Brief*, vol. 13, no. 15, 25 July 2013, <www.jamestown.org/single/?tx_ttnews%5Btt_news%5D=41175&no_cache=1#.Vfjj1xGqpBc> (accessed 1 July 2014).

51 A. Chubb, 'Propaganda as Policy? Explaining the PLA's 'Hawkish Faction' (Part Two)', *China Brief*, vol. 13, no. 16, 9 August 2013, <www.jamestown.org/programs/chinabrief/single/?tx_ttnews%5Btt_news%5D=41254&cHash=57de84de0f8841ac12c795fa4fadffbc#.VfjkIBGqpBc> (accessed 1 July 2014).
52 Ibid.
53 Reilly, *Strong Society, Smart State*, pp. 130–31.
54 D. Shambaugh, 'Containment or Engagement of China? Calculating Beijing's Responses', *International Security*, vol. 21, no. 2, Autumn 1996, p. 209.
55 Ibid.
56 While in the U.S., diplomat-in-chief refers only to the president; it has a broader meaning in China.
57 For a more detailed version of this section, see Q. Zhang, 'Towards an Integrated Theory of Chinese Foreign Policy: Bringing Leadership Personality Back In', *Journal of Contemporary China*, vol. 23, no. 89, 2014, pp. 902–22.
58 T.J. Christensen, A.I. Johnston, and R.S. Ross, 'Conclusions and Future Directions', in Johnston and Ross (eds.), *New Directions in the Study of China's Foreign Policy*, p. 391.
59 M.G. Hermann, 'How Decision Units Shape Foreign Policy: a Theoretical Framework', *International Studies Review*, vol. 3, no. 2, 2001, pp. 64–65.
60 Ibid., p. 56.
61 X. Deng, *Selected Works of Deng Xiaoping*, vol. 2, Beijing: Renmin Chubanshe, 1994, p. 128.
62 Ibid., pp. 127–28.

4 Crises as impetus for institutionalization

Maritime crisis management mechanisms in China's Near Seas

Gaye Christoffersen

Introduction

This chapter examines China's search for a maritime strategy during a time of tension in the East and South China Seas. Chinese efforts to manage tensions might be understood through two models: the bureaucratic politics model of foreign policy making and the unitary actor model. The chapter's hypothesis is that the Chinese state as unitary actor, guided by a maritime strategy, is a strategic priority ideal that Chinese organizations strive for, but that various maritime incidents, domestic debates over maritime strategies, center-local bureaucratic differences, and civil-military differences can best be explained with a bureaucratic politics model. The chapter compares the United States of America-China and China-Japan crisis management mechanisms [危机管理机制] created in response to maritime incidents.

Defining China's maritime strategy

As China's strategic priorities shift from an identity of land power to maritime power, there have been numerous domestic debates over what its maritime strategy should be.[1] Consequently, these debates have prevented the formation of a coherent maritime strategy.[2] Beijing has never published an official maritime strategy,[3] which has created a vacuum that is filled with nationalistic, unofficial Chinese writings.[4] Beijing's failure to coordinate maritime policy and its conflicting directives allow the provincial level wide discretion on how it will implement policy with much confusion as to which directive to implement. This confusion in local level maritime administration impacts how China interacts with Southeast Asian nations in the South China Sea.[5]

Beijing's inability to maintain command and control over the five civilian maritime agencies – the Chinese Coast Guard, Maritime Safety Administration, China Marine Surveillance, Fisheries Law Enforcement Command, and China Customs – leads analysts to call them the "Five Dragons Stirring Up the Sea."[6] Their implementation of Beijing's maritime policies was highly decentralized in 2010–12. According to a Chinese interlocutor at the East Asia Security Symposium and Conference, the maritime agencies' implementation of the center's policies was too decentralized and confused, with too many coastal provinces and municipalities having their own sea patrols.[7] This Chinese analyst noted that maritime policy formulation was centralized but implementation was highly decentralized. He suggested that the five dragons could only be coordinated through international mechanisms, such as including them in the China-ASEAN (Association of Southeast Asian Nations) Code of Conduct, rather than domestically.[8]

In May 2009, Chinese maritime experts were calling for an overhaul of China's maritime strategy due to numerous maritime incidents in the East and South China Seas.[9] Authority over China's coastal waters was divided between the State Council and the Central Military Commission, with coordination carried out by the State Commission of Border and Coastal Defense. Administrative responsibility is shared between the People's Liberation Army (PLA) and local authorities. Each military region, coastal province, and county has a border and coastal defense committee that combines military and civilian agencies.[10]

The National Committee on Border and Coastal Defense of the People's Republic of China (PRC) met January 29–31, 2010, to consider a new coastal defense strategy and better coordination among the center and localities. China had completed a technological hardening of its coastal defense capabilities that would allow for a more a unified leadership. There were several competing understandings of coastal defense and competing perspectives on problems of civil-military integration in coastal defense.[11]

In March 2011, Yin Zhuo noted, "China lacks a clear maritime strategy and its approach was over compartmentalized," fragmented among numerous bureaucratic agencies.[12] A new maritime strategy could manage civil-military relations in peripheral territorial disputes in China's Near Seas. Luo Yuan claimed that further construction of infrastructure to defend China's expanding maritime interests would span civil-military and local-center organizations.[13] A survey of Chinese naval literature in 2011 found a greater than expected diversity of Chinese views on the proposed Chinese maritime strategy, from moderate to belligerent.[14] In mid-2011, the Chinese leadership took two measures: the PLA was ordered to adopt more moderate behavior, and the Chinese Foreign Ministry was ordered to provide stronger policy guidance to the numerous maritime actors. The maritime law enforcement agencies were ordered to inform the foreign ministry of their plans to engage foreign ships or enter disputed territories.[15] Yang Mingjie, vice president of the China Institute of Contemporary International Relations in Beijing, noted the continuous domestic debates on China's maritime strategy, and the need to coordinate the maritime civilian agencies into a more coherent maritime organization to counter bureaucratic competition and better coordinate military and civilian agencies.[16]

In November 2012, at the 18th Party Congress of the Chinese Communist Party (CCP), Hu Jintao announced that China should make itself into a maritime power; this appeared to indicate that domestic debates over China's maritime strategy were over.[17] Although debates over maritime strategy might have subsided, the comprehensive maritime strategy had not yet been revealed, and coordination problems between center-local, civil-military, and multiple maritime agencies still required administrative reorganization.

US–China crisis management mechanism

The United States of America (US) government, when communicating with the PRC during a crisis, would want one point of contact that is in communication with all significant actors. The assumption is that all states are operating under the rational actor model with clear understandings of national interests and strategies, and without inputs from bureaucratic politics, center-local differences, civil-military differences, and domestic debates over interests and strategies. The choice of this analytical model as an ideal type predetermines the type of crisis management mechanism constructed.

Some analysts view Beijing as possessing a carefully managed strategy using numerous instruments, including civil maritime law enforcement agencies.[18] Other observers have questioned China as a unified actor. Admiral Michael Mullen has pointed out the lack of coherence, stating: "Sometimes it's difficult for me to connect the dots, you know, inside China in terms of how the military – the PLA or PLAN [PLA Navy] is tied to its leadership in terms of the strategic objectives."[19] Mullen has pointed out the need for better maritime mechanisms.[20]

Chinese perceive the US as responding to a crisis with a rational actor model with controlled escalation and a strategy of brinkmanship. In contrast, they claim Chinese responses to crises are based on principles – "on just grounds, to our advantage, and with restraint" ["有理, 有利, 有節"] – a defensive strategy with limited goals. The implication is that there are huge US-China differences in how each side manages a crisis.[21] Since the crisis in 1999 after the bombing of the Chinese embassy, Americans and Chinese have jointly worked on closing the gap and identifying principles of crisis management.[22]

Wu Xinbo notes that lower-level rogue elements, military or civilian, can initiate a crisis, presenting a fait accompli to the civilian leadership.[23] One Chinese lesson learned from the 1999 Belgrade bombing was to not assume that the US government is a unitary actor.[24] The Chinese leadership applied this lesson in its response to the EP-3 crisis in 2001 by assuming it had been an accident rather than a deliberate action. Chinese bureaucratic politics had delayed Beijing's response due to civil-military differences and lack of center-local coordination. It was not until the third day of the crisis that Beijing developed its plan on how to respond because information flows through the Chinese bureaucracy were exceedingly slow, and because there was no crisis management mechanism in place prior to the crisis. One had to be created temporarily to manage the crisis.[25] Wang Jisi and Xu Hui argue that the numerous crises China has faced produced a learning curve as Beijing improved its response to crises.[26]

One reform Chinese analysts recommended was a Chinese national security council to replace the CCP leadership's use of the Leading Group style of crisis management. This was undertaken somewhat in November 2013 with the formation of the National Security Commission (NSC) at the 3rd Plenary Session of the 18th Party Central Committee. Whilst its function is to be verified, analysts anticipate that greater institutionalization internationally, through mechanisms, required increased institutionalization domestically. The NSC should also give civilian leaders greater control in a crisis.[27]

Wu Xinbo identifies distinctive characteristics of Chinese crisis management: much time is spent assigning responsibility for the crisis and much effort is put into symbolic gestures, leading to a relatively slow response. Only after a delay is the Foreign Ministry eventually put in charge of crisis management.[28] Foreign analysts have speculated about the difficulties in civil-military interagency coordination and its impact on crisis management.[29] Some analysts have noted that the most complex civil-military interactions in China are at the local level, being both competitive and cooperative.[30]

The US–China Security & Economic Dialogue (S&ED), which first met in 2009, is a type of crisis management mechanism created by the US and China that assumes the rational actor model but that implicitly recognizes that there might be fissures between civil and military actors by giving the S&ED an economic and a strategic track. Shen Dingli has identified the S&ED as a framework that could stabilize US–China relations, although it was not a "solve-all mechanism."[31] Further institutionalization, *zhiduhua* [制度], was needed to transform it into a mechanism.

At the S&ED, the US and China agreed to resume military contacts under the Military Maritime Consultative Agreement first initiated in 1998. It had always been an on-again, off-again mechanism, suspended by Beijing during crises rather than functioning as a crisis management mechanism. In November 2010, at the East Asian Summit held in Hanoi, Secretary of State Clinton reiterated a US offer to host trilateral talks that would address Sino-Japanese territorial disputes. Beijing immediately rejected the idea, worried it would involve the Diaoyu/Senkaku dispute.[32]

However, sometime in 2010, Beijing unilaterally decided that it needed a US–China crisis management mechanism.[33] It is not clear when during 2010 Beijing decided it needed a crisis management mechanism with the US, but it is certain it was in response to the 2010 tensions in the East and South China Seas. This indicates a distinct shift in the evolution of China's strategic priorities. During the January 2011 summit of Barack Obama and Hu Jintao, the Chinese president asked the US for a crisis management mechanism. At first the US was reluctant because it wanted a Japan–US–China trilateral mechanism but later agreed.[34]

During the 3rd US–China S&ED on May 11, 2011, State Councilor Dai Bingguo announced the creation of the requested mechanism, the U.S.-China Consultations on the Asia-Pacific.[35] This mechanism met for the first time on June 25, 2011, in Honolulu, headed by Kurt Campbell, assistant secretary of state for East Asian and Pacific affairs, and Cui Tiankai, vice minister of foreign affairs. They agreed that peace and stability in the South China Sea was their common security interest. They discussed their respective objectives for upcoming meetings of the ASEAN Regional Forum, Asia-Pacific Economic Cooperation, and the East Asia Summit. The US indicated its support for strengthening these regional institutions, which meant support for multilateralization of the issues.

The bilateral mechanism at the level of assistant secretary of state and vice minister of foreign affairs was based on the rational actor assumption that the Chinese Foreign Ministry should be the point of contact during a crisis. Working with the Foreign Ministry should strengthen its role to take charge sooner during a crisis.

The rational actor model holds the Chinese Foreign Ministry accountable for all maritime incidents irrespective of which Chinese organization initiated them.

Chinese reported that this mechanism worked as a confidence building measure for them and, in general, Chinese felt much calmer afterwards. Cui Tiankai afterwards reported that the mechanism had achieved more than he had expected. The idea of a trilateral mechanism is still under consideration. In 2011 Chinese were considering a Track 1 Japan–US–China trilateral mechanism with 2+2 format (Ministries of Defense and Foreign Affairs), but preferred to first hold a Track 1.5 trilateral conference before venturing into Track 1.[36] Whether the mechanism is institutionalized sufficiently to survive beyond the Campbell-Cui personal relationship has yet to be seen. By 2013, Campbell had left the US Department of State, and Cui Tiankai had been reassigned as China's ambassador to the US.

Sino-Japanese crisis management mechanisms

The turning point in Sino-Japanese relations occurred in September 2010 with the Japanese Coast Guard arrest of a Chinese fishing boat captain after he rammed his boat into the Japanese boat, near the Diaoyu/Senkaku Islands. It was just one incident in a long series of incidents in the East China Sea, but this one appeared to change the status quo. China and Japan had agreed to joint development of hydrocarbon resources in the East China Sea in June 2008, which might have initiated a conflict resolution process. However, there were no further negotiations on implementing the agreement, and there was no mechanism in place to resolve the 2010 dispute. Wen Jiabao had suggested in June 2010 that Beijing and Tokyo establish a hotline for better communication during a crisis, especially in the East China Sea. Premier Wen wanted to establish a mechanism for maritime crisis management.[37]

The ongoing Chinese debates over maritime strategies, and the inability to devise a unified maritime strategy, leads to the assumption that different views have found different institutional homes. The Ministry of Foreign Affairs (MFA) of Japan, in managing disputes with China over the Diaoyu/Senkaku Islands, has moved toward the bureaucratic politics model in understanding Chinese foreign policy behavior. Japan itself has divided bureaucracies on the issue of China to the point of political immobilism. The Japanese recognized the numerous challenges to the Chinese MFA as new foreign policy actors complicated policy coordination: local level administrations, a more vocal PLA, Chinese national oil companies, and a more nationalistic public (as discussed further in Chapter 3).

Inclusion of local level administrations and center-local differences over maritime strategies draws on an approach to Chinese foreign relations that claims economic decentralization and globalization have led to China's border provinces developing their own distinctive foreign relations initiatives, and at the least, implementing the center's policy unevenly and according to provincial preferences.[38] The Chinese bureaucratic politics model draws on the Chinese historical experience with the problem of *tiaotiao-kuaikuai* [条条块块], where the vertical lines of authority (*tiao*) conflict with the local-provincial level of authority (*kuai*), and neither has authority over the other.

Chinese analysis of the need for Sino-Japanese crisis management mechanisms claims that the appropriate mechanism should be based on mutual understanding of each other's crisis behavior and management modes. One Chinese analyst felt that Sino-Japanese bilateral crisis management helped in de-escalating a crisis. The Chinese analyst suggested the use of a multilevel, multichannel mechanism.[39]

Japanese recognition of China's search for a maritime strategy was published by the National Institute for Defense Studies (NIDS) in the *NIDS China Security Report 2011*. According to the report, China's large number of maritime agencies, each with its own management system, needed to be rationalized with a "basic ocean law" that defined each agency's responsibilities. The law was a prerequisite for devising a comprehensive maritime strategy but there was too much competition between maritime agencies and too many conflicts over jurisdiction, including competition to take the lead in formulating a maritime strategy.[40]

Some analysts argue that a formal mechanism is not needed due to an institutionalized pattern in Sino-Japanese disputes over the Diaoyu/Senkaku Islands. There have been repeated rounds of incidents since 1968, with a predictable pattern: an escalation phase led by ultranationalist activists and politicians, and a de-escalation phase led by both leaderships using reciprocity and bargaining.[41] This pattern over time contributed to institutionalization of dispute resolution, although no formal mechanism was created. The September 2010 incident appeared to break this pattern of reliance on leadership bargaining.

In September 2010, it was Japan that changed the old pattern. Japan could have chased the fishing boat away as it had routinely done in the past. However, Coast Guard Minister Seiji Maehara, entrepreneurial and rightist, decided to arrest the Chinese captain. The Japanese government at the time was divided, with the prime minister distracted by domestic politics. The prime minister hesitated to approve Maehara's initiative but then acquiesced to it.[42]

This local level maritime incident became a serious diplomatic crisis between China and Japan. In an environment of China's broadly evolving strategic priorities, Beijing and Tokyo rapidly escalated rhetoric and threat perceptions, with both sides reading strategic intent into the incident. Japanese rightist politicians took a hard line, linking it to a Chinese shift from coastal defense to offshore defense. *Asahi Shimbun*, in an alarmist manner, linked the East China Sea incident with incidents in the South China Sea.[43] Shinzo Abe linked the incident to an assumed Chinese grand strategy, claiming China had a more assertive policy over territorial disputes because of "Lebensraum" in its Near Seas.[44]

Prime Minister Naoto Kan appointed Maehara foreign minister, perceived by Beijing as a reward for Maehara changing the status quo. A Japanese crew member had filmed the incident and secretly given the videotape to members of the Diet. In November 2010, the videotape was posted on YouTube by a coast guard official, further inflaming Japanese public opinion.

More moderate Japanese analysts questioned Japan's departure from the status quo, and criticized the linkage of the Daioyu/Senkaku incident with incidents in the South China Sea. They felt it was unnecessary to securitize a fishing boat incident into a "world-level maritime dispute."[45] The US may have played a mediating role in the dispute, while China and Japan came out of the crisis looking more belligerent.[46] This US mediating role demonstrated the need for a trilateral framework for crisis management.

At the September 23–24, 2010, Singapore Global Dialogue, former Chinese Foreign Minister Tang Jiaxuan claimed Japan had initiated the incident because it harbored a strategic intent, "a special agenda," while China had merely reacted to Japan's change in the status quo. Former Deputy Foreign Minister Hitoshi Tanaka denied strategic intent, insisting that the incident was an "accident" that was influenced by a political transition in Japan.[47] Japanese acknowledgment of domestic politics as a factor emphasized that Japanese bureaucratic politics explained the September 2010 events.

At a May 2011 Track 2 conference, Chinese, Americans, Japanese, and others shared views on common maritime security interests such as sea lines of communication (SLOC) security and nontraditional security issues. Admiral Yang Yi stated that China did not yet have a national maritime strategy but it did have a separate SLOC strategy, a South China Sea strategy, and a Taiwan strategy. On the need for a mechanism for crisis management, a Chinese participant noted that even if Japan and China could agree on the formation of a mechanism, "it is not clear which agency within the Chinese government would have the authority to settle the issue."[48]

At the Track 2 Beijing-Tokyo Forum in August 2011, Tang Jiaxuan stated the two countries "should establish a crisis management mechanism to prevent unexpected maritime incidents."[49] Zhang Tuosheng commented that "the mechanism needs to be multi-level, involving national leaders, the foreign ministries, the defense ministries and think tanks in both countries, and should focus on crisis prevention more than conflict resolution."[50] This kind of multilevel mechanism would not require better domestic coordination on the Chinese side in the form of a national security council, and would anticipate that continuous unexpected incidents, initiated by local actors, would be the norm.

Japan's Foreign Minister Koichiro Gemba formally proposed a bilateral mechanism for maritime issues and the East China Sea in late November 2011 to Premier Wen Jiabao.[51] In mid-December, Gemba announced Japan's hope to create a trilateral Japan–US–China dialogue that would be part of a multilayered regional network that would not exclude China. Secretary of State Hillary Clinton supported the trilateral concept.[52] In December 2011, during Prime Minister Yoshihiko Noda's trip to Beijing, China and Japan signed an agreement to create a maritime crisis management mechanism, which would be referred to as the "Japan-China High-Level Consultation on Maritime Affairs." Beijing and Tokyo also agreed in principle to the "Japan-China Maritime Search and Rescue Cooperation."

The mechanism is a multilevel mechanism, involving representatives from numerous agencies: foreign ministry officials, defense ministry officials, agencies representing fisheries and energy, and coast guards. This mechanism was designed for a bureaucratic politics model where center-local coordination is still lacking and civil-military differences are ongoing.

As Sino-Japanese tensions rose in spring 2012 over the Diaoyu/Senkaku Islands, there was no mention of the multilevel mechanism. In March 2012, Yin

Zhuo noted that disputes in the Near Seas would not be resolved by military means but rather through diplomatic, legal and economic means.[53] Luo Yuan called for the formation of a Chinese coast guard for the Near Seas that would unify the numerous civilian maritime agencies that operated under lax coordination, and also called for a special South China Sea administrative zone.[54]

The possibility of de-escalation appeared with the announcement that General Guo Boxiong, vice chairman of China's Central Military Commission, planned to visit Japan in April 2012 to meet with Japan's defense minister and prime minister to try to restart military exchanges that had been stopped after the September 2010 incident.[55] The Chinese military's preference appeared to focus on military-to-military rather than to draw on the newly created multilevel crisis management mechanism. General Guo's visit was subsequently postponed due to Japan's military preparations for the North Korean missile launch in mid-April 2012.

An indication that de-escalation might begin was Tokyo's announcement on April 5, 2012, that it would convene the first meeting of the multilevel crisis management mechanism in late May.[56] To arrange for the May 2012 meeting, the Japanese Foreign Minister Koichiro Gemba and Chinese Foreign Minister Yang Jiechi met on April 7, 2012. The possibility of a Japan-US-China dialogue was broached by Gemba. According to the Japanese Foreign Ministry's website, "Minister Gemba referred to Japan's expectation to hold a Japan-US-China dialogue as soon as possible. Mr. Yang replied that China was now studying the matter in earnest."[57]

The multilevel crisis management mechanism met in Hangzhou on May 16, 2012. Chinese and Japanese officials discussed maritime security and the Diaoyu/Senkaku issue, referred to as the Japan-China High-Level Consultation on Maritime Affairs [海上危机管理机制, or 海事に関する日本と中国のハイレベル協議]. A Chinese Foreign Ministry spokesman expressed China's hope that the mechanism would be an effective platform for managing bilateral maritime affairs. Chinese experts on maritime law felt the new mechanism could resolve maritime disputes.[58]

Just before the mechanism would meet for the first time, Japanese rightists promoted a meeting of the World Uyghur Congress in Tokyo, and a subsequent visit to the Yasukuni Shrine by the Uyghur delegates.[59] Ignoring this provocation, the Japan-China High-Level Consultation on Maritime Affairs was held nevertheless, and the two sides agreed to meet again at the end of 2012 in Japan.

According to Japanese reports, the May 2012 multilevel meeting achieved a Japanese goal, which was to establish contact with representatives from the five Chinese maritime law enforcement agencies. Japanese felt there was no clear division of labor and responsibilities among them, and no clear line of authority over them, which left them embroiled in a nasty power struggle and turf war. Because of this organizational chaos, Japanese felt these five maritime agencies, when they appeared in the vicinity of the Senkaku, were not under clear lines of authority from Beijing.[60] The International Crisis Group had made a similar analysis on China in the South China Sea – it was the lack of coordination among the five maritime agencies that produced increasing Chinese assertiveness over territorial claims.[61]

Japanese Foreign Minister Gemba, at his press conference following the meeting, indicated that the multilayered mechanism was important, stating, "both Japan and China have seven, eight, or nine such organizations. It is important that those organizations can communicate well to prevent accidental incidents . . . all these maritime organizations come together in one forum, for close communication each other" within the multilayered crisis management mechanism.[62]

On June 23, 2012, the Sino-Japanese Friendship Association met in Shanghai, with Tang Jiaxuan attending as President of the Association. Some brainstorming took place on how to establish confidence building measures (CBM). The meeting called for a maritime crisis management mechanism to be institutionalized as soon as possible, one that would contain disputes within a controllable range. In particular, the group thought a hotline should be established quickly to facilitate a rapid response to a maritime crisis.[63]

On July 27, 2012, Prime Minister Noda hinted at using force, the Japanese Self-Defense Forces, to guard the Diaoyu/Senkaku Islands.[64] However, Chief Cabinet Secretary Osamu Fujimura clarified that Noda was only responding to a hypothetical or theoretical possibility, and stressed the importance of using a regular crisis management mechanism instead of using force.[65]

Ken Jimbo, a professor at Keio University, criticized the Japanese government for being so slow in responding to the problem. Two years had passed since the September 2010 fishing trawler incident, and the government had still not developed a domestic crisis management mechanism. He claimed that tensions had escalated because of the failure to establish a functioning bilateral dispute mechanism. The old-style methods of managing Sino-Japanese relations, close personal relations and personal communication channels between Chinese and Japanese leaders, no longer were functional, but nothing had been created to fill the vacuum. Thus, as a strategic priority a mechanism was needed that would function as the personal ties had once done.[66]

China also continued to rely on older organizational forms, despite the fact the Leading Group on Coastal Defense had not satisfactorily coordinated the numerous maritime actors in China's Near Seas, and the Leading Group's *xitong* (system under the Leading Group) appeared to be not functioning. Rather than create a new type of mechanism such as a national security council, the Chinese solution was to create a new Leading Group – the Leading Group for Maritime Security. Despite its shortcomings, there was no indication that Beijing's leaders realized the Leading Group system itself needed reorganization. Leading Groups are policy-making groups for the Central Committee of the CCP, assuring the CCP control over policy, and are being increasingly used in foreign policy issues.

In mid-2012, Xi Jinping was put in charge of the new Leading Group for Maritime Security that would govern the Near Seas and the numerous incidents between China, Japan, the Philippines, and Vietnam. By September 2012, Xi was in charge of the "Office to Respond to the Diaoyu Crisis," which also included Dai Binguo and senior military officials. It was within this office that foreign observers believe Beijing's senior civilian and military leadership carefully escalated Chinese maritime forces in the Diaoyu crisis of autumn 2012 in a step-by-step approach that could be explained by the rational actor model. Other analysts claim Xi did not attend meetings after November 2012 when he was appointed CCP general secretary and became too busy, implying central control might not have been that strong.[67]

Bilateral expectations that the China-Japan mechanism might be functional continued in 2012. In the summer of 2012, as Sino-Japanese relations worsened over territorial disputes, a Track 1.5 seminar was held on August 29, 2012, to commemorate the 40th anniversary of the normalization of China-Japan relations. This seminar was organized and supported by the Japanese embassy, the Japan Foundation, the Institute of Japanese Studies of the Chinese Academy of Social Sciences, the Chinese Association for Japanese Studies, and the National Assembly of the Japanese Economy from Tokyo.[68] The seminar found both sides calling for "a crisis management mechanism to cool down the heated bilateral spats."[69] The seminar referred to the first meeting of the Sino-Japanese crisis management mechanism in May 2012 and hoped a second meeting would be held at the end of 2012. *China Daily* quoted an unnamed scholar as stating "the weakened strategic mutual trust of the Japan–US–China trilateral ties is in 'desperate need' of crisis management."[70] Hideo Tarumi, minister of political affairs at the Japanese embassy in China, called for the use of the crisis management mechanism as a means to ease tensions that he claimed was absent during the current crisis. He worried about the mechanism's "breakdown."[71]

In September 2012, the Japan Institute of International Affairs (JIIA) (affiliated with the MFA) presented recommendations to the Japanese MFA on what actions should be taken to keep the Senkaku situation under control. One of the JIIA recommendations was for the Japanese government to more seriously follow up on the May 2012 meeting of the Japan-China High-Level Consultation on Maritime Affairs in order to develop maritime CBMs and crisis management mechanisms.[72]

Despite the mechanism not yet being institutionalized, the Japanese media claimed the mechanism was being violated in October 2012. The *Sankei Shimbun* claimed Chinese ships passing through the Miyako Strait without prior notification had violated agreements made within the May 2012 meeting for a crisis management mechanism. The Chinese Ministry of Defense denied the existence of the maritime crisis mechanism.[73] There in fact was no violation of international law by the Chinese ships as they passed through international waters, which Japanese Foreign Minister Gemba later confirmed.

The idea of a mechanism was mentioned again during Chen Jian's talk to the Foreign Correspondents' Club of Hong Kong on October 30, 2012. Chen is a former ambassador to Japan and former under-secretary general of the United Nations. His talk had been organized by the Chinese MFA with several Chinese diplomats in attendance. Chen claimed there was a need for China and Japan to form a mechanism to avoid maritime incidents or clashes near the Diaoyu Islands between their patrol vessels. He offered several principles on how to resolve the crisis. Chen claimed that Beijing did not seek to recover all lost territory but instead would engage in give-and-take, and called for the US to urge Japan to come to the negotiating table. The first priority for negotiations would be to form the mechanism to prevent maritime clashes.[74]

At the December 28, 2012, Lanting Forum, *Asahi Shimbun* quoted Chinese Vice Foreign Minister Zhang Zhijun as stating, "China and Japan should find crisis management methods through dialogue." *Asahi* claimed that Zhang was willing to create a framework that might prevent clashes around the Diaoyu/Senkaku Islands from escalating into a military clash.[75] The official transcript of Zhang's presentation only mentions the need for Beijing and Tokyo to have negotiations and consultations.[76]

In January 2013, General Shigeru Iwasaki, chief of staff of Japan's Self-Defense Force Joint Staff, stressed the need for a maritime contact mechanism especially in the case of an emergency. He emphasized that Tokyo had "never closed our window for dialogue and defense exchanges."[77] General Iwasaki was concerned that "unintended scuffles" could escalate into "full-scale crises" without the mechanism.

On January 30, 2013, a Chinese frigate locked its radar onto a Japanese destroyer – usually a prelude to an attack. The Chinese Defense Ministry claimed it was normal surveillance and denied fire control radar was used. This radar "lock-on" incident represented a significant escalation of the conflict. Some accounts of the incident portrayed the local commander of the frigate as acting independently. Some Japanese scholars thought Xi had given his approval only after the incident, implying civilian control over the military was weak.[78] Other accounts claimed there were electronic intercepts indicating Xi Jinping, as head of the Leading Group for Maritime Security, was personally in control of the Chinese side during the incident.[79]

In February 2013, after the radar lock-on incident, Japan's Parliamentary Secretary for Defense Masahisa Sato stated that the initiative for a crisis mechanism had been stalled since June 2012, although Japanese and Chinese foreign ministry officials continued to try to restart the talks.[80] It was the Japanese MFA that had promoted the multilayered mechanism based on a bureaucratic politics model with the assumption that the Chinese MFA is not in full control of all Chinese maritime actors.

The Japanese Ministry of Defense had a different explanation as to why Chinese local level civilian maritime and military agencies appeared uncoordinated. A NIDS report argued that the apparent lack of coordination between Chinese local level civilian and military maritime agencies did not mean there was no control by the center. The CCP had strong top-down operational control over both the civilian and military local level. The problem was that civilian and military agencies did not have good local level coordination because of this CCP control.[81] The NIDS analysis focused more on policy implementation within a Leninist party-state rather than bureaucratic politics. However, many analysts argue that the PLA is straining under the traditional arrangement of party control.[82] Government "stovepiping" is standard in Leninist systems, where vertically organized government agencies do not communicate with one another.

Two American scholars in February 2013 suggested a list of CBMs that Tokyo and Beijing should consider as a means to de-escalate the Diaoyu/Senkaku crisis.

The list included restarting the crisis management mechanism begun in 2012, something Tokyo had repeatedly called for but Beijing had resisted, although both sides recognized the need for a mechanism.[83]

On April 26, 2013, Japanese and Chinese defense officials met for the first time since September 2012. The Japanese participants, motivated by the radar lock-on incident, urged the Chinese to build a "bilateral maritime communications mechanism for crisis management" as soon as possible.[84] That same day a Chinese Foreign Ministry spokeswoman, Hua Chunying, labeled the Diaoyu Islands a "core interest" of China for the first time.[85] The Foreign Ministry later retreated from that claim, expunging reference to core interest from the written transcript, although the official recording still contained it.[86] This mixed message implied Chinese policy on the Diaoyu was subject to bureaucratic infighting that made a unified statement difficult.

Recognizing the need for command-and-control reform, Beijing had announced a reorganization of maritime agencies in March 2013. Four of the civilian maritime agencies would be placed under the State Oceanic Administration (SOA), and formed into a Chinese Coast Guard including China Marine Surveillance (already under the SOA), the Border Control Department, the Fisheries Law Enforcement Command, and the General Administration of Customs. The Maritime Safety Administration remained under the Ministry of Transportation. This Chinese Coast Guard would not be under the command of the provincial border defense force.

On July 22, 2013, Beijing announced the SOA had been reorganized and the new Chinese Coast Guard had gone into operation. The Coast Guard was more heavily armed than the previous maritime agencies with a greater capacity for patrolling disputed waters. Within days, Chinese Coast Guard ships were spotted near the Diaoyu/Senkaku Islands.[87] Zhang Junshe, military researcher often on China Central Television and in the *PLA Daily*, thought administrative reform would strengthen maritime management and command and control with unified maritime law enforcement, which would better protect Chinese maritime rights. Zhang also thought it would further international cooperation with the US, Japanese, and South Korean coast guards.[88] With the coast guard, Chinese capacity to pressure Japan would be stronger, but the US and Japan would be better able to hold Beijing accountable for the actions of the new coast guard.

An international conference on the new Chinese Coast Guard, cohosted by the China Institute of International Studies and the University of California Institute of Global Conflict and Cooperation, brought together numerous organizations including China Maritime Safety Administration, Chinese MFA, SOA of China, the US Coast Guard, and the US Naval War College.[89] Japanese participation was not apparent although Japan had a strong interest in the new Coast Guard.

This bureaucratic unification would strengthen China's capacity for a stronger, more coordinated response in the East China Sea. However, it would only slightly change the structure of the China-Japan crisis management mechanism. There would be fewer civilian maritime agencies to deal with, but the civil-military coordination issue would remain.

Conclusion

This chapter has focused on the years 2010–13 because of China's perceived assertiveness at this time and the sporadic maritime incidents in China's Near Seas. These maritime incidents were the drivers for greater institutionalization in the form of maritime crisis mechanisms in Japan-China relations. Japanese drew on the bureaucratic politics model of foreign policy making, assuming the absence of a coherent Chinese maritime strategy. This was based on the ongoing Chinese domestic debates over maritime strategies and core interests, and center-local bureaucratic differences and civil-military organizational differences. The challenge of China's evolving strategic priorities was apparent.

The numerous times the crisis management mechanism was brought up during China-Japan tensions over the Diaoyu/Senkaku Island dispute is in contrast to the fragility of the mechanism that had not yet been institutionalized. Japanese government frequently mentioned the new and not yet institutionalized mechanism but with sporadic interest by Chinese officials, who only occasionally mentioned it.

Instead, the Chinese and Japanese governments relied on the old style of conflict resolution, drawing on personal ties between former leaders in visits during 2012 and 2013, and relied on back channel diplomacy, but this had no apparent impact on the escalating tensions. The appointment of Wang Yi, former ambassador to Japan, as China's foreign minister appears to be an effort to revive the old-style method of leadership ties. Wang Yi, a Japan specialist fluent in Japanese, is expected to repair leadership ties.

In summer 2013, Chinese analysts continued to call for the Chinese leadership to further develop the "basic principles and policies of crisis management" and to further develop awareness of the importance of a mechanism as a tool to prevent war.[90] Especially in relations with the US and Japan, Chinese analysts have called on the leadership to strengthen crisis management mechanisms – domestic, bilateral, and multilateral.[91] The hoped-for domestic mechanism would be a national security council.

Despite analytical discussions of the need for domestic and bilateral mechanisms, the Chinese leadership appeared to rely on older styles of governance that maintained CCP control, such as Politburo study sessions and the Leading Group for Maritime Security led by Xi Jinping.

On July 30, 2013, Xi Jinping led a study session of the Politburo of the Communist Party of China. The session discussed construction of a roadmap for China's transition to emergence as a maritime power.[92] This was the Politburo's 8th study session, an indication that China had not yet achieved consensus on a coherent and comprehensive maritime strategy. The session heard reports from China National Offshore Oil Corporation and the SOA. Xi stressed using peaceful negotiations with other countries, identifying common or converging interests, while never giving up China's maritime core national interests.[93] There was no announcement of a maritime strategy.

Given the diverging models that the US and Japan use with China, which has resulted in different configurations for crisis management mechanisms, the construction of a Japan–US–China trilateral crisis management mechanism would need to contend with these differences. As a strategic priority a trilateral mechanism should recognize escalating tensions as a consequence of bureaucratic politics but strive for a rational actor model as an ideal that promotes de-escalation.

Notes

1 L. Mingjiang, *Chinese Debates of South China Sea Policy: Implications for Future Developments*, RSIS Working Paper no. 239, 17 May 2012.
2 Y. Hailin, 'Safety at Sea', *Beijing Review*, 15 April 2009.
3 C.H. Sharman, *China Moves Out: Stepping Stones toward a New Maritime Strategy*, China Strategic Perspectives 9, Washington, DC: National Defense University, April 2015.
4 Y. Hailin, 'Securing SLOCs by Cooperation – China's Perspective of Maritime Security in the Indian Ocean', International Maritime Conference 3, National Maritime Policy Research Center, Bahria University Karachi, Pakistan, 7 March 2009, <www.iapscass.cn/english/Articles/showcontent.asp?id=1233> (accessed 12 June 2015).
5 Z. Daojiong, 'Localizing the South China Sea Problem: The Case of China's Hainan', *Pacific Review*, vol. 14, no. 4, December 2001, pp. 575–98.
6 L.J. Goldstein, 'Five Dragons Stirring Up the Sea: Challenge and Opportunity in China's Improving Maritime Enforcement Capabilities', China Maritime Study, no. 5, Newport, RI: China Maritime Studies Institute, U.S. Naval War College, April 2010.
7 Chinese interlocutor, East Asia Security Symposium and Conference, Beijing, June 2011.
8 Ibid.
9 'Change Tack with Sea Strategy: China Experts', *China Daily*, 13 May 2009.
10 Information Office of China's State Council. *China National Defense White Paper 2010*, released 31 March 2011, pp. 15–16, <www.china.org.cn/government/whitepaper/node_7114675.htm> (accessed 12 June 2015).
11 高新生. 中国共产党领导集体海防思想研究 (1949–2009) [G. Xinsheng, *Study on Coastal Defence Thought for the Chinese Communist Party's Leading Group*]. (北京市: 时事出版社, 2010).
12 R. Hsiao, 'Military Delegates Call for National Maritime Strategy to Protect Expanding Interests', *China Brief*, vol. 11, no. 4, 10 March 2011, <www.jamestown.org/single/?no_cache=1&tx_ttnews%5Btt_news%5D=37629#.VfjnphGqpBc> (accessed 23 March 2011).
13 'Military Call for National Maritime Strategy to Protect Expanding Interests', *People's Daily*, 14 March 2011.
14 L. Goldstein, 'Chinese Naval Strategy in the South China Sea: An Abundance of Noise and Smoke, But Little Fire', *Contemporary Southeast Asia*, vol. 33, no. 3, December 2011, pp. 320–47.
15 International Crisis Group, 'Stirring Up the South China Sea, Part I', Asia Report no. 223, 23 April 2012, pp. 32–33.
16 Y. Mingjie, *Global Review October 2011*, Shanghai Institute of International Studies, (accessed 12 June 2015).
17 'Hu Calls for Building China into Maritime Power', *China Daily*, 8 November 2012.
18 T. Fravel, 'Maritime Security in the South China Sea and the Competition over Maritime Rights', in Patrick Cronin (ed.), *Cooperation from Strength: The United States, China and the South China Sea*, Washington DC: Center for a New American Security, January 2012, pp. 33–50, <http://taylorfravel.com/documents/research/fravel.2012.CNAS.maritime.security.SCS.pdf>; A. Erickson and G. Collins, 'Year of The Water Dragon: 12 Chinese Maritime Developments to Look for in 2012', China Realtime Report, *Wall Street Journal*, 23 January 2012 (accessed 12 June 2015).

19 Admiral M. Mullen, Chairman, Joint Chiefs of Staff, 'U.S.-China Relations: Security and the Military-to-Military Exchange', Washington, DC: Center for American Progress, 1 December 2010.
20 Admiral M. Mullen, 'A Step Toward Trust with China', *New York Times*, 25 July 2011.
21 X. Liping, 'Crisis Management in China and in the United States: A Comparative Study', in M.D. Swaine and T. Zhang (eds.), *Managing Sino-American Crises: Case Studies and Analysis*, Washington, DC: Carnegie Endowment for International Peace, 30 November 2006, pp. 156–59.
22 M. Swaine, 'Understanding the Historical Record', in Swaine and Zhang (eds.), *Managing Sino-American Crises*, pp. 4–8.
23 W. Xinbo, 'Understanding Chinese and US Crisis Behavior', *Washington Quarterly*, vol. 31, no. 1, Winter 2007–8, p. 62.
24 Ibid., p. 66.
25 Ibid., p. 72.
26 W. Jisi and X. Hui, 'Pattern of Sino-American Crises: A Chinese Perspective', in Swaine and Zhang (eds.), *Managing Sino-American Crises*, pp. 143–44.
27 Y. Fu, 'What Will China's National Security Commission Actually Do?', *Foreign Policy*, 8 May 2014, <http://foreignpolicy.com/2014/05/08/what-will-chinas-national-security-commission-actually-do/> (accessed 4 June 2015).
28 W. Xinbo, 'Understanding Chinese and US Crisis Behavior', p. 71.
29 N. Li, 'Chinese Civil-Military Relations in the Post-Deng Era: Implications for Crisis Management and Naval Modernization', China Maritime Study, no. 4, Newport, RI: China Maritime Studies Institute, U.S. Naval War College, January 2010.
30 D.M. Finkelstein, 'Introduction', in D.M. Finkelstein and K. Gunness (eds.), *Civil-Military Relations in Today's China: Swimming in a New Sea*, Armonk, NY: M.E. Sharpe, 2007, xii–xv.
31 S. Dingli, 'Incrementally Stabilizing China-US Relations at the 2011 S&ED', *Asia-Pacific Bulletin*, no. 112, 20 May 2011, <www.eastwestcenter.org/publications/incrementally-stabilizing-china-us-relations-2011-sed> (accessed 12 June 2015).
32 'China Decries Any U.S. Involvement in Japan Dispute', *Reuters*, 2 November 2010.
33 Chinese interlocutor, East Asia Security Symposium and Conference, Beijing, June 2011.
34 Chinese interlocutor, East Asia Security Symposium and Conference, Beijing, June 2011.
35 Ministry of Foreign Affairs of the PRC. *Remarks by State Councilor Dai Bingguo at Joint Press Conference of the Third Round of the China-US Strategic and Economic Dialogues*, Washington, DC, 10 May 2011, <www.fmprc.gov.cn/eng/wjdt/zyjh/t823968.htm> (accessed 12 June 2015).
36 Chinese interlocutor, East Asia Security Symposium and Conference, Beijing, June 2011.
37 A. Rowley, 'Looking Beyond the Obvious: Few Reports Have Mentioned the Extraordinary Context in Which the Recent Sino-Japanese Spat Has Taken Place', *Business Times Singapore*, 29 September 2010.
38 A.I. Johnston and R.S. Ross, *New Directions in the Study of China's Foreign Policy*, Stanford, CA: Stanford University Press, 2006, p. 410.
39 矫正, 中日关系:结构冲突还是博弈合作——从危机管理的视角进行分析, 长春理工大学学报(社会科学版) [J. Zheng, 'Sino-Japan Relations: Structural Conflict or Gambling Collaboration – Analyzing from the Perspective of Crisis Management', *Journal of Changchun University of Science and Technology*, Social Sciences Edition], vol. 2, no. 1, January 2009, pp. 8–10.
40 National Institute for Defense Studies, Japan (NIDS), *NIDS China Security Report 2011*, Tokyo: NIDS, February 2012, pp. 12–14.
41 M.G. Koo, *Island Disputes and Maritime Regime Building in East Asia: Between a Rock and a Hard Place*, New York: Springer, 2009, pp. 103–36.

42 Y. Tiberghien, 'The Diaoyu Crisis of 2010: Domestic Games and Diplomatic Conflict', *Harvard Asia Quarterly*, vol. 12, no. 3/4, p. 74.
43 'Seas Fill with Tension over China's Moves', *Asahi Shimbun*, 2 October 2010.
44 'China Seeking "Lebensraum", Says Abe,' *AFP*, 19 October 2011.
45 T. Sakai, 'Rekindling China-Japan Conflict: The Senkaku/Diaoyutai Islands Clash', *Japan Focus*, September 2010, <http://japanfocus.org/-Tanaka-Sakai/3418> (translation by K. Selden from *Tanaka News* on 17 September 2010 with a follow-up story on 21 September 2010) (accessed 12 June 2015).
46 W. Xiangwei, 'Diaoyu Dispute Marks a Win for Washington', *South China Morning Post*, 27 September 2010.
47 Y.R. Kassim, 'Singapore Global Dialogue: Heated Start to Strategic Debates', RSIS Commentaries, No. 123/2010, 27 September 2010.
48 'Maritime Strategy: Security and Governance', organized by Carnegie-Tsinghua Center and Institute for Asia Pacific Studies, May 2011, Shanghai, <http://carnegietsinghua.org/events/?fa=3558> (accessed 12 June 2015).
49 'Crisis Management Mechanism Will Enhance Mutual Trust', *China Daily*, 22 August 2011.
50 Ibid.
51 'Japan to Propose Crisis Mechanism', *Global Times*, 24 November 2011.
52 'Gemba Hoping to Launch Japan-China-U.S. Trilateral Dialogue', *Mainichi*, 15 December 2011.
53 'China Navy Officer Rejects Joint Development Agreement,' *Asahi Shimbun*, 7 March 2012, <http://ajw.asahi.com/article/behind_news/AJ201203070027> (accessed 12 June 2015).
54 'Coast Guard Needed for Maritime Disputes', *China Daily*, 5 March 2012, <www.chinadaily.com.cn/china/2012–03/06/content_14762729.htm> (accessed 12 June 2015).
55 M. Chan, 'Military Visit to Japan Amid Diaoyus Tension. General's Trip Seen as Part of High-Level Exchanges, with Both Sides Hoping to Understand Other's Stance', *South China Morning Post*, 24 March 2012.
56 'Japan, China to Begin High-Level Maritime Talks', *Japan Times*, 5 April 2012.
57 Ministry of Foreign Affairs of Japan, *Japan-China Foreign Ministers' Meeting (Overview)*, 23 April 2012, <www.mofa.go.jp/announce/jfpu/2012/04/0423–01.html> (accessed 12 June 2015).
58 Y. Jingjie, 'China, Japan Start Sea Talks', *Global Times*, 16 May 2012, <www.globaltimes.cn/NEWS/tabid/99/ID/709685/China-Japan-start-sea-talks.aspx> (accessed 12 June 2015).
59 'Japan's Tough Posture Masks Its Weakness', *Global Times*, 16 May 2012, <www.globaltimes.cn/NEWS/tabid/99/ID/709669/Japans-tough-posture-masks-its-weakness.aspx> (accessed 12 June 2015).
60 'China's Brooding "Dragons" Complicate Standoffs at Sea', *Sentaku Magazine, Japan Times*, 12 June 2012.
61 International Crisis Group, 'Stirring Up the South China Sea: Part I', *Asia Report*, no. 223, 23 April 2012, <www.crisisgroup.org/en/regions/asia/north-east-asia/china/223-stirring-up-the-south-china-sea-i.aspx> (accessed 12 June 2015).
62 Ministry of Foreign Affairs of Japan, 'Press Conference by Minister for Foreign Affairs Koichiro Gemba', 16 May 2012, <www.mofa.go.jp/announce/fm_press/2012/5/0516_01.html> (accessed 12 June 2015).
63 中国学者：中日两国应建立海上危机管理机制　中国海洋报　2012年08月24日, ['Chinese scholars: China and Japan should establish a maritime crisis management mechanism', 24 August 2012, *China Ocean News*], <http://news.ifeng.com/mil/4/detail_2012_08/24/17073484_0.shtml> (accessed 12 June 2015).
64 'Noda Hints at Using SDF to Defend Senkaku Islands', *Asahi Shimbun*, 27 July 2012, <http://ajw.asahi.com/article/behind_news/politics/AJ201207270060> (accessed 12 June 2015).

65 'Using Self-Defense Forces Only Theoretical Possibility: Japan's Gov't Spokesperson', *English.news.cn*, 27 July 2012, <http://big5.xinhuanet.com/gate/big5/news.xinhuanet.com/english/world/2012–07/27/c_131743697.htm> (accessed 12 June 2015).
66 K. Jimbo, 'The Crumbling of Japan's Status Quo Management', *CNN.com*, 24 August 2012, <http://globalpublicsquare.blogs.cnn.com/2012/08/24/the-crumbling-of-japans-status-quo-management/> (accessed 12 June 2015).
67 L. Jakobson, 'How Involved Is Xi Jinping in the Diaoyu Crisis?', *Diplomat*, 8 February 2013.
68 'Uphold Larger Interest and Manage Crisis for Sound and Steady Development of China-Japan Relations', 30 August 2012, <www.fmprc.gov.cn/eng/zxxx/t980262.htm> (accessed 12 June 2015).
69 'Trust Highlighted in Beijing Forum', *China Daily*, 30 August 2012, <www.chinadaily.com.cn/china/2012–08/30/content_15718113.htm> (accessed 12 June 2015).
70 Q. Zhongwei and Z. Yunbi, 'China Vows to Defend Islands,' *China Daily*, 31 August 2012.
71 'Trust Highlighted in Beijing Forum,' *China Daily*, 30 August 2012, <www.chinadaily.com.cn/china/2012–08/30/content_15718113.htm> (accessed 12 June 2015).
72 'The Senkakus: Actions to Keep the Situation under Control', 24 September 2012, by the Japan Institute of International Affairs (JIIA). In the light of current situation surrounding the Senkaku Islands, JIIA has presented the following recommendations to the government of Japan. The JIIA is under the Japanese Foreign Ministry. <www2.jiia.or.jp/en/pdf/polcy_report/20120924e-recommendations.pdf> (accessed 12 June 2015).
73 'China Says No Japan Maritime Deal in Place', *crienglish.com*, 10 October 2012, <http://english.cri.cn/6909/2012/10/10/2982s726293.htm> (accessed 12 June 2015).
74 'FCC Club Lunch with Ambassador Chen Jian', 30 October 2012, <http://fcchk.org/event/2012–10–30-fcc-club-lunch-ambassador-chen-jian> (accessed 12 June 2015).
75 N. Hayashi, 'Chinese Think Tank: Conflict Inevitable between Japan, China over Senkakus', *Asahi Shimbun*, 31 December 2012.
76 'Stay Committed to Peaceful Development and Win-Win Cooperation', Speech by Vice Foreign Minister Z. Zhijun at the Eighth Lanting Forum of the Ministry of Foreign Affairs, 28 December 2012, <www.fmprc.gov.cn/eng/topics/lantingluntan/t1001499.htm> (accessed 12 June 2015).
77 Y. Hayashi, 'Japanese General Seeks to Reinforce Defenses', *Wall Street Journal*, 13 January 2013.
78 M. Matsumura, 'Praetorian China?', *Project Syndicate*, 26 April 2013, <www.project-syndicate.org/commentary/china-s-loss-of-civilian-control-over-the-military-by-masahiro-matsumura> (accessed 12 June 2015).
79 J. Garnaut, 'Leader's Ploy More than Naval Gazing', *Sydney Morning Herald*, 27 April 2013, <www.smh.com.au/world/leaders-ploy-more-than-naval-gazing-20130426–2ijxx.html> (accessed 12 June 2015).
80 A. Martin, 'Tokyo Seeks Military Hot Line to Beijing', *Wall Street Journal*, 13 February 2013.
81 National Institute of Defense Studies, Japan Ministry of Defense, *NIDS China Security Report 2012*, Tokyo, December 2012.
82 J. Mulvenon, 'Straining Against the Yoke? Civil-Military Relations in China after the Seventeenth Party Congress', in C. Li (ed.), *China's Changing Political Landscape: Prospects for Democracy*, Washington, DC: Brookings Institution, 2008, pp. 267–79.
83 J.J. Przystup and P.C. Saunders, 'Time for China and Japan to Cool It', *Yale Global Online*, 27 February 2013, <http://yaleglobal.yale.edu/content/time-china-and-japan-cool-it> (accessed 12 June 2015).
84 'Japan, China Defense Officials Eye Maritime Hotline', *Japan Times*, 27 April 2013.
85 'China Officially Labels Senkakus a "Core Interest"', *Kyodo*, 27 April 2013.
86 'China-Japan Island Dispute Could Become Flashpoint', *Defensenews.com*, 4 May 2013.

87 'Coastguard Vessels Make First Foray to Diaoyus', *South China Morning Post*, 25 July 2013, <www.scmp.com/news/china/article/1290052/coast-guard-vessels-make-first-foray-diaoyus> (accessed 12 June 2015).

88 喜看'九龙'归一 张军社 [Zhang Junshe, 'Enjoying Watching the "Nine Dragons" Normalized'], *PLA Daily*, <www.chinamil.com.cn/jfjbmap/content/2013-07/23/content_43892.htm> (accessed 12 June 2015).

89 *Northeast Asia Maritime Safety Cooperation Project Held in CIIS*, 18 July 2013, <www.ciis.org.cn/english/2013-07/18/content_6132639.htm> (accessed 12 June 2015). J. Perlez, 'Chinese, with Revamped Force, Make Presence Known in East China Sea', *New York Times*, 27 July 2013, <www.nytimes.com/2013/07/28/world/asia/chinese-with-revamped-force-make-presence-known-in-east-china-sea.html?_r=0> (accessed 12 June 2015).

90 Z. Tuosheng, 'What Should China Do in a Period of Frequent Frictions?', *China-US Focus*, 27 June 2013, <www.chinausfocus.com/foreign-policy/what-should-china-do-in-a-period-of-frequent-frictions> (accessed 12 June 2015).

91 挑战、机遇与对策（中国国际战略研究基金会对外政策研究中心主任 张沱生）[Z. Tuosheng, Director, Chinese Foundation for Strategic and International Studies Foreign Policy Research Center, 'How to Construct a New U.S.-China Great Power Relationship, Part II: Challenges, Opportunities and Strategies', 30 July 2013], NAPSNet Special Reports, <http://nautilus.org/napsnet/napsnet-special-reports/challenges-opportunities-and-strategies/> (accessed 12 June 2015).

92 W. Qian and Z. Yunbi, 'President Xi Vows to Protect Maritime Interests', *China Daily*, 1 August 2013, <http://europe.chinadaily.com.cn/china/2013-08/01/content_16859218.htm> (accessed 12 June 2015).

93 习近平在中共中央政治局第八次集体学习时强调 进一步关心海洋认识海洋经略海洋 推动海洋强国建设不断取得新成就,中国海洋报, 1 August 2013, <www.soa.gov.cn/xw/hyyw_90/201308/t20130801_26776.html> (accessed 12 June 2015). 'Xi Jinping at the CCP Central Committee Politburo's Eighth Collective Study Session Emphasized Further Attention on Maritime Awareness, Maritime Economic Strategy, Promotion of Understanding Maritime Power Construction in Order to Continuously Make New Achievements', China Ocean News, 1 August 2013, <www.soa.gov.cn/xw/hyyw_90/201308/t20130801_26776.html> (accessed 12 June 2015).

5 The US factor in China's dispute with Japan over the Diaoyu/Senkaku islands

Balancing Washington's 'rebalancing' in East Asian waters

Ulises Granados

Introduction

The Diaoyu/Senkaku islands territorial conflict between China (whose historical claim Taiwan shares) and Japan is, particularly since 2009, one of the most worrisome flash points in East Asia, and an important source of insecurity in the region. Frequent incursions from Chinese and Taiwanese ships and boats, submarines and law enforcement aircraft into waters and airspace claimed by Japan as territory and Exclusive Economic Zone (EEZ) – together with official protests already heard from both sides at nonregional fora spanning from New York to Davos – only highlight the need to find realistic confidence-building measures.

China's maritime security strategy has slowly taken shape under the current administration of President Xi Jinping,[1] and forms part of an emerging Chinese national security strategy. In the context of this strategy, the Diaoyu/Senkaku conflict belongs to a group of external threats that involve territorial integrity (such as the South China Sea islands issue, separatism in Xinjiang and reunification with Taiwan).[2] This means that no compromise can be reached; conflict prevention and effective crisis management mechanisms, at most, remain as ideal goals; and, as Gaye Christoffersen develops in Chapter 4, China and Japan have been working for effective crisis management in spite of currently being dragged into a poorly institutionalized process. China has seen a significant deterioration of bilateral ties, particularly with Japan, at least during the last decade. The visits to the Yasukuni Shrine by Prime Minister Shinzo Abe in December 2013, and almost 150 high politicians in April 2014,[3] have only driven the bilateral links to its low ebb, with almost no high-level government-to-government dialogue.

Moreover, one of the most prominent features of this Sino-Japanese conflict is the decision by the United States of America (US) decision to be more actively involved in the dispute, not only by explicitly offering mediation, but by making clear that it would honor the US–Japan alliance against what is denounced as intimidation by China. The 'internationalization' of this conflict has complicated for Beijing the security environment diagnostic of the region. Managing this conflict with Tokyo – without further dragging Washington into a confrontational policy – represents a pressing strategic priority for the Chinese government.

US factor in China's dispute with Japan 81

Today it is not enough to merely explain the process of Sino-Japanese confrontation for these insular formations; the US variable renders it more important than ever to understand how the Diaoyu/Senkaku issue remains a highly securitized issue in the region.

This chapter first overviews Chinese and Japanese central narratives on their own claims, highlighting that both narratives contain important arguments. It further illustrates that these arguments impede reaching clear conclusions over ownership, and have crystallized official positions to the point of no compromise. This is followed by an analysis of US involvement in this conflict since 1951, in spite of years without expressing any position over competing claims, and how since 2009 the Obama administration has engaged this problem as part of its 'rebalancing' strategy for Asia-Pacific. Washington is no longer a passive bystander in the conflict, and its involvement could only deepen further, depending on the regional security environment.

Next, the contrast between China's engagement of the US over the East China Sea conflict and China's galvanized position against Japan is illustrated, pointing out an important level of deference Beijing concedes to Washington vis-à-vis Tokyo. This recognizes not only the G2 partnership, but also that the US–Japan alliance remains the cornerstone of peace and stability in the region, with a direct impact on Chinese strategic thinking regarding Japan. This is followed by discussion of how China has, since 2012, tried to effectively engage the US under a major power relationship model[4] as one of its top priorities. Finally, future scenarios – some potentially constructive – on how to manage this complex conflict for China, Japan and the US are provided.

The dispute

The Diaoyu/Senkaku group, currently under the effective control of the Japanese Coast Guard, is a rather loose cluster of eight main islets (see Table 5.1).

The history of the conflict is contingent on the Chinese (also Taiwanese) and Japanese narratives. Beijing's legal basis rests, among others, on claims that it

Table 5.1 The Diaoyu/Senkaku islands

Japanese Kanji	Japanese Name	Chinese Name	Chinese Hanzi
尖閣諸島	Senkakushoto	Diaoyu Dao	钓鱼岛
魚釣島	Uotsurishima	Diaoyu Dao	钓鱼岛
北小島	Kitakojima	Beixiao Dao	北小岛
南小島	Minamikojima	Nanxiao Dao	南小岛
久場	Kuba	Huangwei Yu	黄尾屿
大正	Taisho	Chiwei Yu	赤尾屿
沖の北岩	Okinokitaiwa	Bei Yu	北屿
沖の南岩	Okinominamiiwa	Nan Yu	南屿
飛瀬	Tobise	Fei Yu	飞屿

was the first to discover, name, and exploit the islands. China recounts that it has exercised jurisdiction since the early Ming dynasty,[5] and placed them under the authority of the local government of Taiwan since the Qing dynasty. Furthermore, Japanese nationals surveyed the islands in 1885, the Meiji government acknowledged Chinese ownership of the islands the same year,[6] and the Chinese government ceded them to Japan in 1895 under the Treaty of Shimonoseki together with the island of Formosa amid the military defeat. Next, the islands were returned to China after World War II,[7] but the US included them among its postwar trusteeships in the 1950s and 'returned' its 'power of administration' to Japan in 1972. Finally, China and Japan reached consensus and understanding at the time of the negotiation of the 1978 Sino-Japanese Treaty of Peace and Friendship on 'leaving the issue to be resolved later'.[8] The Chinese narrative rests on history and is linked to wars of aggression and what has been regarded as illegal occupation after World War II.

The Japanese stance, on the contrary, states that to begin with there is no issue of territorial sovereignty to be resolved, as Japan is the rightful owner. However, Tokyo adds that preventive acts, namely that surveys in 1885 proved that the islands were *terra nullius* at the time, and, as a consequence, the Japanese government issued a cabinet decision on 14 January 1895 to erect a marker on the islands to formally incorporate them into the empire (therefore incorporation by acquisition through occupation). Japan also claims that the islands have never been part of Formosa or the Pescadores, either as territories ceded in the 1895 Treaty of Shimonoseki or included in the 1951 San Francisco Peace Treaty as a territory renounced by Japan at the end of World War II; instead, they were placed under the administration of the US as part of the Nansei Shoto archipelago. The official stance further points out that administrative right over the Senkakus was later restored in 1972 and that Chinese claims emerged only in the early 1970s.[9] Finally, Tokyo denies that in 1972 or 1978 China and Japan ever reached agreement in order to shelve the problem for the future.[10] As it became apparent, Japan has divorced the Diaoyu/Senkaku issue from Taiwan's incorporation and cession after the war with this reinforcing and complementing the absence of any reference to the islands in the 1951 Peace Treaty. It has nonetheless linked the issue with the US administration over the area since 1972, thus placing Washington in the eye of the storm.

Four of the eight main islands that constitute the Diaoyu/Senkaku group, namely Taisho, Okinokitaiwa, Okinominamiiwa and Tobise, have remained state-owned since the late 1890s; Kuba, even though its ownership was until 1972 transferred between Japanese citizens, then became part of the US military facilities and areas under the US Status of Forces Agreement. Until recently, members of the Kurihara (栗原) family from Saitama Prefecture possessed property documents of Kuba and the other three islets (Kitakojima, Minamikojima and Uotsurishima). They bought the four islands (Kitakojima and Minamikojima in 1972, Uotsuri in 1978, and Kuba in 1988) from Zenji and Hanako Koga, whose family (Tatsushiro Koga) had managed them since the 1890s.[11] Excluding Kuba, the remaining three islands were leased to the Japanese state on 1 April 2002.[12] Currently only Kuba island is privately owned, while the remaining seven are state-owned.

The conflict between China and Japan remained relatively dormant until a decade ago.[13] In recent years, however, the number of incidents near the Senkakus has been on the rise (notably since 2006), and particularly since September 2010 when a Chinese fishing trawler rammed two Japan Coast Guard patrols. And yet, 2012 was by far the tensest year, a turning point in the conflict. In March 2012 the Chinese government published the names of all the seventy-one geological formations of the group,[14] and in April governor Shintaro Ishihara responded in Washington that the Tokyo metropolitan government intended to purchase three islands from the Kurihara family.[15] In spite of a public donation campaign that received some 1.5 billion yen by January 2013, the Kuriharas rather decided in September 2012 to sell the islands to the central government, a much desired 'nationalization' in Japanese ultranationalist circles, for a price tag of 2.05 billion yen (then roughly $26 million).

In sharp response, Taiwan and China resorted to their own policies in order to defend rights, including escorting fishing boats toward the area.[16] On September 17, 2012, a flotilla of around 1,000 Chinese fishing boats approached the islands;[17] on April 23, 2013, eight Chinese patrol ships from the China's State Oceanic Administration[18] entered waters near the islands,[19] after ten boats carrying members of the Japanese ultranationalist group Ganbare Nippon and Japanese Coast Guard ships were in the area. The event alone prompted Japanese Prime Minister Shinzo Abe to publicly vow to expel by force any Chinese landing on the islands.[20]

Reasons for the involvement of the US

Until recently, Washington had kept a low profile in this conflict, and in fact had shown clear neutrality, but Washington's involvement in fact dates back some decades. The US's first involvement was in 1951 with the San Francisco Peace Treaty, when the allies shaped the extent of the postwar Japanese territory.[21] In 1951 Taisho and Kuba islands were designated by the US for artillery ranges. Two years later, the United States Civil Administration of the Ryukyu islands designated the geographical boundaries of the Ryukyu islands in the Civil Administration Proclamation No. 27 of December 19, 1953.[22]

It is known that some years later, in 1958, the Koga family leased the islands to the Ryukyu government, which in turn leased them to the US authorities. In 1960 the US–Japan Security Treaty was revised, whereby in Article V it is stipulated that the US is bound to protect 'the territories under the Administration of Japan'.[23]

In the Okinawa Reversion Treaty reached between the US and Japan on June 17, 1971, a provision was included for the return to Japan of 'all and any powers of administration, legislation and jurisdiction' over the Ryukyu and Daito islands, which the US had held under the 1951 peace treaty. Article I of the Okinawa Reversion Treaty defines 'the Ryukyu islands and the Daito islands' as

> all territories with their territorial waters with respect to which the right to exercise all and any powers of administration, legislation and jurisdiction

was accorded to the United States of America under Article 3 of the Treaty of Peace with Japan.[24]

Conceding that the islands were included in Article III, it seems that in 1971 the US eventually resolved the issue of the Japanese administration over the islands without having to address the problem of competing claims of sovereignty – claims well known at the time the Okinawa Reversion Treaty had to be ratified by the US Senate.[25]

The current US official position had until recently rested on three pillars: '(1) strict neutrality; (2) strong support for peaceful resolution; and (3) a disinclination to become publicly or actively involved in the disputes or their resolution'.[26] However, Washington has begun to calibrate some of these principles, first because current US overall involvement in the Asia-Pacific region is now more open and visible as part of the *rebalancing* policy of the Obama administration. Second, subtle changes have occurred partly as a natural reaction of an ally of Japan in view of a more powerful Chinese presence in those waters. Finally, the US government seems to have concluded that inaction and not being a facilitator for dialogue simply sends the wrong message to China and to what is perceived as aggressive Chinese behavior.

On October 27, 2010, Secretary of State Hillary Clinton made clear that the islands are part of the US–Japan mutual treaty obligations.[27] The Obama administration has made the interpretation that the US agreed to in the Okinawa Reversion Treaty, to apply the 1960 Security Treaty to the treaty area, including the Senkakus.[28] In January 2013 Clinton further warned that 'although the United States does not take a position on the ultimate sovereignty of the islands, we acknowledge they are under the administration of Japan and we oppose any unilateral actions that would seek to undermine Japanese administration.'[29] The same official position has been consistently expressed by Secretary of State John Kerry and former Secretary of Defense Chuck Hagel.[30] At the same time, however, the US government has reiterated that dialogue and consultations are the best way to ease tensions between China and Japan.

The recognition of 'Japanese administration' of the islands has been shared by the US Congress. China protested the approved US National Defense Authorization Act in late December 2012, whereby the Congress also recognized, in section 1286, Japan's administration over the archipelago.[31]

Dealing with the US and Japan: a Chinese strategic dilemma?

China, however, recognizes that the US bilateral relationship is her most important one, above that with Japan. Therefore, China's efforts to maintain high-level dialogues with Washington on several issues, including territorial rows with her Asian neighbors, remain a paramount strategic priority. In August 2012, Cai Yingting, deputy chief of staff of the Chinese People's Liberation Army (PLA), heading a military delegation, paid a visit to Washington, Texas, and Hawaii; here issues related to Taiwan, Tibet, the South China Sea, and the Diaoyu/Senkaku islands were discussed. On the territorial row with Japan, Cai said:

> We would prefer to resolve conflicts through peace talks and negotiations. We strongly reject the claim that the Diaoyu Islands fall within the scope of the US–Japan Treaty of Mutual Cooperation and Security. We hope the US will do something good to maintain regional peace and to maintain a good relationship between China and the US.[32]

Since 2013, when a more conciliatory tone could be heard between the militaries of both countries, it seems that the bilateral strategic dialogue has privileged other topics with more global implications such as cybersecurity cooperation, counter-terrorism, and stability of the Korean Peninsula. For instance, in July of the same year, during the fifth US–China Strategic and Economic Dialogue, ninety-one strategic agreements were agreed upon between both countries.[33]

As for Japan, however, China's response has been particularly strong, and the improvement of relations seems decidedly pessimistic. As of May 2015 both leaders have not met in any constructive, purposeful, or directed manner where the bilateral relationship has been the central matter. Since taking office they have only met briefly four times, on the sidelines of two summits (2015 Asian-African and Asia-Pacific Economic Cooperation) and at brief encounters often in the midst of negative actions (such as Abe's sending of a gift to the Yasukuni Shrine).[34] Beijing promulgated the baselines of the territorial sea of the islands and affiliated features and published the chart of those baselines on September 10, 2012, and later a list of geographical coordinates of points and a chart of features. On September 21, the government deposited the maritime Zone Notification M.Z.N. 89.2012.LOS at the United Nations (UN) with the list of geographical coordinates of points and a chart of features,[35] an action quickly responded to by Japan. Further declarations were advanced at the 67th Session of the UN General Assembly, the same month by the Chinese Foreign Minister Yang Jiechi and Japanese Ambassador to the UN Kazuo Kodama.[36] A Chinese government White Paper on the Diaoyu islands was quickly issued on the September 29.[37]

Beyond the diplomatic front, Beijing has since autumn 2012 deployed China Maritime Surveillance (CMS) and Fisheries Law Enforcement Command (FLEC) ships to patrol near the islands and has stepped up other activities. On January 30 a radar-guided weapon was directed from a Chinese Navy vessel to an escort vessel of the Japanese Maritime Self-Defense Force, which led to an official protest and a Japanese proposal for an inquiry over the incident (see Chapter 4 by Gaye Christoffersen). Furthermore, on November 23, 2013, China declared creation of the East China Sea Air Defense Identification Zone (ADIZ). Sea and air incursions were reported throughout the year, through 2014 and into 2015.[38]

Even though speaking outside of government circles, the Chinese academic community has even raised the question of the status of Okinawa and its historical links to Japan. Zhang Haiping and Li Guoqiang, attached to the Chinese Academy of Social Sciences, suggested through a People's Daily commentary on May 8 that 'it may be time to revisit the unresolved historical issue of the Ryukyu Islands', questioning in fact Japan's Okinawa ownership.[39]

China's approach to Japan contrasts with that of Taiwan, which has tried to defuse some tension by focusing on a small window of opportunity that bilateral cooperation with Tokyo might present, without compromising Taiwan's historical claim. Tokyo and Taipei signed a fishery agreement, for the first time in four years, in April 2013. Both parties will designate an area in Japan's EEZ (excluding waters within a 12-nautical-mile radius of the Senkakus) as jointly managed waters, or a 'special cooperation zone'.[40]

The US–Japan alliance factor

The aforementioned Chinese approach, which sharply contrasts Beijing's relationship with the US and Japan, should overshadow the fact that these latter two countries sustain an alliance precisely for this type of environment of insecurity. The US–Japan alliance and its evolution have shaped Chinese and Japanese mutual perceptions of security in the East China Sea, in particular since the fall of the Berlin Wall.[41] Conversely, the recent deterioration in the bilateral Sino-Japanese links has increased pressure on an even more complex US–Japan alliance that now needs more coordination, particularly when Japan has already shown signs of a more autonomous foreign policy against China and North Korea at the expense of the US.[42]

From the purely military perspective, since 2011 the US–Japan defense alliance has started to evolve under the framework of a so-called dynamic defense cooperation (DDC), even though important issues on military cooperation remain unsolved – such as the level of relocation of Marines from Okinawa to Guam and the deployment of MV-22 Osprey to Okinawa.[43] Washington has been in fact struggling to have enough assurances from Tokyo that a more active Japanese commitment to the alliance is possible. In a 2012 Center for Strategic and International Studies joint report, Richard Armitage and Joseph S. Nye even warned that Japan might be drifting into a tier-two status, something the US deems detrimental to the stability of the whole Asia-Pacific region.[44] Washington has been struggling to receive enough assurances from Tokyo (at least before the Obama–Abe summit in April 2014) that a more active Japanese commitment to the alliance is possible.

In the meantime, however, Washington is assuring Beijing that the US–Japan alliance is as strong as ever, warning repeatedly that the Senkakus are in fact covered by the 1960 security treaty.[45] On September 19, 2012, then US Secretary of Defense Leon Panetta met with then vice chairman of the Chinese Communist Party (CCP), Xi Jingping, and stated that the Senkakus are covered by the security treaty.[46] Later, an unofficial, bipartisan US delegation traveled to Japan and China in October 2012, before the US presidential election. The delegation was headed by former administration official Armitage, former Deputy Secretary of State James Steinberg, Joseph Nye, and former national Security Adviser Stephen Hadley. Armitage again warned China by clarifying the Obama administration's current policy: 'We're not neutral when our ally is a victim of coercion or aggression or intimidation.'[47] At his meeting in Beijing with Chinese Vice Premier Li Keqiang, Armitage conceded that 'there is no quick solution' to the territorial row, but quickly accused China of 'trying to drive a wedge' between the US and Japan. The Obama administration, while maintaining its neutrality on the competing claims, had made clear that the US agreed in the Okinawa Reversion Treaty to apply the 1960 Security Treaty to the treaty area, including the Senkakus. Here, a crucial difference was thus made clear by the US between Japanese 'sovereignty' and 'administration' over the islands, without changing the application of the 1960 Security Treaty to the Diaoyu/Senkakus. Such a distinction also allows the US some space on the diplomatic front by not directly challenging China's sovereignty claims over the islands or by openly supporting Japan.

As the US makes the clear distinction between administration and sovereignty, Tokyo has concluded that there is no need, at least for now, to pressure Washington further over a military commitment to Japan against China on the matter. In February 2013, Prime Minister Abe, while assuring that his country will never fall as a tier-two nation, warned that Japan will not allow China to change the status quo (namely, Japanese effective control over the islands), adding that 'on the Senkaku issue, our intention is not to ask the United States to do this or that or to say this or that.'[48] But there is no doubt that Japan has welcomed US deterrence versus China and hopes for a more active role in maritime East Asia.

One of China's strategic priorities in East Asian waters: managing the US relationship

An important underlying objective for the US–Japan alliance is how to cope with a more assertive China. Washington has to balance its own interests with both players, the world's second and third strongest economies. For China, currently the South China Sea and East China Sea conflicts have become one her most important foreign policy challenges (together with Taiwan, Xinjiang, and Tibet as 'core interests'); at the same time, Beijing has seen an increasing US involvement in both regional disputes. Chinese leadership's recent approaches to pro-China Japanese politicians reveals that in their eyes much of the bilateral deterioration has to do with the nationalistic credentials of Prime Minister Abe on Yasukuni and the Senkakus, and that one way to defuse tensions is to foster good relations with Liberal Democratic Party lawyers and the Japanese private sector and companies.[49] Yet, the CCP leadership might evaluate that the strategic priority is to stabilize and promote the growth of the overall relationship with the US, Japan's main ally.

This is particularly relevant as China perceives more coordination in maritime policies between Japan and the US. Since 2012, Washington and Tokyo policies over the Diaoyu/Senkaku look more coordinated within the frame of the bilateral alliance. The Armitage-Nye report summarized the challenges ahead:

> The alliance must develop capabilities and policies to respond to China's rise. The alliance has much to gain from a peaceful and prosperous China, but

continued high economic growth and political stability are not assured. Allied policies and capabilities should be adaptable to China's possibly expanding core interests, changing trajectory, and a broad range of possible futures.[50]

Starting with the message from Secretary of State Hillary Clinton at the Association of Southeast Asian Nations (ASEAN) Regional Forum meeting in Hanoi in 2010, Beijing has had to deal with Washington's demands for restraint, stability, freedom of the sea lanes of communication, and peaceful measures among neighbors with vested interests in East and Southeast Asian waters. But while the US has kept strict neutrality in the South China Sea,[51] now the Obama administration has recognized on several occasions, as mentioned earlier, that Japan maintains 'administration' over the Diaoyu/Senkakus, which in China's eyes means taking a clear side with Japan. On April 25, 2014, while on his state visit to Japan, President Obama bluntly declared for the first time:

> We stand together in calling for disputes in the region, including maritime issues, to be resolved peacefully through dialogue. We share a commitment to fundamental principles such as freedom of navigation and respect for international law. And let me reiterate that our treaty commitment to Japan's security is absolute, and Article 5 covers all territories under Japan's administration, including the Senkaku Islands.[52]

While China has adamantly opposed the US move to place the Diaoyu/Senkaku islands under the cover of the US–Japan security treaty,[53] it has become increasingly obvious that the overall bilateral US–China relationship has to be invigorated; Washington not only has denounced the high level of distrust and tension between China and Japan, but now has made clear which side it is taking in case of conflict. To enhance confidence, China has shown interest in a more cooperative partnership with the US.

What had been characterized since 1997 as a 'strategic partnership' or 'constructive partnership' (using Su Hao's name for potential strategic rivals),[54] China now regards as a Major Country Relationship (*xinxing daguo guanxi*). Starting in 2012 Beijing has engaged the US through this framework as a cooperative relationship characterized by 'mutual understanding and strategic trust', 'respect of each other's "core interests," and major concerns', 'mutually beneficial cooperation', and 'coordination and cooperation in international affairs and on global issues'.[55] The ultimate aim for China is to build a new relationship – including an informal 'shirt-sleeve summit' between Xi and Obama in 2013 – to work through differences and maximize opportunities. In this new Sino-US relationship it is believed that Japan has little leverage, and the model itself remains not yet ripe for strategic deployment within the Tokyo-Beijing relationship dynamic.[56] Through this model, China can send a message to the US that the Diaoyu/Senkaku dispute is a threat to the overall Sino-US bilateral relationship and thus undermine the Japanese position against China.

Moreover, having in place the US–China Strategic and Economic Dialogue since 2009 has allowed high-level officials from the two nations to discuss important economic, political, and geostrategic issues. China now relies on a high level forum to engage in dialogue with Washington. Even though the concept of Major Country Relationship is in the early stages of formation, and the trade and investment aspects of the dialogue are more prominent than the strategic one, both countries recognize that 'complex relationships call for sustained, high-level engagement' in order to sort out differences.[57]

Future scenarios

It is clear that the dispute, regardless of whether Japan recognizes there is one or not, will not be solved in the foreseeable future with China or Taiwan. Complex legal, historical, ideological, and nationalistic factors blend together to make it impossible to untie the knot. Considering peace and stability in the region is the ultimate goal, how to manage crystallized narratives and turn a conflict of interests into a sea of opportunities of cooperation among allies, strategic partners, and adversaries? No doubt neither China, nor Taiwan, nor Japan wants to pay the political price of ordering a military solution for the East China Sea dispute.

Moreover, what possible role should the US have in the future as an actor already dragged into the dispute? Washington is in a delicate, albeit privileged position to use its political capital with both Tokyo and Beijing as part of the power triangle in the Asia-Pacific region – a triangle that could, as Inoguchi and Ikenberry hope, 'transform Asia and set the world on a stable path of growth and peace'.[58] It is in the national interest of the US to promote good relations between China and Japan and not to be dragged further into this territorial conflict.

Perhaps the most welcomed scenario for the US is to see China and Japan easing tensions by themselves and adhering to the joint statement issued by both governments on May 2008, when they committed to enhance mutually beneficial cooperation by working together to make the East China Sea a 'Sea of Peace, Cooperation and Friendship'.[59] However, increasing mistrust on both sides, with ultranationalism rising in Japan (personified by Ishihara and Abe) and the Chinese military buildup, prevent this path from occurring. In fact, both sides' militaries have long contemplated the idea of a military clash if tensions continued to escalate.[60] Interestingly enough, however, is the initiative of Taiwan. Its current administration has laid out a 5-point proposal for the conflict, called the 'East China Sea Peace Initiative', that focuses on (1) refraining from taking any antagonistic actions, (2) shelving controversies and not abandoning dialogue, (3) observing international law and resolving disputes through peaceful means, (4) seeking consensus on a code of conduct in the East China Sea, and (5) establishing a mechanism for cooperation on exploring and developing resources in the East China Sea.[61]

How to perceive and evaluate future scenarios depends largely on what side the policy maker or academic takes in the dispute. Japan's approach on how to defuse and contain what are considered Chinese ambitions in the Diaoyu/Senkakus includes a more active American participation through the following actions: (1) acknowledge Japanese sovereignty over the islands; (2) encourage China to accept arbitration (which might include submitting the dispute to the International Court of Justice [ICJ]);[62] and (3) promote the Code for Unalerted Encounters at Sea.[63]

For Washington, however, the Japanese proposals present a dilemma. Now that the government, including President Obama himself, and the Congress have publicly expressed that 'administration' and not 'sovereignty' is being recognized for Japan, the idea that suddenly Washington officials are supporting the opposite is rather wishful thinking.

On the other side are China's more realistic proposals to defuse tensions. Fudan and Nottingham University professor Guo Dinping, for example, envisions three possible scenarios for the future of the conflict: (1) the establishment of a crisis management mechanism between China and Japan; (2) wisdom and courage by Chinese and Japanese leaders to put the bilateral relationship on track; and (3) a more balanced triangular relationship among China, Japan, and the US, as well as substantial progress to be 'made in regional cooperation and community-building in East Asia'.[64] Because of the absence of a crisis management mechanism, both countries should try to create new and more stable communication channels, as well as a military-to-military hotline.[65] Understandably, both proposals are qualitatively different, as one country has effective control over the islands while the other tries to reverse decades of status quo.

Taking into account that the US has been an actor with a shared history in the conflict, and even though it has repeatedly said that it does not take a position in the merits of the claims, it in fact has a role to play in order to help defuse tensions. Washington is in a privileged position to use its political capital, with both Tokyo and Beijing as part of this power triangle in the Asia-Pacific. Unlike its purely passive neutrality on the Dokdo/Takeshima island conflict between South Korea and Japan (totally refraining even to comment on the dispute between its two allies), and the 'proactive neutrality' shown since 2010 in the South China Sea territorial conflict between China and some ASEAN countries (expressing its 'national interest'), the US has more options to assert its leadership in Northeast Asia between China and Japan for the Diaoyu/Senkaku islands. Some of these options are the following:

(1) An increasingly hands-off policy. This would leave China and Taiwan, on one side, and Japan, on the other, to lead their own bilateral relations back on track regarding the issue. That would mean 'shelving the dispute for future generations' through a joint declaration, even though that must entail for Japan recognizing there is a dispute to begin with. This is probably the most ideal scenario for the US, but difficult to realize as tensions are already high and because Washington has publicly stated that Japan has 'administration' over the islands – further fueling animosity in political circles in Beijing. An important step to be taken by the US administration might be to craft a joint declaration by China and Japan agreeing that the dispute and negotiations be put aside for the future.[66] This hands-off approach will largely depend, however, on the political will of Chinese and Japanese leaders. However, not taking the initiative would also mean for the US a loss of prestige in the region,

similar to the damage that resulted from the absence of President Obama in October 2013 during the Asia-Pacific Economic Cooperation and the East Asia summits. Washington cannot ignore the conflict anymore, and should devise a more constructive policy.

(2) Military support for Japan, which is the least desired scenario but nonetheless the most prepared given the US and Japanese alliance through the US–Japan Security Consultative Committee. It remains to be seen, however, whether Washington would accept damage in the G2 relationship with China. Defense cooperation has been focused during the last few years on the Realignment Roadmap for US bases in Japan. Eventually American military presence is to provide a deterrence needed for the defense of Japan and mainly for the maintenance of peace, security, and economic prosperity in the Asia-Pacific region, in particular in the Korean Peninsula.[67] During his September 2012 trip to Japan, Secretary of Defense Leon Panetta stated: 'It is in everybody's interest ... for Japan and China to maintain good relations and to find a way to avoid further escalation.'[68]

(3) US mediation, track-two diplomacy initiatives, and third-party arbitration. This is a more proactive and constructive approach that may include preparations for a Northeast Asian summit to discuss ways to enhance confidence-building measures and the creation of a functional crisis management mechanism to defuse tensions, not only between Japan and China, but also with South Korea.[69] It would open channels of communication at the highest level, both political and military. The US may also encourage through Taiwan further agreements with Japan on search and rescue operations in areas close to the islands. Track-two diplomacy might also include official funds allocated by the US Department of State to universities and think tanks to facilitate informal meetings among Chinese, Taiwanese, and Japanese officials to discuss maritime crisis management. Third-party arbitration (which may not include the US itself) could be the most difficult task in this scenario – as Washington first has to induce Japan to recognize the existence of a dispute – but mostly because of China's poor record of accepting any sort of arbitration (including ICJ advisory opinions) involving territorial disputes.

Careful and timely implementation of these options might result in defusing tensions, thus proving that, even though not desired by Beijing, the role of the US as a mediator might be the most pragmatic option, as its rebalancing policy is creating strong resonances in the international system specifically in the Asia-Pacific region.

Overall, constructive mediation by the US might help to revive the idea put forward in 2008 by China and Japan of the East China Sea as a 'Sea of Peace, Cooperation and Friendship',[70] recently rephrased by Taiwan as a five-point proposal – the so-called East China Sea Peace Initiative. Also, US mediation efforts may be placed between the somehow more idealistic Chinese proposals of coexisting with the status quo and those more radical Japanese proposals (including for Washington to acknowledge Japanese sovereignty over the Senkakus and pressing China to accept arbitration that may also hopefully include submitting the dispute to the ICJ). Washington has the responsibility and the power, through its own bilateral relations with Beijing and Tokyo, to help de-securitize the Diaoyu/Senkaku issue and lower tensions. Because China promulgated the East China Sea ADIZ in November 2013[71] and increased patrols and incursions in waters near the islands, it is imperative that new, creative measures are found. Even though more declaratory than effective in nature, the aforementioned Code for Unalerted Encounters at Sea has taken shape in the form of a Code for Unplanned Encounters at Sea when it was recently adopted during the 14th Western Pacific Naval Symposium held in late April 2014 in Qingdao, China.[72] For Beijing, such international agreements, if fully implemented, might also be the best way to defuse further tensions with Tokyo in the East China Sea now that the Diaoyu/Senkaku imbroglio has dangerously escalated and effective crisis management mechanisms are yet to be found.

Notes

1 Central to this developing strategy are the creation of the National Security Commission [中央国家安全委员会], first proposed during the 3rd Plenary Session of the 18th CCP Central Committee in November 2013; the reorganization of the five Chinese civil maritime agencies in March 2013; and the Leading Group for Maritime Security in 2012 under the leadership of Xi Jinping (see Chapter 4).
2 The South China Sea and East China Sea conflicts are not officially included in the 'core interest' category by the Chinese government, even though hints have been advanced recently.
3 T. Osaki and R. Yoshida, '149 Lawmakers Visit Yasukuni', *Japan Times*, 22 April 2014, <www.japantimes.co.jp/news/2014/04/22/national/politics-diplomacy/149-lawmakers-visit-yasukuni/#.U2zpllfN4TA> (accessed 22 April 2014).
4 This concept was first mentioned by then Vice President Xi Jinping in his 15 February 2012 speech in Washington, DC. See D.M. Lampton, 'A New Type of Major-Power Relationship: Seeking a Durable Foundation for U.S.-China Ties', *Asia Policy*, 2013, vol. 16, pp. 51–68.
5 The first records came from the Shun Feng Xiang Song records (1403) from the early Ming dynasty. The waters surrounding the Diaoyu, the official narrative recounts, have been traditional fishing grounds for Chinese fishermen.
6 N. Kristof, 'The Inconvenient Truth behind the Diaoyu/Senkaku Islands', *New York Times*, 19 September 2012, <http://kristof.blogs.nytimes.com/2012/09/19/the-inconvenient-truth-behind-the-diaoyusenkaku-islands/> (accessed 6 August 2013).
7 Taken as basis the 1943 Cairo Declaration and the 1945 Potsdam Proclamation.
8 PRC State Council Information Office, 'Diaoyu Dao, and Inherent Territory of China', White paper, 29 September 2012, <www.gov.cn/english/official/2012-09/25/content_2232763_2.htm> (accessed 6 August 2013).
9 The dispute ignited after the United Nations ECAFE Commission suggested earlier in 1968 the potential of huge deposits of hydrocarbons in the area.
10 Japan Ministry of Foreign Affairs, *The Basic View on the Sovereignty over the Senkaku Islands*, May 2013, <www.mofa.go.jp/region/asia-paci/senkaku/basic_view.html> (accessed 3 May 2015). Recent statements to the contrary, however, have been revealed to the Japanese press. See J. Hofilena, 'Ex-Cabinet Secretary: Japan, China Agreed to "Shelve" Senkaku Territorial Dispute in 1970s', *Japan Daily Press*, 4 June 2013, <http://japandailypress.com/ex-cabinet-secretary-japan-china-agreed-to-shelve-senkaku-territorial-dispute-in-1970s-0429996> (accessed 18 May 2014).

US factor in China's dispute with Japan   93

11 Masami Ito, 'Senkaku Owners Prefer Selling Islets to Tokyo, Hope All Nations Can Benefit, *Japan Times*, 21 July 2012, <http://info.japantimes.co.jp/text/nn20120721a9.html> (accessed 6 August 2012).
12 Ministry of Foreign Affairs, *The Senkaku Islands*, March 2013, <www.mofa.go.jp/region/asia-paci/senkaku/pdfs/senkaku_en.pdf> (accessed 6 August 2012).
13 In 1996 Hong Kong activist David Chan Yuk-cheung, one leader of the Hong Kong–based *Baodiao Movement* advocating Chinese sovereignty over the islands, drowned while trying to reach one island. 'Thousands Mourn Drowned Protester', *Chicago Tribune*, 30 September 1996. Mike Mochizuki identifies 2004 as the beginning of renewed tensions in the East China Sea. M. Mochizuki, 'Dealing with a Rising China', in T. Berger, M. Mochizuki, and J. Tsuchiyama (eds.), *Japan in International Politics. The Foreign Policies of an Adaptive State*. Boulder, CO: Lynne Rienner, 2007, p. 248.
14 Published originally online by the Chia State Oceanic Administration, it has been printed in *Guojia Haiyangju, Zhongguo diaoyudao dimingce*, Beijing: Haiyang Chubianshe, 2012, pp. 29–32.
15 It is known that the owners wanted to sell them to the Tokyo government, rather than the central government, in order not to inflame tensions between China and Taiwan against Japan. M. Ito, 'Senkaku Owners Prefer Selling Islets to Tokyo, Hope All Nations Can Benefit', *Japan Times*, 21 July 2012, <http://info.japantimes.co.jp/text/nn20120721a9.html> (accessed 6 August 2012).
16 M. Blake, 'Duel by Water Cannon: Japanese and Taiwanese Coastguards Blast Each Other with Spray in Row over Disputed Islands', *Daily Mail Online*, 25 September 2012, <www.dailymail.co.uk/news/article-2208305/Senkaku-Islands-Japan-Taiwan-boats-attack-spray.html#ixzz2WpeML8s0> (accessed 3 May 2015).
17 D. Alexander, 'In Everybody's Interest for Japan, China to Maintain Good Relations, Panetta Says as Beijing Launches Flotilla of 1,000 Fishing Boats to Disputed Islands', *Reuters*, 17 September 2012, <http://news.nationalpost.com/2012/09/17/china-japan-leon-panetta/> (accessed 23 October 2013).
18 The marine surveillance ships Haijian 51, 23 and 46, later joined by the Haijian 50, 15, 49, 66 and 137.
19 'Eight Chinese Vessels Enter Senkaku Area', *Japan Times*, 24 April 2013, <www.japantimes.co.jp/news/2013/04/24/national/eight-chinese-vessels-enter-senkaku-area/#.Uh-XKT_9zbw> (accessed 10 May 2013).
20 A. Westlake, 'PM Abe Vows to Expel Any Chinese Landing on Senkakus with Force', *Japan Daily Press*, 23 April 2013, <http://japandailypress.com/pm-abe-vows-to-expel-any-chinese-landing-on-senkakus-with-force-2327530/> (accessed 25 April 2013).
21 While not mentioning the Diaoyu/Senkaku group at all in Article II, Article III of the 1951 San Francisco Peace Treaty did stipulate the following: 'the United States as the sole administering authority, Nansei Shoto south of 29 deg. north latitude (including the Ryukyu Islands and the Daito Islands), Nanpo Shoto south of Sofu Gan (including the Bonin Islands, Rosario Island and the Volcano Islands) and Parece Vela and Marcus Island'. <www.taiwandocuments.org/sanfrancisco01.htm/> (accessed 3 May 2015).
22 H. Moteki, *The Senkaku Islands Constitute an Intrinsic Part of Japan*, Tokyo: Society for the Dissemination of Historical Fact, 2010, <http: //www.sdh-fact.com/CL02_1/79_S4.pdf> (accessed 3 May 2015).
23 'Each Party recognizes that an armed attack against either Party in the territories under the administration of Japan would be dangerous to its own peace and safety and declares that it would act to meet the common danger in accordance with its constitutional provisions and processes.' Article V, *Treaty of Mutual Cooperation and Security between the United States and Japan*, Ministry of Foreign Affairs of Japan, <www.mofa.go.jp/region/n-america/us/q%26a/ref/1.html> (accessed 3 May 2015).
24 M.E. Manyin, *Senkaku (Diaoyu/Diaoyutai) Islands Dispute: U.S. Treaty Obligations*, Washington, DC: Congressional Research Service, 22 January 2013, p. 4.

25 Ibid.
26 D. Keyser, 'The Senkaku/Diaoyu Dispute: The U.S. Policy Perspective and Japanese PM Abe's Visit', *China Policy Institute Blog*, 21 February 2013, <http://blogs.nottingham.ac.uk/chinapolicyinstitute/2013/02/21/the-senkakudiaoyu-dispute-the-u-s-policy-perspective-and-japanese-pm-abes-visit/> (accessed 25 February 2014).
27 *Secretary Clinton Joint Press Availability with Japanese Foreign Minister Seiji Maehara*, Honolulu, HI, 27 October 2010, <www.state.gov/secretary/rm/2010/10/150110.htm> (accessed 3 May 2015).
28 Manyin, *Senkaku (Diaoyu/Diaoyutai) Islands Dispute*, p. 5.
29 *Remarks by Secretary Clinton with Japanese Foreign Minister Fumio Kishida after Their Meeting*, 18 January 2013, <www.state.gov/secretary/rm/2013/01/203050.htm> (accessed 3 May 2015).
30 K. Mori, 'Kerry Spells Out Policy on Senkaku Islands', *UPI*, 15 April 2013, <www.upi.com/Top_News/World-News/2013/04/15/Kerry-spells-out-policy-on-Senkaku-Islands/UPI-20751366006285/> (accessed 1 February 2014). Also see 'U.S. Warns against "Coercive Action" over Senkaku Issue', *Asahi Shimbun*, 30 April 2013, <http://ajw.asahi.com/article/behind_news/politics/AJ201304300129> (accessed 18 May 2014).
31 C. Billones, 'China Opposes US Decision to Recognize Japan as Owner of Senkaku Islands', *Japan Daily Press*, <http://japandailypress.com/china-opposes-us-decision-to-recognize-japan-as-owner- of-senkaku-islands-2620423> (accessed 3 May 2015).
32 'China Seeks New Military Relationship with U.S.', *Xinhua*, 26 August 2012, <http://english.sina.com/2012/0825/500028.html> (accessed 27 April 2015).
33 D. Shambaugh, 'A Big Step Forward in U.S.-China Relations', *China US Focus*, 19 July 2013, <www.chinausfocus.com/foreign-policy/a-big-step-forward-in-u-s-china-relations/> (accessed 3 May 2015).
34 A. Panda, 'Fourth Time's the Charm: Xi Jinping and Shinzo Abe Meet Again', *Diplomat*, 22 April 2015, <http://thediplomat.com/2015/04/fourth-times-the-charm-xi-jinping-and-shinzo-abe-meet-again/> (accessed 27 April 2015).
35 United Nations Office of Legal Affairs, *Circular Communications from the Division for Ocean Affairs and the Law of the Sea*, <www.un.org/depts/los/LEGISLATIONANDTREATIES/PDFFILES/mzn_s/mzn89ef.pdf (accessed 3 May 2015).
36 Ministry of Foreign Affairs of Japan, *Statements Made by H.E. Mr. Kazuo Kodama . . . at the General Debate of the 67th Session of the UN General Assembly on 27 September, 2012*, <www.mofa.go.jp/announce/speech/un2012/un_0928.html> (accessed 3 May 2015).
37 State Council Information Office, The People's Republic of China, *Diaoyu Dao, an Inherent Territory of China*, White paper, 29 September 2012, <http://losangeles.china-consulate.org/eng/topnews/t975371.htm> (accessed 1 May 2013).
38 Kyodo News International, '3 Chinese Ships Intrude into Japanese Waters Near Senkaku Islands', *Global Post*, 29 April 2014, <www.globalpost.com/dispatch/news/kyodo-news-international/140429/3-chinese-ships-intrude-japanese-waters-near-senkaku-i> (accessed 7 May 2014).
39 'China Questions Okinawa Ownership', *Japan Times*, 8 May 2013.
40 Kyodo, Staff Report, 'Japan to Let Taiwanese Fish near the Senkakus', *Japan Times*, 10 April 2013, <www.japantimes.co.jp/news/2013/04/10/national/japan-to-let-taiwanese-fish-near-the-senkakus/#.UcOWAZyk9x0> (accessed 3 May 2015).
41 Michael Green points to an important redefinition of the alliance since the mid-1990s. M. Green, 'Japan in Asia', in D. Shambaugh and M. Yahuda (eds.), *International Relations of Asia*, Lanham, MD: Rowman & Littlefield, 2008, p. 181.
42 Japan-North Korea secret meetings on October 2013 in Dalian and January 2014 in Hanoi, as well as the December 2013 visit by the Japanese prime minister to the Yasukuni Shrine, seem to confirm this trend. M. Fackler, 'Japan: Report of Possible Talks with North Korea to Thaw Ties', *New York Times*, 28 January 2014,

<www.nytimes.com/2014/01/29/world/asia/japan-report-of-possible-talks-with-north-korea-to-thaw-ties.html> (accessed 3 March 2014). 'Japan Held Secret Talks with N. Korea Last Year', *Chosun Ilbo*, 12 February 2014, <http://english.chosun.com/site/data/html_dir/2014/02/12/2014021201947.html> (accessed 18 February 2014).
43 T. Satake, 'US Rebalancing toward the Asia-Pacific and Japan-US Dynamic Defense Cooperation', *The National Institute for Defense Studies News*, Tokyo: NIDS, October 2012, <www.nids.go.jp/english/publication/briefing/pdf/2012/briefing_e169.pdf> (accessed 10 March 2014).
44 R.L. Armitage and J.S. Nye, 'The U.S.-Japan Alliance: Anchoring Stability in Asia', Washington, DC: Center for Strategic and International Studies, August 2012, p. 5.
45 S. Harner, 'Is the U.S. Committed to Defend the Senkakus? Text of Article 5 of the U.S.-Japan Treaty', *Forbes*, 23 September 2013, <www.forbes.com/sites/stephenharner/2012/09/23/is-the-u-s-committed-to-defend-the-senkakus-text-of-article-5-of-the-u-s-japan-treaty/> (accessed 10 March 2014).
46 Ibid.
47 P. Landers, 'U.S. Not Neutral about Japan, Armitage Told Beijing', *Wall Street Journal*, 29 November 2012, <http://blogs.wsj.com/japanrealtime/2012/11/29/u-s-not-neutral-about-japan-armitage-told-beijing/> (accessed 10 March 2014).
48 *Statesmen's Forum: Shinzo Abe, Prime Minister of Japan*, Washington, DC: Center for Strategic and International Studies, 22 February 2013.
49 'Yasukuni, Senkakus Impeding Better Ties, Top Chinese Politician Says', *Japan Times*, 9 May 2014.
50 Armitage and Nye, 'The U.S.-Japan Alliance', p. 17.
51 Even though a pattern distancing from traditional neutrality and towards a 'proactive neutrality' is already visible.
52 Joint Press Conference with President Obama and Prime Minister Abe of Japan, April 24, 2014, <www.whitehouse.gov/the-press-office/2014/04/24/joint-press-conference-president-obama-and-prime-minister-abe-japan> (accessed 10 June 2014).
53 Z. Yunbi, 'Obama Criticized for Diaoyu Islands Remarks', *China Daily USA*, 24 April 2014, <http://usa.chinadaily.com.cn/world/2014-04/24/content_17458845.htm> (accessed 3 May 2015).
54 R. Li, *A Rising China and Security in East Asia*, London: Routledge, 2009, p. 182.
55 D.M. Lampton, 'A New Type of Major-Power Relationship: Seeking a Durable Foundation for U.S.-China Ties', p. 53. Video of then Vice President Xi Jinping's speech at the National Committee on United States-China Relations, 15 February 2012, <www.ncuscr.org/programs/luncheon-honor-vice-president-xi-jinping> (accessed 3 May 2015).
56 Amy King, 'Where Does Japan Fit in China's *New Type of Great Power Relations*?', *Asian Forum*, 20 March 2014, <www.theasianforum.org/where-does-japan-fit-in-chinas-new-type-of-great-power-relations/> (accessed 10 May 2015).
57 Remarks by Vice President Joe Biden and President Xi Jinping of the People's Republic of China, Great Hall of the People, Beijing, PRC, 4 December 2013, <www.whitehouse.gov/the-press-office/2013/12/04/remarks-vice-president-joe-biden-and-president-xi-jinping-peoples-republ> (accessed 3 May 2015).
58 T. Inoguchi and G.J. Ikenberry, *The Troubled Triangle: Economic and Security Concerns for the United States, Japan, and China*, New York: Palgrave Macmillan, 2013, p. 2.
59 Joint Statement between the Government of Japan and the Government of the People's Republic of China on Comprehensive Promotion of a 'Mutually Beneficial Relationship Based on Common Strategic Interests', Tokyo, Japan, 7 May 2008, <www.mofa.go.jp/region/asia-paci/china/joint0805.html> (accessed 17 April 2014).
60 Some scenarios have been envisioned by PLA Navy Rear Admiral Yin Zhou, while information in March 2013 suggested that the US and Japan defense officials have contingency plans involving cooperation from both militaries. See K. Spitzer, 'Chinese

View of Islands Conflict: "Make It Quick"', *Time Online*, 20 February 2013, <http://nation.time.com/2013/02/20/chinese-view-of-islands-conflict-make-it-quick/> (accessed 3 May 2015). See also J.E. Barnes, 'U.S. Japan Update Plans to Defend Islands', *Wall Street Journal*, 21 March 2013. Online. Available HTTP: <http://online.wsj.com/article/SB10001424127887324373204578373230195065860.html> (accessed 6 August 2014).
61 *2012 Report to Congress of the U.S.-China Economic and Security Review Commission*, Washington, DC: U.S. Government Printing Office, 2012, p. 258, <http://origin.www.uscc.gov/sites/default/files/annual_reports/2012-Report-to-Congress.pdf> (accessed 21 June 2014).
62 Proposal by Masashi Nishihara, President of the Research Institute for Peace and Security (RIPS). See M. Nishimura, 'Japan Should Stand Firm in the Senkaku Islands Dispute', *AJISS Commentary 164*, 6 November 2012, <www2.jiia.or.jp/en_commentary/pdf/AJISS-Commentary164.pdf> (accessed 21 June 2014).
63 T. Kotani, 'The Senkaku Islands and the U.S.-Japan Alliance: Future Implications for the Asia-Pacific', *Project 2049 Institute*, p. 8, <http://project2049.net/documents/senkaku_kotani.pdf> (accessed 18 April 2015).
64 D. Guo, 'Three Scenarios for the Diaoyu/Senkaku Dispute', *China Policy Institute Blog*, 21 February 2013, <http://blogs.nottingham.ac.uk/chinapolicyinstitute/2013/02/21/three-scenarios-for-the-diaoyusenkaku-dispute/> (accessed 3 May 2015).
65 Such proposals have been already mentioned by S. Kleine-Ahlbrandt, 'Navigating Tensions in the East China Sea', *Huffington Post*, 17 April 2013, <www.huffingtonpost.com/stephanie-t-kleineahlbrandt/china-japan-islands_b_3093882.html> (accessed 12 March 2015).
66 The agreement of putting disputes aside for the future has proven not to be as easy as it seems. Currently Japan has officially denied that during the 1972 and 1978 normalization process with China it accepted to put aside the dispute. Unless there is an official joint communique on the issue, a similar conflict of interpretation may also occur for future generations.
67 Japan Ministry of Defense, *Joint Statement of the Security Consultative Committee*, 27 April 2012, <www.mod.go.jp/j/approach/anpo/js20120427.html> (accessed 3 May 2015).
68 '"In Everybody's Interest" for Japan', *Reuters*, 17 September 2012, <http://news.nationalpost.com/2012/09/17/china-japan-leon-panetta/> (accessed 21 January 2015).
69 On June 25, 2013, South Korea and Japan announced the suspension of a swap financial agreement.
70 Joint Statement between the Government of Japan and the Government of the People's Republic of China, <www.mofa.go.jp/region/asia-paci/china/joint0805.html> (accessed 3 May 2015).
71 Kyodo, 'China Eyeing Contentious Air Defense Zone in East China Sea: Paper', *Japan Times*, 10 November 2013, <www.japantimes.co.jp/news/2013/11/10/national/china-eyeing-contentious-air-defense-zone-in-east-china-sea-paper/#.UowBrKQMSo> (accessed 27 April 2015).
72 This symposium, even though not East Asian in nature, nonetheless received the attention of twenty-five countries including China, Japan, and the U.S.

6 China's relations with India
Great power statecraft and territory

Jonathan H. Ping

Introduction

Within a statecraft-based approach, and with a concentration on great power statecraft, this chapter discusses relations between the People's Republic of China (PRC or China) and the Republic of India (India). In an age broadly described as globalised (or globalising), the potential of operative relations between these states means, first, effective governance over a significant portion of humanity; and second, guidance and stabilisation of the globalising system through the precedent of their independent and combined great power statecraft. Inversely – and correspondingly – tribulations between China and India are inevitably global in their effect.

Empirical data and predicted trends make plain the relative size and systemic impact of China and India. Approximately 36 per cent of the world's population is governed by these two great power states.[1] This relative population weight has significant implications for the global political economy (GPE). For example, nearly half of all increased demand for oil is predicted to be from China up to the year 2040, and demand from India will likely shadow that of China.[2] In addition, China and India – presently the second- and fourth-highest oil-consuming states – have a far lower per capita consumption than the leading consumer, the United States of America (US).[3] If oil is considered an example of the effect on all scarce and nonrenewable resources, when China and India reach per capita parity with the US, the supply and price implications will be immense.

Energy generated from oil and other fossil fuels add to total global CO_2 emissions. China ranks first and India third (behind the US), but similar to oil, their emissions per capita are far lower.[4] China and India are presently the main drivers of global growth – China by size and India by rate.[5] In summary, China and India are the returning centre of the GPE. Consequently, China and India, and their ability to conduct and maintain a stable relationship, affect us all – whether a business looking to profit, a nongovernmental organisation concerned with the environment or human rights, or a consumer managing petrol and energy prices for the family budget.

The domestic characteristics of the two great powers, and the forms of power they hold, provide insight, as these are the basis of their statecraft and thus critical to their relations and the effects of their statecraft upon the GPE. In contrast to the *leading* statistics, they are profoundly and only developing states, presently grappling with the management of an industrial revolution. Both have nuclear weapons and effective ballistic missile delivery systems.[6] They practise politics through extremely different systems of governance, India being a democracy and China a single-party socialist state. China has successfully created a unique development model – socialist state–directed market capitalism[7] – that has a strong emphasis on infrastructure and manufactured exports. India, in searching for an effective development path, chose the import substitution model following independence, which has resulted in it presently having 33 per cent of the world's extremely poor who live on less than $1.25 per day.[8] Ominously, China and India have a common – but disputed – 4,047-kilometre land border over which they fought a military war in 1962, and along which presently incidents and provocations are commonly reported.[9]

The relations between China and India are thus critical to each state, to all other states, and to the GPE. In order to study this decisive relationship, this chapter identifies and considers the China-India border dispute as a strategic priority; even though it has been consistently mishandled postindependence, ignored following war, downplayed, and then side-lined for decades within unique closed forums – within the relationship, and particularly within China's foreign policy. At the East Asia Security Symposium and Conference held annually in Beijing, it is one of only a few subjects, such as Tibet, which are politely yet forcefully avoided by Chinese presenters, and about which different presenters provide an extremely similar curt *party* line.

Since the formation of the Xi and Modi governments' significant trade, cultural, and personal leadership affinity has been publically celebrated, and these forms of expanding links have been posited as potential paths to solve the intractable border dispute. However, these are seemingly enfeebled when confronted with the border issue. Many scholars, such as Malik and Chellaney, and mercantilist/realist thinkers generally, reason that economic growth – rather than quelling tensions – may actually inflame them.[10] Greater political and cultural bilateral ties and interaction may not improve relations either, as Holslag found that public perceptions of China in India are not necessarily improved.[11] Garver argues that even if the leaders take a positive approach, the border dispute is a deliberate Chinese policy of deterrence to ensure India remains sober and clear of China's core interests such as Tibet. Settlement would thus be opposed by the People's Liberation Army and Chinese nationalists, and thus be derailed by China's domestic politics (see Chapter 3).[12]

Why does this chapter identify the border dispute as a strategic priority if the matter is of little public concern to the claimants? It is seen to be a matter to be resolved with time, privately, through bilateral negotiations which have been ongoing for more than three decades without success; or via the indirect routes of trade, cultural, and personal leadership affinity.

First, the potential benefits of resolving the territorial problems are significant for the GPE as a whole, and not simply for the two great powers. Second, the consequences of failing to effectively recreate the two great powers, and the returning centre of the GPE, leave it flawed, as increasing population size, obligatory economic growth, resource scarcity, and environmental concern add political pressure and complexity to global governance.

Essentially, this chapter is about China's strategic priorities with regard to India, but it also accounts for the complex global reality of great power issues having consequences for many actors. The thesis leads to the disturbing and theorised idea of Western strategic scholars, that of China being a revisionist power. The border dispute may require India and China to embrace thorough revision of the system, and given a structural power capacity and historical rationale, it may be entirely practical and consummate to their broader common global interests.[13]

This chapter is not a detailed historical record of the Sino-Indian border dispute. The history from before and after the iconic Simla Convention of 1914 is well documented by many other publications, including my own, but notably in books – recently Eric Hyer's *The Pragmatic Dragon* – and in articles such as published in a special issue of the *China Report*.[14] Hence this chapter provides a strategic rationale and suggests methods for solving the China-India border dispute through a theoretical approach.

Global political economy and critical theory

This theoretically orientated approach is practical and viable through the use of the eccentric discipline of the GPE. The chapter's thesis employs this subfield of international relations as canonically acknowledged in works such as *Global Political Economy*.[15] It holds that domestic and international politics and economics are not independent, and being symbiotic are necessarily consulted to gain practical policy and outcomes in matters of the GPE such as states, markets, and society. Within the GPE, and to subdue the ideological schisms, it is possible to focus on concepts which underpin the system and which are human creations that change, and thus effect change, in the system as a whole – such as statecraft, the classification of states, or sovereignty.

Statecraft is the creation and recreation of the state.[16] Arising from differentiated resource endowments, geographic location, or the size or endeavour of the population of the 195 states is their differentiated capacity to conduct international relations and a hierarchical international system.[17] Each individual state pursuing its own (re)creation in cooperation and contest with others results in the creation and recreation of the GPE.

The disparity between states' relative power gives a few great powers a larger influence over the form of the international system and the (re)creation of the GPE. Great powers thus may be characterised as being at the pinnacle, dominant, and most liberated from systemic constraint, whilst having the greatest capacity to remake the GPE in their own image – by design, mere existence, or incompetence. Middle powers have a limited capacity to impose and resist via hybridisation, whilst small powers have little or no capacity to impose or resist through their statecraft on the GPE.[18] The three categories of state describe the differentiated power and thus the capacity of states to conduct international relations. Identifying the different capacity of different-sized states to conduct international relations successfully, as measured by the ability to achieve their goals, acknowledges that different sizes require different forms of statecraft. Great powers, such as China and India, have a superior opportunity to make the system work best for them.

A statecraft-based approach is also useful, as it allows for change unhindered by ideological limits, emphasising innovation beyond current precedent and allowing the creation of functional policy to achieve a state's goals within an evolving GPE. It thus pays attendance to Coxian political economy. Cox wrote: 'Theory is always *for* someone [a specific state] and *for* some purpose [to achieve goals set by that state]'.[19] Furthermore,

> Critical theory is theory of history . . . concerned . . . with a continuing process of historical change [the (re)creation of the state through statecraft and the evolving GPE]. Problem-solving theory is non-historical . . . since it . . . posits a continuing present.'[20]

Via ongoing negotiations and other routes, methods for solving the border dispute may be understood as being based on problem-solving theory.

The thesis of this chapter is that critical theory would be a valuable addition to the use of problem-solving theory presently being used in creating policy to seek resolution of the China-India border dispute. China has an opportunity, as a great power, to pursue this strategic priority through critical theory, which will allow for historical change beyond the continuing present, specifically with regard to sovereignty.

Theoretically, through a GPE statecraft-based approach China, as a great power, has the capacity to employ statecraft to form policy with the aim of achieving its own goals that impose change on the GPE and concepts of human creation such as sovereignty. As great powers, India and China have the capacity to impose change on the GPE as a path to solving their territorial dispute and to embrace theory so they achieve their purpose. A purposeful, controlled, and adept management of a seemingly intractable problem via mature great power statecraft is, hypothetically, a better path than an uncontrolled, unplanned, incompetent collapse into crisis management by incapable developing states.

Why territorial assurance as a strategic priority?

The outcome of sovereignty is territorial assurance, and the outcome of territorial assurance is security. Security is the foundation of states and the GPE. The Peace of Westphalia sought peace within a defined geographic space, and the subsequent standardisation of political units as being only states within a defined geography provided a functional basis for a global system.[21] Without the threat of violence, or the threat of violence being held legitimately only by states, the daily lives of citizens stabilised and was assured, so pursuits other than security became viable and persistent. Landed farming, factories, health care, education, infrastructure, currencies, and all manner of human invention were brought into being, once their destruction or loss by theft or death became an anomaly. These artefacts are political and economic goods.[22]

Hence, without global security, no other global political or economic public goods may be persistently provided.[23] Yet alarmingly, the creation of China and India in the 1940s as Westphalian 'European' sovereign states was flawed and is incomplete. They do not hold supreme legitimate authority within their territory, as they have ill-defined territory. The extent of this is significant.

The major disputes are:

> *Between China and India*: (1) Aksai Chin, approximately 38,000 sq. km; (2) Arunachal Pradesh, approximately 83,743 sq. km; (3) the Trans-Karakoram Tract, approximately 5,800 sq. km, ceded by Pakistan to China in 1963 and claimed by India.[24]
>
> *Between India and Pakistan*: (1) Kashmir, approximately 308,000 sq. km (Azad Jammu and Kashmir and Gilgit-Baltistan are occupied by Pakistan but claimed by India; Jammu and Kashmir are occupied by India but claimed by Pakistan); (2) Sir Creek, a 92-km strip of water that divides the Pakistani province of Sindh from the Indian state of Gujarat; (3) Siachen Glacier, a 76-km-long glacier in the Karakoram range.[25]
>
> *Between India and Bangladesh*: The recently resolved issue of Indian and Bangladeshi enclaves which existed in each other's territories (India and Bangladesh signed an historic territory swap deal in June 2015).[26]
>
> *Between Pakistan and Afghanistan*: The Durand Line, the 2,640-km border between Afghanistan and Pakistan.[27]

The most important strategic priority between China and India for the GPE thus concerns territorial assurance. Stability of the GPE is gained through a dynamic process of creation and recreation.[28] Without rectification of the territorial dispute, the twenty-first-century GPE is being built on a broken foundation. This is because great powers and their domestic statecraft are the most significant contributing influence of the GPE. A territorial dispute between middle or small powers would be of lesser consequence to the system. Thus the GPE is not viable or persistent, or at best it is guarded and limited, if the border dispute which previously caused war between two great powers (now armed with nuclear weapons) remains unresolved. Whilst China and India may assume to proceed, without repair, their growing significance within the GPE, and the knowledge of all states and other actors in the system of the dispute, give rise to doubt and a lack of trust in the security of the system as a whole.

It may be the case that China and India are holding productive and successful annual talks on the border dispute, having conducted fruitful negotiations – most recently the 2005 agreement *Political Parameters and Guiding Principles for the Settlement of the India-China Boundary Questions*.[29] These annual talks should be made far more transparent, as this may enamour the system with a promise of a process underway towards a practical outcome. However, as Kumar stated following President Xi's 2014 visit to India: 'Without further momentum or compulsion, maintaining the status quo along the border seems to be the best that can be hoped for in the foreseeable future.'[30] This is a common view echoed by many scholars and practitioners.[31]

Without a substantive pronouncement, the GPE is adrift in troughs of negative media hype and memories of 1962[32] and peaks of trade agreement numbers and transformative leadership.[33] President Xi and Prime Minister Modi may be able to share the delights of their hometowns, despite the fact that the systemic flaw exists, but we may well ask, will all Chinese and Indian leaders?[34] Thus their domestic politics around international relations problems, unless resolved formally, transparently, and institutionalised, are the concern of all states within the globalised twenty-first-century system.

To progress the present problem-solving theory-based status quo negotiations, there are two critical theory possibilities drawn from historical periods of systemic change: back to the 1940s, and beyond the 1640s. Back to the 1940s wouldn't entail resolving the claims to territory by fixing the disputed border at the Line of Actual Control (LAC), known as the package deal, where each state accepts to swap claims made since independence (China gets Aksai Chin and India Arunachal Pradesh).[35] Back to the 1940s would ideally include resolving the India-Pakistan dispute over Jammu-Kashmir, as Pakistan ceded part of this territory to China in 1963.[36] Back to the 1940s would thus occasion revisiting the partition of British India, an unravelling which was advocated by Mao in the 1950s when he refused to recognise unequal treaties, including the McMahon Line. The status quo negotiation would be overcome through continuance of the independence process and the common rally against European intervention in Asia, rather than by focusing on the decades of failure and conflict which followed independence.

Beyond the 1640s would involve the redefinition of the contemporary European-derived relationship between geography and politics – the Westphalian system of states holding sovereignty.[37] China and India are not European, and yet both have inherited seemingly intractable issues of European design, or design failure. At the core, thus, would be a bold initiative to step beyond, if only by narrative, to jointly replace European Political Economy (EPE) (politics through sovereign states and economics through markets) to move beyond colonialism and imperialism, beyond the century of humiliation. The goal would be to reclaim the pre-European by not returning to the past, but instead building something fundamentally new that creates the same outcome of assurance of territory. As great powers, within their bilateral relationship, theoretically this is entirely possible. In practice, this would be a concerted and intense negation – one which began from a borderless map and would place new borders. The Indian constitution and its ability to create new states is a precedent for India, and as will be discussed later, China has a remarkable and practical ability to modify sovereignty to overcome historical problems.[38] Further, symbolically, the resolution of the territorial dispute is also only an initiating step within a larger requirement for China and India, as responsible and unhindered great powers, to gain knowledge of how to contribute to management of the system as a whole.

Historic realignment in the global political economy as a strategic imperative

Prior to the arrival of European maritime powers in Asia, the Industrial Revolution in Europe, and the American Revolution, the Indian and Chinese political economies were the largest and most productive.[39] Their contribution to global gross domestic product (GDP) declined until the later part of the twentieth century, and since then it has been growing rapidly. The principle reasons for decline include endogenous explanations such as political machination, inefficient production, or lack of an epistemic base. Exogenous reasons include the capture or imposition of trade by rival states, and colonialism and imperialism.[40] Chinese recollect this bitterly within their national psyche as culminating in the century of humiliation between the First Opium War that began in 1839 and the formation of the PRC in 1949.[41]

The century, within the thousands of years of China's civilisational history, marks a rapid and significant shift from an internally derived political economy to one externally imposed – a shift from a Chinese tributary system of international relations to the European Westphalian model. In the present, this is arguably expressed in territorial disputes and debates, such as between the United Nations Convention on the Law of the Sea and the Nine-Dash Line in the South China Sea, or between the McMahon Line/LAC and pre-European agreements between China and India.[42]

Eric Hyer, co-author of Chapter 3, states in his book *The Pragmatic Dragon: China's Grand Strategy and Boundary Settlements*:

> Although the Sino-Indian dispute remains unresolved, a stable status quo exists along the Line of Actual Control and negotiations continue. This will remain the case until a large and strategic imperative sets the context for a final resolution.[43]

The general thesis of Hyer's book emphasises systemic change as the 'decisive factor influencing Beijing's policy toward its territorial disputes and boundary settlements'.[44] The return of China and India to their historically dominant position in the GPE is a large and strategic imperative. A final resolution of the border is required, and great power statecraft could be employed to set the context in a controlled and managed manner. An unforeseen strategic imperative – such as mercantilist power balancing, warfare, economic collapse, or a nontraditional security threat (e.g. water,[45] terrorism, or unregulated population movements) – may lead to a larger, more intractable problem, such as occurred with the partition of British India. Similar to the present border dispute, although partition was negotiated and debated for decades, it was hastily resolved, arguably erroneously, due to the calamity of World War II and its effect on the British Empire that precipitated its rapid quit from India.[46]

If we accept the present GDP percentage growth trajectory, combined with the relative population size of China and India – and accept that it is possible for states with over a billion people to successfully industrialise – it is inevitable that through relative productivity and time, China and India will be the largest economies, have the largest consumer markets, and be the principal consumers of raw materials. The return to dominance, however, unlike as envisioned by various Chinese scholars and commentators, does not mean a return to the pre-European tributary system, as the PRC is interdependent with all other states on the GPE.[47] Twenty-first-century globalisation has been achieved on the basis of an EPE model: Westphalian sovereign states and market capitalism. If this present global system is to be sustained and expanded to account for the higher levels of development and consumption, it theoretically requires the continuance of the same model of domestic and international relations. China and India thus must gain the ability to maintain the contemporary GPE in order to sustain themselves, and all states, as it is, or overcome their domestic and bilateral issues so as to be able to carry global confidence in any systemic revisions they may wish to make.

The issues of the stateless territory

The LAC begets many problematic issues and holds China and India to old ways, methods and powers, hobbling them, limiting their statecraft, and squandering opportunity. The second section of this chapter aims to state a list of problems to be overcome and identify the potential benefits of resolution of the border dispute. This section also considers the strategic consequences of not resolving the dispute for both India and China within the GPE versus other states and actors. Finally, the chapter considers potential mechanisms for implementing either back to the 1940s or beyond the 1640s methods of resolution.

The three direct problems of the LAC are Aksai Chin and Kashmir,[48] Tibet and the Tibetan government-in-exile,[49] and Arunachal Pradesh.[50] Each of these matters is uniquely complex, but all are linked to the failure of China and India to answer the boundary questions. Secondary matters include the China-India-Pakistan strategic nexus,[51] Afghanistan,[52] the modern phenomenon of global terrorism, and nuclear weapons proliferation.[53] Each of these matters complicates China and India's ability to pursue their core interests. The first group of issues is linked directly to the geography of the dispute, and while peripheral to the geographic centre of China and India, it nevertheless disrupts relations disproportionately. The secondary matters would all be lessened by resolution of the border dispute, and again, although peripheral to the core issues of the GPE, they affect it disproportionately.

Are the subjects related to the three direct problems easily negotiated through the use of problem-solving theory? The Aksai Chin and Kashmir issue is a combination of *terra nullius* (nobody's land), the displacement of native political economies by colonialism, the extension of the European states system globally, postcolonial states seeking security through assured territory, and the nascent realist strategies of new states within the ideological contestation of the middle twentieth century. The issue of Tibet and the Tibetan government-in-exile is a combination of these, as well as religious affinity, human rights, self-determination, and stateless nations in a world of states and hard borders. Arunachal Pradesh is a corollary of these. This is an extremely simplistic overview of these subjects, and yet they are obviously already unfathomably complex to resolve through problem-solving theory alone.

The potential benefits that would result from resolving the border dispute include a significant increase in state power. This would be achieved through the unique bilateral relationship capacity of having two billion-plus population size states pursuing common interests, either via mercantilism/realism or liberalism. China and India are both developing states that have to answer the same unique question, that is how to successfully develop over one billion people through an industrial revolution. The scale and volume of development is far beyond previous experiences, and cooperation on policy, products, and services development would be beneficial.

In answering their own development questions both separately and together, the two great powers have the potential to act as test cases or models that may be followed by all states – in particular with regard to global infrastructure and global public goods. The global demographic transition begun in the 1800s will end with a planet holding approximately ten billion people.[54] Projects such as Myanmar's oil and gas pipelines,[55] Sri Lanka's Hambantota port,[56] Pakistan's China-Pakistan Economic Corridor linking Gwadar-Karakorum Highway-Xinjiang,[57] or the proposed Nepal extension to the Qinghai-Tibet railway[58] are all essential for global development. This is borne out by the broad acceptance and wide membership of China's initiative, the Asian Infrastructure Investment Bank,[59] and factually supported as viable by the infrastructure investment-led development of China itself.[60] China's complementary Belt and Road Initiative would be furthered by settlement of the border dispute, and the resolution would enable a faster uptake of Chinese investment in India and replication of China's infrastructure-led development style by India.[61]

Gaining of global structural power is also possible if China and India collaborate. Their combined consumption levels can lead to the development of markets, resources, and mining projects, as well as determine emissions and other global common, regulatory questions.[62] Thus, in pursuit of their own interest, their activity and relative capacity potentially gives them the ability to establish rules and norms of the system, where all other states would define themselves in relation to them.

Failure to address this strategic priority will potentially result in numerous unavoidable challenges, the principle of these being the inability to pursue domestic development. Stagnant economies give rise to political turmoil. A lack of coordination between them and fear of conflict does not encourage markets and firms domestically or internationally. Resource and market constraints would result from political and military instability, undermining economic growth. The resultant relative loss of power versus other states or groups of states (such as the US, Japan, Russia, the European Union, or the Association of Southeast Asian Nations) would curtail China and India's ability to pursue global statecraft to recreate the GPE towards their own interests, and would constitute a strategic failure.

The need to power balance as geopolitical rivals against each other at best results in dependence on extra-regional powers, and at worst invites external intervention – examples being the cyclical US–Pakistan relationship, the International Security Assistance Force in Afghanistan led by the US and North Atlantic Treaty Organization, or the persistent attention on Tibet and the Dalai Lama.[63] States as well as multinational corporations, intergovernmental organisations, and nongovernmental organisations think and act globally, but not necessarily for a broader common global good, or take into account Chinese or Indian national interests. Finally, instability of the GPE due to conflict between China and India would be a disaster for all states, but foremost for China and India.

Back to the 1940s

Are nations truly independent if they have become so through other terms and processes? The back to the 1940s process would entail, first, agreeing to reset the post-British India borders, and second, negotiating for a practical outcome. How would this be undertaken? The present negotiation method has been via Bilateral Joint Working Groups such as the India-China or Bhutan-China precedents.[64] Additional methods could be considered, such as a multiparty talks method including the regional great, middle and small powers, and optionally, an extra-regional great power such as the US or Russia. Precedents include the Six-Party Talks or P5+1 talks, as has been utilised to negotiate nuclear weapons proliferation issues with the Democratic People's Republic of Korea and Islamic Republic of Iran.[65]

Working through a regional forum, such as the Shanghai Cooperation Organisation (SCO) or the South Asian Association for Regional Cooperation (SAARC), is a possibility. However, whereas the SCO has been relatively successful in surviving territorial disputes, it has not been successful in resolving them (see Chapter 8). Its focus on the common interests of states is instructive, in the SCO's case these being opposition to terrorism, separatism, and religious extremism.[66] The SAARC model has been equally inept at dealing with territorial disputes, choosing to avoid contentious issues by focusing on economic growth.[67]

China and India have both solved border disputes with other states, and these may be indicative of what may be successfully merged to find a method that works between the great powers. China's resolution of other border disputes may be instructive, particularly between Russia and China; and yet Hyer's finding links the numerous successes to broader systemic imperatives, as quoted earlier. Nonetheless, China's unique method of solving border disputes in South Asia could be considered a tributary model, as displayed in the successful resolution of the China-Burma border dispute. This was defined in a different, less public era of the 1950s and 1960s and entailed avoiding internationalisation; a willingness to remake (border) issues; regular vassal-like trips to Beijing; the use of New Era concepts (Five Principles, Kin Folk Concept); negotiated settlement; and joint military operations to remove opposition.[68] India too has solved many of its border disputes – most recently settling with Bangladesh – through negotiation, as opposed to the use of warfare and stalemate with regard to Pakistan.[69]

Beyond the 1640s

The beyond the 1640s concept seems to be an excessive mechanism for solving the border dispute. It also may seem unequivocally threatening to the present global order of sovereign states, given that it is critical theory–based and would make China and India revisionist great powers. However, the system is far more flexible than it appears. The concept of sovereignty is a human invention and has been evolving through norms and precedent since it was first employed in 1648. In addition, the practical expression had been theorised for ninety-three years prior to that.[70] Thus, over extended periods of time significant changes may be made less threatening, as long as they provide the same utility of sovereignty: territorial assurance.

Historical materialism provides a wide lens through which to consider systemic change over time. The basic tenet is that the economy ('mode of production' could also be used) gives rise to social relations. Technological change from invention or necessity changes the economy, which changes relations between people and requires new social relations. If it is accepted that technological change is inevitable and required for the survival of the human species, then it follows that sovereignty as an organising principle of human social relations will also change slowly over time.[71]

The reinvention of sovereignty in line with historical materialism to suit a more interconnected (e.g. jet engines, satellites, the Internet) and crowded (ten billion plus population) planet is already ongoing. Europe's regionalism, presently named the European Union, has been evolving and reworking territorial assurance for decades.[72] Its precedent of regionalism has been adopted in North America (the North American Free Trade Agreement, or NAFTA) as well as in numerous other locations, to varying degrees of complexity and success.[73] Shortly after independence, China and India took an idealistic attempt at designing norms of sovereignty with the Five Principles (Panchsheel) Agreement, which was followed by the Non-Aligned Movement; these were revisited and revamped in the 1990s as the New Security Concept.[74] We may theorise that they didn't affect the GPE's recreation, as China and India were not great powers, whereas the US and the Soviet Union were.

With more power in the later part of the twentieth century, China solved its own legacy territorial assurance issues and built its development model through revision of sovereignty. The Special Administrative Regions of Hong Kong and Macau are unique geopolitical spaces created by Chinese great power statecraft. They redefined the relationship between geography and political economy to produce a policy and outcome most suitable to the PRC to solve the European leases.[75] The one country, two systems policy enables a unique solution through adaption of concepts rather than kowtowing to them, which may ultimately find Hong Kong as well as Taiwan reunifying with the PRC.[76] The four Special Economic Zones of the Open-Door policy from December 1978, in Guangdong and Fujian provinces (Shenzhen, Xiamen, Shantou, and Zhuhai), are a similar, deliberate Chinese mutation of sovereignty to seek success.[77]

108 *Jonathan H. Ping*

Revision of sovereignty through critical theory, when backed by great power statecraft, is thus practical to achieve outcomes often unobtainable through problem-solving theory. In each of the above cases, if the principal of supreme legitimate authority had been applied rigorously within a problem-solving theory approach, and not challenged by accounting for the continuous process of historical change, the outcomes would not have been obtainable. The requirement of territorial assurance, however, has been adhered to, and this helps find the limits of revision. The global ramifications of undermining sovereignty, making it dysfunctional, would potentially lift nations from the arbitrary colonial division of geography into states that don't meet nationalist desires as undertaken by European great powers. Nonetheless, to disallow the sanctuary of a nation with an exclusive geographic space entirely would have a potentially significant and negative impact on self-determination and human rights.

Conclusion

This chapter has identified the China-India border dispute as a strategic priority for China. The rapid development of China, its relative size, and its dependence on the GPE result in the border dispute constituting a systemic failure and threat to the stability and further development of the GPE. Without repair, the border dispute between the two great powers is a hazard to all states; but first to China, as its economic development would be stalled, leading to political turmoil.

The increased stability afforded to the GPE by resolution of the border dispute is not only ideal but requisite, as the increasing global population, required economic growth, and problematic environmental management make global governance more complex. This chapter has thus provided a strategic rationale for China and India to resolve the border dispute.

Problem-solving theory leads to recommendations identified by many scholars of continued trade, economic, cultural, political, or leadership interaction. This chapter has argued that whilst these are useful, they should be supported by a far greater level of transparency of the ongoing negotiations, and these negotiation should be placed within the broader relationship rather than being side-lined. However, whilst this may ensure a continuing status quo, it does not entail an assured resolution to the dispute. In addition, unforeseen events such as changes in leadership, nontraditional security threats, or demographic change may destabilise the presently insubstantial relationship.

As great powers, China and India have the capacity to pursue a resolution in a purposeful, directed manner, rather than continue with the decades-long stalled negotiations. In addition, they have the ability to begin negotiations from any point, rather than proceeding from the McMahon Line or the LAC, which are both historically problematic for China (as an unequal treaty) and India (due to the 1962 border war). To overcome the present status quo, this chapter has employed the discipline of GPE and critical theory to propose two theoretical alternatives. As great powers, China and India have the capacity to pursue unique statecraft that reinvents key components of the contemporary system, such as sovereignty. They attempted this postindependence, but lacked the great power status to remake the GPE. In the present, they have both developed ample capacity to influence the system as a whole, and this power could be used to push for solutions which seek policies best suited to their interests.

The first approach is to reset the borders pre-independence and revisit the partition of British India. The benefit of doing this is that it includes the Pakistani-ceded parts of Jammu-Kashmir, and avoids enshrining the results of decades of mistrust and conflict which has led to the present LAC. The second critical theory approach envisions remaking the concept of sovereignty and builds upon numerous examples of modification of the European Westphalian ideal of sovereignty by Europeans, and indeed India and China themselves. China and India's great power statecraft has the capacity to solve the border dispute through the additional use of critical theory to supplement problem-solving theory. This would enable both states to build an assured, stable, and viable GPE primarily for their benefit, but in a global, public good manner to benefit all states.

Notes

1 World population 7.32 billion, China 1.39 billion, India 1.26 billion. <www.worldometers.info/> (accessed 8 June 2015); D. Anand, 'Revisiting the China-India Border Dispute: An Introduction', *China Report*, vol. 47, May 2011, pp. 65–69, <http://chr.sagepub.com/content/47/2/65> (accessed 9 June 2015).
2 International Energy Agency, FAQs: Oil, <www.iea.org/aboutus/faqs/oil/> (accessed 8 June 2015).
3 'The 10 Biggest Oil Consuming Countries', hydrocarbons-technology.com, <www.hydrocarbons-technology.com/features/featurethe-10-biggest-oil-consuming-countries-4141632/> (accessed 8 June 2015); 'Petroleum Consumption', World by Map, <http://world.bymap.org/OilConsumption.html> (accessed 8 June 2015).
4 International Energy Statistics, *Total Carbon Dioxide Emissions from the Consumption of Energy (Million Metric Tons)*, <www.eia.gov/cfapps/ipdbproject/iedindex3.cfm?tid=90&pid=44&aid=8> (accessed 8 June 2015); World Bank, CO_2 emissions, <http://data.worldbank.org/indicator/EN.ATM.CO2E.PC> (accessed 8 June 2015).
5 World Bank 2015, GDP (current US$), <http://data.worldbank.org/indicator/NY.GDP.MKTP.CD?order=wbapi_data_value_2013+wbapi_data_value+wbapi_data_value-last&sort=desc>; 'World GDP', *Economist*, 21 March 2015, <www.economist.com/news/economic-and-financial-indicators/21646778-world-gdp?zid=295&ah=0bca374e65f2354d553956ea65f756e0> (accessed 8 June 2015).
6 M. Malik, 'India Balances China', *Asian Politics & Policy*, vol. 4, no. 3, 2012, p. 348; J. Holslag, 'The Persistent Military Security Dilemma between China and India', *Journal of Strategic Studies*, vol. 32, no. 6, 2009, pp. 834–35.
7 B. McCormick and J.H. Ping, *Chinese Engagements: Regional Issues with Global Implications*, Robina, Queensland: Bond University Press, 2011, p. 169.
8 P. Olinto, K. Beegle, C. Sobrado, and H. Uematsu, 'The State of the Poor: Where Are the Poor, Where Is Extreme Poverty Harder to End, and What Is the Current Profile of the World's Poor?', *Economic Premise* (The World Bank), no. 125, October 2013.
9 L.M. van der Mey, 'The India-China Conflict: Explaining the Outbreak of War 1962', *Diplomacy & Statecraft*, vol. 5, no. 1, 1994, pp. 183–99; B. Chellaney, 'India's Intractable Border Dispute with China', in B. Elleman, S. Kotkin and C. Schofield, *Beijing's Power and China's Borders: Twenty Neighbors in Asia*, Hoboken, NJ: Taylor & Francis, 2014, pp. 47–59.

10 M. Malik, 'India Balances China', *Asian Politics & Policy*, vol. 4, 2012, pp. 345–76, doi:10.1111/j.1943–0787.2012.01360.x; Chellaney, 'India's Intractable Border Dispute with China', p. 53.
11 J. Holslag, 'Progress, Perceptions and Peace in the Sino-Indian Relationship', *East Asia: An International Quarterly*, vol. 26, no. 12009, 41–56.
12 J. Garver, 'The Unresolved Sino-Indian Border Dispute: An Interpretation', *China Report*, vol. 47, May 2011, pp. 99–113, <http://chr.sagepub.com/content/47/2/99.full.pdf+html> (accessed 10 June 2015).
13 S. Strange, *States and Markets* (2nd ed.), London: Pinter, 1994, p. 25: Structural power is 'the power to decide how things shall be done, the power to shape frameworks within which states relate to each other, relate to people or relate to corporate entities'.
14 'State Council of the People's Republic of China, Tibet: Its Ownership and Human Rights Situation', *Chinese Journal of International Law*, vol. 2, no. 2, 2003, pp. 747–90; S.K. Mitra, *Politics in India: Structure, Process and Policy*, London: Routledge, 2011; E. Hyer, *The Pragmatic Dragon: China's Grand Strategy and Boundary Settlements*, Contemporary Chinese Studies, Vancouver: UBC Press, 2015; Anand, 'Revisiting the China-India Border Dispute'.
15 R. O'Brien and M. Williams, *Global Political Economy: Evolution and Dynamics* (4th ed.), Basingstoke: Palgrave Macmillan, 2013.
16 J.H. Ping, *Middle Power Statecraft: Indonesia, Malaysia, and the Asia Pacific*, Aldershot: Ashgate, 2005, p. 17.
17 U.S. Department of State, *Independent States in the World*, <www.state.gov/s/inr/rls/4250.htm> (accessed 8 June 2015).
18 Ping, *Middle Power Statecraft*, p. 226.
19 R.W. Cox and T.J. Sinclair, *Approaches to World Order*, Cambridge: Cambridge University Press, 1996, p. 87.
20 Ibid., p. 89.
21 H.M. Schwartz, 'The Rise of the Modern State: From Street Gangs to Mafias', in *States Versus Markets: History, Geography, and the Development of the International Political Economy*, New York: St. Martin's Press, 1994, pp. 10–42; D. Philpott, 'Sovereignty: An Introduction and Brief History', *Journal of International Affairs*, vol. 48, no. 2, 1995, pp. 352–68.
22 For a definition and discussion of political goods, see R.I. Rotberg (ed.), 'The Failure and Collapse of Nation-States: Breakdown, Prevention and Repair', in *When States Fail: Causes and Consequences*, Princeton, NJ: Princeton University Press, 2004, <http://press.princeton.edu/chapters/s7666.pdf> (accessed 11 June 2015).
23 For a discussion and definition of public goods, see I. Kaul, 'Rethinking Public Goods and Global Public Goods', in E. Brousseau, T. Dedeurwaerdere, and B. Siebenhüner (eds.), *Politics, Science, and the Environment: Reflexive Governance for Global Public Goods*, Cambridge, MA: MIT Press, 2012. Also see B. McCormick and J.H. Ping, *Chinese Engagements: Regional Issues with Global Implications*, Robina, Queensland: Bond University Press, 2011, p. 180.
24 N.S. Jamwal, 'Management of Land Borders', *Strategic Analysis*, vol. 26, no. 3, 2002, pp. 406–26.
25 'Kashmir Profile', *BBC News*, 26 November 2014, <www.bbc.com/news/world-south-asia-11693674> (accessed June 10, 2015); R. Mishra, 'The "Sir Creek" Dispute: Contours, Implications and the Way Ahead', *Strategic Analysis*, vol. 39, no. 2, 2015, pp. 184–96; R.S. Khosa, 'The Siachen Glacier Dispute: Imbroglio on the Roof of the World', *Contemporary South Asia*, vol. 8, no. 2, 1999, pp. 187–209.
26 'India and Bangladesh Sign Historic Territory Swap Deal', *BBC News*, 6 June 2015, <www.bbc.com/news/world-asia-33033342> (accessed 10 June 2015).
27 A. Rahi, 'Why the Durand Line Matters', *Diplomat*, 21 February 2014, <http://thediplomat.com/2014/02/why-the-durand-line-matters/> (accessed 10 June 2015).

28 Ping, 'China's Relations with India's Neighbours: From Threat Avoidance to Alternative Development Opportunity', Asian Journal of Political Science, vol. 21, no. 1, pp. 25–26.
29 Hyer, *The Pragmatic Dragon*, p. 63.
30 V. Kumar, 'India-China Border Dispute: A Study of Joint Working Group', figshare, 2014, <http://dx.doi.org/10.6084/m9.figshare.1167445> (accessed 9 June 2015).
31 A general reading of the subject offers many similar findings.
32 M. Haider, 'Pakistan and Kashmir Are Inseparable: General Raheel Sharif', *Dawn*, 3 June 2015, <www.dawn.com/news/1185928> (accessed 10 June 2015); R.H. Laskar, 'India, Pakistan Spar over Economic Corridor Passing through PoK', *Hindustan Times*, 1 June 2015, <www.hindustantimes.com/india-news/india-pakistan-spar-over-46-billion-pak-china-economic-corridor-passing-through-pok/article-1353486.aspx> (accessed 10 June 2015).
33 M.N.M. Walsh, 'Xi Xinping and Shinzo Abe Show Australia How to Reform', *Australian Financial Review*, 20 May 2015, <www.afr.com/news/world/asia/narendra-modi-xi-xinping-and-shinzo-abe-show-australia-how-to-reform-20150520-gh5t8v> (accessed 20 May 2015).
34 NDTV, 'Chinese President Xi Skips Protocol, Gives PM Narendra Modi "Highest-Level Reception" in His Hometown Xian', *NDTV*, 14 May 2015, <www.ndtv.com/india-news/chinese-president-xi-jinping-skips-protocol-gives-prime-minister-narendra-modi-highest-level-recepti-763063> (accessed 16 May 2015).
35 Hyer, *The Pragmatic Dragon*, p. 57; Chellaney, 'India's Intractable Border Dispute with China', p. 52.
36 B.M. Jain, 'India-China Relations: Issues and Emerging Trends', *Round Table: The Commonwealth Journal of International Affairs*, vol. 93, no. 374, 2004, pp. 253–69.
37 D. Philpott, 'Sovereignty: An Introduction and Brief History', *Journal of International Affairs*, vol. 48, no. 2, 1995, pp. 352–68.
38 S.K. Mitra, 'The Federal Structure', in *Politics in India*, pp. 87–108.
39 H.L. Wesseling, 'Globalization: A Historical Perspective', in *Cape of Asia: Essays on European History*, Amsterdam: Leiden University Press, 2011; D. Thompson, 'The Economic History of the Last 2,000 Years in 1 Little Graph', *Atlantic*, 19 June 2012, <www.theatlantic.com/business/archive/2012/06/the-economic-history-of-the-last-2-000-years-in-1-little-graph/258676/> (accessed 9 June 2015); 'Share of World GDP Throughout History', infogr.am, <https://infogr.am/Share-of-world-GDP-throughout-history> (accessed 9 June 2015).
40 W. Thompson and R. William, 'The 1490s: A Question of Evolution (Dis)continuity', *Emergence of the Global Political Economy*, London: Routledge, 2000, pp. 39–53.
41 D. Scott, *China and the International System, 1840–1949: Power, Presence, and Perceptions in a Century of Humiliation*, Ithaca: State University of New York Press, 2008.
42 United Nations Convention on the Law of the Sea, 10 November 1982; Z. Gao and B.B. Jia, 'The Nine-Dash Line in the South China Sea: History, Status, and Implications', *American Journal of International Law*, vol. 107, no. 1, 2013, pp. 98–124.
43 Hyer, *The Pragmatic Dragon*, p. xi.
44 Ibid., p. 15.
45 Chellaney, 'India's Intractable Border Dispute with China', p. 58.
46 S. Tejani, 'The Colonial Legacy', in A. Guneratne and A.M. Weiss (eds.), *Pathways to Power: The Domestic Politics of South Asia*, Plymouth: Rowman & Littlefield, 2014, pp. 21–103; S. Bose and A. Jalal, *Modern South Asia: History, Culture and Political Economy* (2nd ed.), London: Routledge, 2007.
47 L. Jing, 'China's Rise Will Restore History of Peaceful Benefits for Its Neighbors', *Global Times*, 15 February 2015, <www.globaltimes.cn/content/907832.shtml> (accessed 10 June 2015).
48 R. Egreteau, 'The China-India Rivalry Reconceptualized', *Asian Journal of Political Science*, vol. 20, no. 1, 2012, p. 8.

49 P. Mehra, 'India's Border Dispute with China: Revisiting Nehru's Approach', *International Studies*, vol. 42, no. 3–4, 2005, p. 357.
50 Holslag, 'The Persistent Military Security Dilemma between China and India', p. 812.
51 P.J. Smith, 'The Tilting Triangle: Geopolitics of the China-India-Pakistan Relationship', *Comparative Strategy*, vol. 32, no. 4, 2013, pp. 313–30.
52 A. Saikal, 'Securing Afghanistan's Border', *Survival: Global Politics and Strategy*, vol. 48, no. 1, 2006, pp. 129–42.
53 C.B. Primiano, 'China under Stress: The Xinjiang Question', *International Politics*, vol. 50, no. 3, 2013, pp. 455–73.
54 'World Population Could Soar to 12 Billion by 2100: Demographers', *ABC News*, 19 September 2014, <www.abc.net.au/news/2014–09–19/world-population-could-hit-12b-by-2100-demographers/5755148> (accessed 16 June 2015).
55 H. Zhao, 'China-Myanmar Energy Cooperation and Its Regional Implications', *Journal of Current Southeast Asian Affairs*, vol. 30, no. 4, 2011, pp. 89–109; 'China-Myanmar Oil-Gas Pipeline Section Breaks Ground in China', *China Chemical Reporter*, vol. 21, no. 20, 2010, p. 10.
56 P. Barta, 'In Sri Lanka's Post-Tsunami Rise, China Is Key', *Wall Street Journal*, 18 December 2014, <www.wsj.com/articles/in-sri-lankas-post-tsunami-rise-china-is-key-1418938382> (accessed 10 January 2015); N. Samaranayake, 'Are Sri Lanka's Relations with China Deepening? An Analysis of Economic, Military, and Diplomatic Data', *Asian Security*, vol. 7, no. 2, 2011, pp. 119–46.
57 'Is China-Pakistan "Silk Road" a Game-Changer?', *BBC News*, 22 April 2015, <www.bbc.com/news/world-asia-32400091> (accessed June 10, 2015); 'Pakistan-China Trade Corridor: Construction of Karakoram Highway', *Pakistan Construction & Quarry*, 27 April 2015, <www.pcq.com.pk/pakistan-china-trade-corridor-construction-of-karakoram-highway/> (accessed 10 May 2015).
58 'Qinghai-Tibet Railway to Reach Nepal in 2020', *China Daily*, 7 April 2015, <http://usa.chinadaily.com.cn/china/2015–04/07/content_20016584.htm> (accessed 10 April 2015); T. Mathou, 'Tibet and Its Neighbors: Moving Toward a New Chinese Strategy in the Himalayan Region', *Asian Survey*, vol. 45, no. 4, 2005, pp. 503–21.
59 C. Huang, '57 Nations Approved as Founder Members of the China-Led AIIB', *South China Morning Post*, 27 April 2015, <www.scmp.com/news/china/diplomacy-defence/article/1766970/57-nations-approved-founder-members-china-led-aiib> (accessed 5 May 2015).
60 P. Chakraborty and Y. Zhang, 'Economic Reforms and Infrastructure Spending: Evidence from China and India', Research Paper No. 2009/43, Helsinki: United Nations University World Institute for Development Economics Research, 2009.
61 X. Jinping, 'Towards a Community of Common Destiny and A New Future for Asia', Keynote Speech, Boao Forum for Asia Annual Conference, 28 March 2015, <http://news.xinhuanet.com/english/2015–03/29/c_134106145.htm?utm_content=buffer4cf1e&utm_medium=social&utm_source=twitter.com&utm_campaign=buffer> (accessed 11 June 2015).
62 J.P. Vazhayil and R. Balasubramanian, 'Copenhagen Commitments and Implications: A Comparative Analysis of India and China', *Energy Policy*, vol. 38, no. 11, 2010, pp. 7442–50; S. Breslin, 'China's Emerging Global Role: Dissatisfied Responsible Great Power', *Politics*, vol. 30 (S1), 2010, pp. 52–62; V. Vivoda, 'China Challenges Global Capitalism', *Australian Journal of International Affairs*, vol. 63, no. 1, 2009, pp. 22–40.
63 N. Hynek and P. Marton, *Statebuilding in Afghanistan: Multinational Contributions to Reconstruction*, London: Taylor & Francis, 2011; C.B. Kelly and V.B. Francis, *Pakistan and U.S. Relations*, New York: Nova Science, 2009; C. Hatton, 'China Resettles Two Million Tibetans, Says Human Rights Watch', *BBC News*, 27 June 2013, <www.bbc.com/news/world-asia-china-23081653> (accessed 23 December 2014).

64 'Joint Statement between the Republic of India and the People's Republic of China on Building a Closer Developmental Partnership', Ministry of External Affairs – Government of India, 19 September 2014, <www.mea.gov.in/bilateral-documents. htm?dtl/24022/Joint+Statement+between+the+Republic+of+India+and+the+Peoples+Republic+of+China+on+Building+a+Closer+Developmental+Partnership> (accessed 10 June 2015).
65 R.P. Pardo, 'China and Northeast Asia's Regional Security Architecture: The Six-Party Talks as a Case of Chinese Regime-Building?', *East Asia*, vol. 29, 2012, pp. 337–54.
66 J. Yuan, 'China's Role in Establishing and Building the Shanghai Cooperation Organization (SCO)', *Journal of Contemporary China*, vol. 19, no. 67, 2010, pp. 855–69.
67 R. Jetly, 'Conflict Management Strategies in ASEAN: Perspectives for SAARC', *Pacific Review*, vol. 16, no. 1, 2003, pp. 53–76; G. Zhang, 'China and South Asian Regionalism: SAARC and Beyond', in R. Dossani, D.C. Sneider and V. Sood (eds.), *Does South Asia Exist? Prospects for Regional Integration*, Stanford, CA: Walter H. Shorenstein Asia-Pacific Research Center, 2010.
68 Ping, 'China's Relations with India's Neighbours', pp. 33–36.
69 'India and Bangladesh Sign Historic Territory Swap Deal', *BBC News*, 6 June 2015, <www.bbc.com/news/world-asia-33033342> (accessed 12 June 2015).
70 Ping, *Middle Power Statecraft*, pp. 24–25.
71 I. Buchanan, 'Historical Materialism', in *A Dictionary of Critical Theory*, Oxford: Oxford University Press, 2010.
72 M. Avbelj, 'Theorizing Sovereignty and European Integration', *Ratio Juris*, vol. 27, no. 3, 2014, pp. 344–63.
73 S. Sehgal, 'The Evolution of NAFTA: An Experience in Regionalism', *India Quarterly*, vol. 66, no. 3, 2010, pp. 303–16; NAFTANOW.org, <www.naftanow.org/> (accessed 12 June 2015).
74 China Report, 'China's Position Paper on the New Security Concept, 31 July 2002', *China Report*, vol. 39, no. 1, 2003, pp. 128–31; S. Singh, 'Three Agreements and Five Principles between India and China', in T. Chung (ed.), *Across the Himalayan Gap: An Indian Quest for Understanding China*, New Delhi: Indira Gandhi National Centre for the Arts, 1998, <www.ignca.nic.in/ks_41062.htm> (accessed 12 June 2015); M.A. Vieira, C. Alden, and S. Morphet, *The South in World Politics*, Basingstoke: Palgrave Macmillan, 2010; S. Randol, 'How to Approach the Elephant: Chinese Perceptions of India in the Twenty-First Century', *Asian Affairs: An American Review*, vol. 34, no. 4, 2008, pp. 211–88.
75 B. Chou, 'Local Autonomy in Action: Beijing's Hong Kong and Macau Policies', *Journal of Current Chinese Affairs*, vol. 42, no. 3, 2013, pp. 29–54.
76 'One Country, Two Systems', *China through a Lens*, 22–23 June 1984, <www.china.org.cn/english/features/dengxiaoping/103372.htm> (accessed 12 June 2015).
77 K.T. Liou, *Managing Economic Reforms in Post-Mao China*, Westport, CT: Greenwood, 1998, p. 77; X. Zhang, B. Krug, and P. Reinmoeller, *Historical Attitudes and Implications for Path Dependence: FDI Development and Institutional Changes in China*, Rotterdam: Erasmus University, Rotterdam School of Management, <http://down.cenet.org.cn/upfile/36/2005121184837120.pdf> (accessed 12 June 2015).

7 US–China cooperation

The role of Pakistan after the death of Osama bin Laden

Timothy D. Hoyt[1]

Introduction

South Asia emerged as a regional system from 1947, with the partition of Britain's Indian Empire into several states, the two largest being the Republic of India and the Islamic Republic of Pakistan. The region remains a hotbed of conflict, both internal and interstate, but the security dynamic is complicated by the existence of two major outside powers with significant interests and a history of intervention in the region: the United States of America (US) and the People's Republic of China. Each state has a long and complicated relationship with India, including a still unresolved border issue between India and China that sparked a war in 1962 and remains a sore spot even today (see Chapter 6). The US and China each has a long history of alliance with Pakistan, although these relationships are very different.[2]

The twenty-first century has, in some ways, only exacerbated the South Asian security dilemma. India's economic rise has been accompanied by a widening military imbalance between India and Pakistan. As India and China continue their remarkable economic development, their demand for the energy resources of the Persian Gulf increases, making the sea lines of communication across the Indian Ocean a vital interest for both.[3] The US invasion of Afghanistan not only drove the Taliban into neighboring Pakistan, but also created an unprecedented and semi-permanent presence of US and North Atlantic Treaty Organization (NATO) troops in the region. Indo-Pakistani tensions remain, and Pakistani-based and supported terrorist groups have sparked two major crises that almost led to war in 2001–2 and 2008.[4] Sino-Indian tensions have increased, the US–India relationship has turned much more positive than at any time in history, and the US–Pakistan relationship is in a dangerous decline after US forces killed Osama bin Laden in Abbottabad, Pakistan, without informing the Pakistanis of the raid.[5]

Nevertheless, the current environment offers new strategic opportunities as well as challenges which may be given priority. With the US and International Security Assistance Force withdrawal in 2014, the security challenges posed by the Western force structure in Afghanistan will recede. The slow emergence of nonmilitary actors in Pakistani domestic politics offers the possibility of a gradual shift away from traditional hostility towards India and opportunities for normalization of relations over time.[6] In addition, the emergence of a deadly antigovernment

Islamist militancy in Pakistan creates incentives for the security services to reprioritize and focus more on internal threats.[7] Finally, the US and China have important shared interests in the region: good order at sea, combating regional terrorist threats, nuclear nonproliferation, and the establishment of a stronger, more stable Pakistani state. South Asia, in fact, offers a significant strategic opportunity for China and the US to cooperate in areas of common interest and build the kinds of patterns of trust and cooperation that will facilitate better relations between the two in periods of future tension and in other regions.

The US–Pakistan relationship

The US–Pakistan relationship might best be described as a sine curve – a wave pattern with high peaks and deep valleys. The US pursues a close relationship with Pakistan when it perceives vital interests are at stake. It also has a sad history of devaluing or terminating that relationship in response to changes in the economic and security environment, or in response to specific Pakistani actions that violate US laws or norms. These have included the use of US military equipment to invade India in 1965, the acceleration of Pakistan's nuclear weapons program in violation of the Pressler Amendment in 1990, support for multiple militant groups that engage in regional and transnational acts of terror, and (perhaps) Pakistan's unacknowledged but obvious tolerance of Taliban leadership in Baluchistan and the Federally Administered Tribal Areas.

Pakistan, on the other hand, seizes opportunities to capitalize on US interest, while recognizing (perhaps too cynically) that these opportunities might be short-lived.[8] The US has resources that Pakistan desperately needs, including foreign aid and assistance with international lending institutions and creditors. Equally important, for a Pakistan that remains dominated by a military-driven, India-centric perspective on security, the US is a source of top-of-the-line military hardware *and* of military assistance programs that can fund Pakistani purchases. Access to US resources, however, has not affected Pakistan's perspective on core interests nor its approach to securing regional security. Despite occasional statements suggesting the possibility of change, Pakistan remains committed to a volatile mix of militant allies, using them as assets in both regional and domestic policy.[9] The large, deeply politicized army is increasing its influence over the domestic economy and maintains virtual control over foreign policy.[10] Finally, Pakistan has the most rapidly expanding nuclear arsenal in the world, and has remained resistant to efforts to improve security and prevent the proliferation of nuclear weapons technology.[11]

The history of the US–Pakistan relationship, therefore, is one of roughly ten year cycles of cooperation and alienation. From 1947–54, the US was largely absent from the subcontinent, engrossed in the Cold War and Korea. From 1954–65, the US provided large amounts of military and economic aid to Pakistan, and Pakistan provided air bases and intelligence facilities for the US to monitor the Soviet Union.[12] The relationship collapsed with Pakistan's two-phase attack on Indian-held Kashmir in 1965, which prompted US sanctions on both Pakistan and

India – and which coincided with an increased US commitment in Vietnam that distracted it from South Asia for years. There was a brief rapprochement in 1970 when the Nixon administration used Pakistan as an intermediary in its approach to China, but this ended almost immediately after the war that liberated Bangladesh in 1971. US–Pakistan relations warmed again in 1980 after the Soviet invasion of Afghanistan put the Red Army on Pakistan's border.[13] For ten years Pakistan was the recipient of vast quantities of US aid in return for acting as a conduit and coordinator to Afghanistan's mujahideen. The end of the Cold War, and Pakistan's violation of US nonproliferation laws, led to another downturn in relations, which was further exacerbated by Pakistan's 1998 nuclear tests and open support for the Taliban regime. After 9/11, Pakistan again became an essential partner for the US, being granted the status of Major Non-NATO Ally and receiving billions of dollars in aid and compensation from 2001 to 2011.

The discovery of Osama bin Laden in Abbottabad, Pakistan – site of Pakistan's prestigious military academy – and the US raid that killed him created another crisis in US–Pakistan relations.[14] Although both sides have made efforts to prevent the relationship from collapsing, as it did in 1965 and 1990, relations remain rocky and vulnerable. This uncertainty poses both a strategic challenge and opportunity for cooperation, and a possibility that the US and China, for the first time since 1971, can jointly cooperate on policies in the region that help to advance common interests with and in Pakistan.

The Sino-Pakistan relationship

China's relationship with Pakistan has been much less volatile than US–Pakistani ties. Pakistan recognized the People's Republic of China while a member of the South East Asian Treaty Organization – an action that prompted an explanatory statement by senior Chinese officials to the effect that this was not viewed as incompatible.[15] In 1962, Pakistan transferred several thousand square kilometers of disputed territory to Chinese control,[16] and the bilateral economic and security relationship deepened in the 1960s after sanctions were imposed on Pakistan by the US.

Sino-Pakistani ties were critical in President Nixon's initial efforts to reestablish a relationship between the US and China. China became the major supplier of arms to Pakistan, providing the tanks and aircraft that make up most of the Pakistani Army and Air Force arsenals today. In addition, China reportedly provided significant assistance to Pakistan's nuclear weapons program and its missile delivery capability.[17] This assistance included establishing factories for the production of short and medium range ballistic missiles. More recently, Chinese involvement in the nuclear weapons program was revealed in the form of nuclear warhead designs, which Pakistani scientist A.Q. Khan sold to Libya, as well as Khan's more recent revelations that the Chinese government provided shaped nuclear warhead cores to Pakistan in 1986.[18]

China has also made significant investments in Pakistan, particularly in terms of infrastructure. The Karakoram Highway is a striking example of Chinese investment, and is a critical land link between the two countries. China's investments in the new port of Gwadar – in Baluchistan near the Iranian border – have raised concerns in India and elsewhere.[19] China has denied it intends to use the facility as a naval base, and a long-term deal was signed with a firm in Singapore in order to reassure the international community. Nevertheless, in late 2011 Pakistani officials loudly announced that they had held talks with China and had offered China a naval base there.[20] The official Chinese reply politely denied Pakistan's claims.[21]

This unusual and very public episode suggests that China and Pakistan view the relationship very differently. Pakistan consistently refers to China as an 'all-weather friend' and, more privately, as an indispensable ally.[22] China's commitment is much less clear, but certainly less intense than Pakistan would prefer. In virtually every Indo-Pakistani crisis or war, for example, Pakistani delegations have gone to China to ask for support.[23] In each case, they have been politely rebuffed. Pakistan desperately wants military equipment and support to balance out India's larger resources – while China has been willing to sell equipment in peacetime, it has been noncommittal regarding political or military support during crisis or war.

China's restraint is not surprising, in the broader context of Chinese foreign policy. China has not established the kinds of alliance networks that the US created in the Cold War, and approaches bilateral relations with most states on a transactional basis. The One Belt, One Road, concept plus the furtherance of the 2013 proposed Asian Infrastructure Investment Bank through early 2015 proffer a more networked foreign policy through neighboring diplomacy but this is yet to be consolidated.[24] Chinese long-term foreign policy thus has focused on opening or maintaining access to markets, rather than choosing sides in regional competitions or even internal conflicts. Pakistan has received very positive treatment, but China's commitment to Pakistani security, and more importantly its willingness to back Pakistani actions that threaten regional stability, remains pragmatic and limited.

This is particularly important in the context of other regional relationships. China's border with India remains unresolved (see Chapter 6). The Sino-Indian security relationship, which Indians see as fundamentally altered after India's 1998 nuclear tests and deployment, remains deeply asymmetrical. The Indians worry far more about Chinese threats to Indian security than China worries about Indian threats.[25] India does, however, pose peripheral threats to important Chinese interests – its geographic position on the Indian Ocean sea lanes is undeniable, and its relationship with the Dalai Lama and Tibetan exiles is a sensitive matter for Chinese foreign policy. In addition, China has become India's largest trading partner, and holds the possibility of becoming an important market for Chinese goods. China's commitment to Pakistan, regardless of flowery rhetoric, remains pragmatic, and must be balanced against Indian concerns and sensitivities.

Chinese and US interests in South Asia

Although both the US and China have long histories of engagement in the region, and particularly with Pakistan, it is remarkable how rarely the policies of the two states have intersected. The US and China are not actually competing in the region – each has a historically tense relationship with India and a much greater level of engagement with Pakistan – but it would be hard to argue that, with just a few exceptions, there have ever been moments of close coordination or cooperation. Any form of close coordination or cooperation therefore is a strategic opportunity for China. US and Chinese policy for both Pakistan and the region have tended to run on parallel tracks, and common interests have been pursued independently.

The two most important points of intersection occurred in the Cold War. In 1970–71, Pakistan was a critical interlocutor between China and the US. Their independent bilateral ties with Pakistan were instrumental in creating an opportunity to fundamentally change the Sino-American relationship. The opening of informal and later formal diplomatic contacts between the US and China altered the regional security environment *and* the international system and this could occur again. Indian analysts perceived a US–Pakistan-China containment regime – aided by reports of a clumsy attempt by the Nixon administration to 'play the China card' – during the 1971 Indo-Pakistani war that established the independence of Bangladesh.[26] More importantly from a US perspective, the new opening to China provided the US additional leverage in ending the war in Vietnam, and conclusively demonstrated that a two-decade assumption of an unbreakable Sino-Soviet alliance was invalid.

A second episode of cooperation emerged from Soviet actions later in the decade. The Soviet invasion of Afghanistan in 1979 altered both the regional security environment – putting the Red Army on Pakistan's borders – and international perceptions of Soviet behavior. The US and China cooperated, first covertly and later more openly, in arming the mujahideen in Afghanistan, many of whom used Chinese small arms and equipment.[27] Utilizing Pakistan as a staging area, the US and China were able to train and fund a formidable resistance to Soviet rule, and eventually create an environment where Soviet costs far outweighed any benefits of remaining. The result was Soviet withdrawal – a positive outcome – but then a decade of civil war leading to a Taliban takeover of Afghanistan, as both states focused on other more important interests. Such Afghanistan-based cooperation is once again feasible, albeit for an altogether different purpose, and could be viewed presently as one of China's greatest strategic opportunities.

An important episode of noncooperation – indeed, an apparent fundamental difference of interests – emerged during the same period and continued through the 1990s and into the twenty-first century. The US and China took fundamentally different positions on Pakistan's efforts to obtain nuclear weapons.[28] Beginning in the mid-1970s, US policy shifted to attempting to prevent the further proliferation of nuclear weapons technology. In the case of Pakistan, however, this policy was temporarily set aside in the 1980s, until the passage of the Pressler Amendment to the Foreign Assistance Act in 1986.[29] From that point until 1998, when Pakistan tested multiple nuclear devices on May 28 and 30, US efforts to prevent Pakistan from obtaining nuclear weapons accelerated. These included regular efforts to engage China diplomatically and stop what was seen as enabling behavior by the Chinese government.[30]

Chinese policy regarding these issues remains officially opaque. Nevertheless, international reports strongly suggest that Chinese policy actively supported Pakistan's efforts to obtain nuclear weapons and delivery systems, and that this policy was very consistent throughout the 1975–98 period. The fact that Pakistan provided, through A.Q. Khan's illegal network, Chinese nuclear weapons designs to Libya is a diplomatically unpleasant but incontrovertible indicator of the very substantive nature of Chinese support for Pakistan's nuclear program.[31] Statements by Khan himself suggest China provided nuclear weapons cores to the Pakistani military in the mid-1980s, and other reports suggest that China cooperated actively with Pakistan's nuclear efforts.[32] US efforts to pressure China to stop nuclear cooperation were futile, demonstrating that on this issue US and Chinese interests fundamentally diverged.

More recently, the improved US–India relationship has also raised nuclear concerns. A major concession in the US approach to India was the decision to sign a bilateral civilian nuclear deal that granted India the de facto status of a nuclear weapons state without India having to sign the Nuclear Non-Proliferation Treaty. In effect, this legitimizes India's nuclear weapons program, and establishes it as an entity free from international inspection, but allows India to develop a separate commercial nuclear program that will be subject to International Atomic Energy Agency inspections.

Pakistan would like the same deal from the US. Bluntly, this is unlikely until Pakistan demonstrates several decades' worth of responsible nuclear behavior – the specter of the A.Q. Khan affair puts Pakistan's nuclear establishment in a very different position than India's. China, however, continues to provide Pakistan with nuclear reactors and facilities that will contribute to Pakistan's production of weapons grade fissile material – plutonium in particular.[33] Here, again, is evidence of conflict or tension in core national interests, rather than collaboration.

Nevertheless, the next decade actually offers a substantial opportunity for cooperation, as the US realigns both its policy and its force posture in the region. Both Pakistan and Afghanistan have relied on generous US economic and security assistance. These forms of aid will be much more constrained in the future, as will US force presence and capabilities. China will have an opportunity to expand its influence in this sensitive region, but has historically been reluctant to make major commitments in this and other regions. The best opportunity to shape the region to maximize both US and Chinese interests is to identify areas of common concern and to cooperate together, bringing different tools and strengths to bear on common problems.

Opportunities after Bin Laden's death: an increasing coincidence of interests?

Given this background, what points of intersection *do* exist between the US and China in the region? What shared interests could shape cooperation and joint efforts, and why is the current environment particularly promising as a strategic priority?

There are three factors that make this moment particularly promising. The first is, quite simply, the lack of vital national interests for both states in the region, and the absence of major differences or conflicts. Although both China and the US have important interests in South Asia and more particularly in Pakistan, these interests are relatively modest. The region, in essence, is not a cockpit for potential conflict – although, of course, *any* region can eventually become a point of conflict depending on the maturation of the Sino-US relationship. In fact, because relative interests are modest for both states, an argument could be made that there is an opportunity for a natural collaboration in South Asia that can build habits and patterns of trust and cooperation that may help to defuse or limit future conflicts and tensions in regions where the stakes are higher for both states.

This leads to the second point – the US is currently reevaluating its interests and commitment, and revamping its overall strategy and force posture in the region. This should relieve, to some extent, Chinese fears of encirclement or US expansionism. It also provides China with an opportunity to engage in the region to a greater extent than previously, in pursuit of both Chinese interests and broader regional stability. The latter is particularly useful for China, since threats of ethnic unrest are particularly prevalent on China's southern border with Tibetan and Uighur populations.

Finally, this moment is a unique strategic opportunity because it offers an occasion for both China and the US to help Pakistan help itself. The Abbottabad raid created major shocks in the Pakistani system, suggesting that the military and intelligence services were either complicit in or ignorant of Bin Laden's Pakistani sanctuary.[34] It demonstrated the fallibility of the Pakistani military, in terms of defending itself from outside powers. Pakistan is also confronting a series of internal threats that call into question its use of militant groups as foreign policy proxies – at least some of these former assets have declared war against the Pakistani state.[35] Recent reports question Pakistan's nuclear security.[36] Pakistan's military has taken a more restrained political role, the judiciary is asserting itself more aggressively as a force in Pakistani politics, and the 2008 Pakistan People's Party administration became the first freely elected government in Pakistan to serve out a full five-year term without a military intervention.[37] Both the US and China would prefer to see a stable, healthy Pakistan. Regardless of regime type, both would prefer a Pakistan that does not constantly threaten the region. In addition, both have concerns about Pakistan's unique combination of nuclear weapons, hundreds of armed religious militant groups with relative freedom of action inside the country, and continuing revisionist objectives regarding its neighbors to both the east and the west.

As a result, this period may be particularly propitious for Sino-US cooperation. This cooperation could be based around a few common interests, which facilitate both mutual benefit and regional security. The objective would be multi-tiered: cooperation will build trust and enhance Sino-US relations in an area of lesser concern and greater mutual interest; cooperation will ensure regional stability and minimal disruption of trade and commerce; cooperation will facilitate the strengthening and evolution of Pakistan from its current domestic instability to become a stronger and more moderate state.

The first level of mutual interest (and minimal conflict) is related to the political economy of South Asia. Both the US and China have economic interests in the region, particularly in access to valuable resources. China has made expensive investments in Afghanistan's resource base, as well as to the port of Gwadar in Pakistan.[38] In addition, China relies on the free flow of energy resources across the Indian Ocean, not just from the Persian/Arabian Gulf but also from the coast of Africa. Finally, China is also pursuing expensive and vulnerable pipeline projects across South and Central Asia to move oil and natural gas from the source to Western China.

The US is particularly interested in good order at sea, and the free flow of commerce across the global commons. The Indian Ocean rim includes some of the best sources of oil and natural gas in the world. US energy supplies do not rely on these producers, but much of the developing world requires access to inexpensive oil from the Persian/Arabian Gulf region. In addition, the three Asian economic giants (China, India, and Japan) as well as the growing Southeast Asian economies will increase their energy demands. Energy and free commerce are key elements of the global economy. The US, which has a very high stake in that economy, remains committed to preserving both.

The possibility for cooperation in this arena is considerable, and much of it could occur at low cost. Freedom of the seas is guaranteed in international law, and is both a mutual and a common benefit. Assuring energy and commerce flows to China is a mutual interest, given the dependency of the two economies on one another. A foundation for this type of cooperation is already emerging, in the very loose cooperation of US, international, and Chinese naval forces on antipiracy missions around the Horn of Africa. So long as Gwadar is not militarized, and recent Chinese actions have shown great prudence in response to Pakistani offers, cooperation at sea is a natural starting point for this relationship. The Pakistanis play an important role in maritime presence in the Arabian Sea as well, including participation in both antipiracy and counterterrorism missions. This type of cooperation, therefore, comes at a low cost and is easily facilitated. It can, however, serve a number of useful purposes, including the lessening of Sino-Indian and Indo-Pakistani tensions, as China demonstrates its cooperation.

A second concern is regional stability, which is menaced at the interstate and intrastate levels. South Asia is a hotbed of terrorism, and Pakistan is one of the epicenters. Both the US and China have strong concerns about Pakistan's control over militant groups based in its territory. The US is primarily concerned about Al Qaeda, the Taliban, and the Haqqani network.[39] China is primarily concerned about Uighur separatist groups.[40] Both states, however, have a common concern in other groups in Pakistan that act to destabilize the region: Uzbek militants could risk commercial ties of interest to China, and both Punjabi and Kashmiri groups have created dangerous crises that almost led to wars between India and Pakistan. Because of the unique concentration of these groups in Pakistan, and the mutual concerns of China and the US for regional stability, counterterrorism is an area where collaboration makes sense.

Collaboration on counterterrorism should be a higher priority, however, because of the emergence of a threat to Pakistan itself. Many of Pakistan's militant groups have interacted with Al Qaeda, including Lashkar-e-Taiba and Jaish-e-Mohammed (two of Inter-Services Intelligence's [ISI] most favored militant groups).[41] Tehrik-e-Taliban Pakistan (TTP, or the 'Pakistani Taliban') emerged as a powerful coalition of allied militant groups, and in 2007 it committed itself to overthrowing the Pakistani state and imposing Islamic rule.[42] Al Qaeda has called for the overthrow of the Pakistani regime. Attacks on Pakistani security forces and intelligence headquarters have increased, including high-profile attacks on General Headquarters in Rawalpindi and key ISI sites in Lahore and Peshawar. Recent attacks on Pakistani naval facilities suggest the possibility of Al Qaeda infiltration into the military.[43] The fact that factions in Pakistan were able to keep Osama bin Laden's presence there secret for ten years suggests a very high level of sympathy for Islamist extremism – an extremism which now targets Islamabad as well as Pakistan's neighbors.

Regional terrorism therefore threatens China, the US, *and* Pakistan, both directly and indirectly. It threatens stability in neighboring states, raises the risks of regional war, and has moved, on occasion, into the maritime realm.[44] Pakistan is extremely sensitive to accusations that the state or the military actively support terrorist groups – a sensitivity that is only heightened because of the fact that at least some of these accusations are correct. Use of militants has been an important tool in Pakistan's regional policy – but for at least five years Pakistan has been seeing significant blowback, leading to the deaths of thousands of security personnel and tens of thousands of citizens. It appears that Pakistan is still mustering the will to confront the consequences of this policy. US and Chinese support are crucial in helping Pakistan to gain time for this cognitive shift to occur. It is also in the best interests of both states.

A third concern is the stability of Afghanistan as the US draws down forces. Given China's economic investments in Afghanistan, it has a strong financial incentive to ensure that it can maintain access to those resources. In addition, as China and the US have experienced, an Afghanistan that serves as a terrorist or militant haven is a significant concern both in the region and abroad. China has natural reasons to be suspicious of a continued US presence in Afghanistan, but at the same time this presence may be the best guarantor of Chinese interests – and collaboration on the terms and objectives of the ongoing US mission may be a useful area for discussions. This, again, overlaps with Pakistan, which desperately wants to determine the outcome of any talks, but Pakistani objectives may not coincide with those of the US and China. Cooperation is the key to arriving at a stable outcome that benefits all players, including Afghanistan.

Finally, the US and China both have strong incentives to prevent regional interstate war. The most risky of these potential conflicts is war between India and Pakistan – rivals who on at least seven occasions since 1984 have engaged in some form of nuclear brinkmanship.[45] Unresolved territorial disputes, issues of self-definition and existential threat dating back to Partition, and the existence of potential ethnic separatists in each country make this relationship particularly dangerous. Both the US and China have some influence and history with Pakistan, and some interests in engaging India. Neither wants to see a regional war that could escalate. At the same time, as outsiders, each must act carefully in order not to inflame the suspicion of one or both South Asian powers. But the close relationship each has built with the Pakistani military does provide influence and leverage, and cooperating to reassure Pakistan of its security while simultaneously lowering the overall tension in the region is clearly a mutual interest.

This leads to a final area for cooperation – one where the Sino-US record is not good, but where the incentives are increasing. The 'nuclear genii' is out of the bottle in South Asia, but Pakistan's reckless proliferation record should not inspire confidence that nuclear weapons technology is secure or contained. The fact that China has been embarrassed publicly by the transfer of its nuclear weapons designs should provide a strong incentive to consider mutually coordinated policies to lower risks. Although the US and China may not agree on all aspects of the nonproliferation question, Pakistan's sale of nuclear technology and materials to Iran and Libya should be a matter for concern – and sales to North Korea have contributed to a series of crises that have often adversely affected Sino-US relations. Second- and third-order consequences of China's nuclear proliferation have contributed to nuclear crises in Iran, Libya, and Syria – something Chinese policy may well wish to prevent in the future.

The problem in Pakistan, of course, is again exacerbated by the multitude of militant groups and the unknown influence radical ideologies may have among the military and nuclear establishments. The possibility of nuclear theft, while presumably remote, is nevertheless plausible, given the participation of military officers in assassination attempts against then President Musharraf, an Islamist coup attempt in 1995, and the uncertain command and control relationship between ISI officers and their militant agents.[46] Islamist militants have attacked Chinese engineers in Pakistan, and expressed support for their Muslim brethren in western China. The idea of a nuclear weapon in such hands should be an incentive for some level of cooperation between the US, China, and Pakistan. This will not reach the levels the US government prefers – China will almost certainly honor agreements for the transfer of nuclear reactors to Pakistan, for example – but it may help put safeguards in place that better address concerns about security.

Although this will be a difficult strategic priority, cooperation is not unprecedented. The US and China have found ways to begin cooperating on North Korea – a particularly difficult proliferation question, given China's alliance with the North and the US alliance with the South. Because the stakes are lower, Pakistan should be an easier cooperative effort. The focus of cooperation should be first on preventing further proliferation. The remnants of the A.Q. Khan network and the institutions that supported Pakistani nuclear proliferation have not disappeared, and as Khan demonstrated there are tangible financial and geopolitical gains to be made from illicit transfer of nuclear technology.[47] A second but related concern should be assuring nuclear security. After the Bin Laden raid, Pakistan's military leadership is certain the US is preparing to seize Pakistan's nuclear assets.[48] This makes cooperating on security particularly difficult – and US–Pakistan cooperation with the Musharraf and following governments has been sensitive and one-sided. China may be able to work as an interested but relatively neutral third party, reassuring the US where appropriate but also helping Pakistan to better secure its most important security assets. This will take time and careful negotiation, but perhaps after all sides are more confident this will also have built enough trust to make other negotiations (arms control, nuclear status) possible.

Conclusion

China and the US have a complicated relationship – one which, as China's startling economic growth continues, generates mutual suspicion and distrust. Each state views the other with concern, based on some combination of fear, honor, and interest.[49] This leads some analysts on both sides to view the relationship as a competition – a zero-sum game in which cooperation is not only unrewarded but actually dangerous. This conception of the relationship is a recipe for misunderstanding and crisis.

The strategic priority opportunities for cooperation identified in this chapter should, under the circumstances, be seized – particularly if cooperation can genuinely be viewed as *mutually* beneficial. South Asia offers a unique opportunity for this type of cooperation. The US and China have shared interests, both states have a history of close and influential relations with Pakistan, and both have concerns about Pakistan's future and its stability.

The timing for such cooperation is particularly ripe at the present. As the US reduces its footprint in South Asia, the potential threat to China is reduced, facilitating cooperation. For the US, China taking some role in the postwar stabilization helps ensure a stable Afghanistan that is not a supporter of regional and international terrorism. A stable Afghanistan may, over time, become an important economic partner for China, particularly if energy pipeline projects become viable.

In addition, both states have a unique opportunity to intercede with Pakistan in ways that promote regional stability *and* help Pakistan at a time of significant domestic change. Transitions from military rule to a more democratic system are difficult in any state, but Pakistan's history is particularly troubled. There is now a brief window in which Pakistan's government can reflect the aspirations of its people. That possible transition, however, is menaced by both the possibility of the military reentering politics *and* by the emergence of significant internal threats to the government which threaten stability and even governance in some of the more remote regions. Since these forces have, in the past, been linked to the military, the new civilian government has had difficulty reasserting control. The result is a government unfairly perceived at home and abroad as weak and ineffective, still locked in a zero-sum security struggle with India, and trying to manage not only political transition at home but also to maintain some say in the ultimate outcome in Afghanistan. The temptation to revert to past policies of confrontation and state-sponsored terrorism will be very high, particularly as supporters of internal violence take increasingly strident positions against the government.

China and the US can help buy Pakistan time through a combination of assistance, reassurance, and coordinated policy. China and the US can reassure Pakistan about perceived threats from India through measures ranging from selective provision of military equipment to creating opportunities for bilateral and multilateral talks. They can include Pakistan in negotiations over the future of Afghanistan, while at the same time stressing that inclusion does not mean Pakistan will be the primary beneficiary or have the final vote. They can put pressure on Pakistan to better control the actions of its proxies in Afghanistan and elsewhere, using economic and security assistance as both a carrot and a stick if necessary. Perhaps the most important strategic priority opportunity is to continue to work with Pakistan on the security of its nuclear technology and weapons.

The benefits of such an approach are significant, both for China and the US and (just as importantly) for Pakistan. China and the US will achieve mutual goals for regional stability and security, will build trust through cooperation and coordinated effort, and will help a war-torn region rebuild itself at modest cost. Pakistan will benefit from regional stability as well, and reduction of tensions with India may create a more favorable climate for increasing economic relations between these two South Asian antagonists. More importantly, Sino-US cooperation will buy Pakistan time. This time can be used to strengthen reemerging political and judicial institutions, for the military to regain its stature in Pakistani society while remaining free of domestic politics, and for regional governments to begin better meeting the needs of their constituents. Stronger, more capable institutions will lead to better governance, which will do much to address the grievances of local populations that contribute to the strength of terrorist groups like the TTP. There is no magic solution through which the US and China can stop terrorism in and from Pakistan, but US–China cooperation can provide Pakistan with the time for recovery and some of the tools that will be necessary for it to reduce internal threats and become a more stable, prosperous, and moderate ally. The death of Osama bin Laden and the substantive end to US operations in Afghanistan has provided a strategic priority opportunity. It would be a shame if China and the US could not take advantage of this chance, both for their benefit and for Pakistan's.

Notes

1 The views contained in this chapter are those of the author alone, and do not represent the official views or policy of the US Naval War College, the US Navy, the Department of Defense, or any other institution of the US government.
2 M. Guruswamy, 'The China Factor', in S.P. Cohen et al. (eds.), *The Future of Pakistan*, Washington, DC: Brookings Institution, 2011, pp. 122–33.
3 J. Garofano and A. Dew (eds.), *Deep Currents and Rising Tides: The Indian Ocean and International Security*, Washington, DC: Georgetown University Press, 2013.
4 S. Tankel, *Storming the World Stage: The Story of Lashkar-e-Taiba*, New York: Columbia University Press, 2011; J.R. Schmidt, *The Unraveling: Pakistan in the Age of Jihad*, New York: Farrar, Strauss & Giroux, 2011.
5 'Pakistan's Bin Laden Dossier', *Al Jazeera*, <www/aljazeera.com/indepth/spotlight/ binladenfiles/2013/07/201378143927822246.html> (accessed 1 September 2013).
6 S.R. Hussain, 'The India Factor', in M. Lodhi (ed.), *Pakistan: Beyond the Crisis State*, New York: Columbia University Press, 2011, pp. 319–47.
7 H. Abbas, *Pakistan's Drift into Extremism: Allah, the Army and America's War on Terror*, New York: M.E. Sharpe, 2005; Z. Hussain, *Frontline Pakistan: The Struggle*

with Militant Islam, New York: Columbia University Press, 2007; A. Lieven, *Pakistan: A Hard Country*, New York: Public Affairs, 2011.
8 H.B. Schaffer and T.C. Schaffer, *How Pakistan Negotiates with the United States: Riding the Roller Coaster*, Washington, DC: US Institute of Peace, 2011.
9 B. Riedel, *Deadly Embrace: Pakistan, America and the Future of Global Jihad*, Washington, DC: Brookings Institution, 2011; I. Gul, *Pakistan before and after Osama*, New Delhi: Roli Books, 2012.
10 Lieven, *Pakistan*, pp. 161–211.
11 J. Goldberg and M. Ambinder, 'Pakistan: The Ally from Hell', *Atlantic*, December 2011, <www.theatlantic.com/magazine/print/2011/12/the-ally-from-hell/8730> (accessed 5 May 2015).
12 R.J. McMahon, *The Cold War on the Periphery: The United States, India, and Pakistan*, New York: Columbia University Press, 1994.
13 D. Kux, *The United States and Pakistan, 1947–2000: Disenchanted Allies*, Baltimore, MD: Johns Hopkins University Press, 2001.
14 In fact, relations had been souring since the previous autumn, when the head of Pakistan's Inter-Service Intelligence Directorate had been subpoenaed in a civil suit in the US, and ISI had retaliated by releasing the name of the CIA chief of station in Islamabad. The situation further deteriorated after a US contractor working at the consulate in Lahore was involved in a shooting incident.
15 A.H. Syed, *China & Pakistan: Diplomacy of an Entente Cordiale*, Amherst: University of Massachusetts Press, 1974.
16 See Chapter 6 in this volume; Guruswamy, 'The China Factor', p. 129.
17 F. Khan, *Eating Grass: The Making of the Pakistani Bomb*, Stanford, CA: Stanford University Press, 2012.
18 R.J. Smith and J. Warrick, 'A Nuclear Power's Act of Proliferation', *Washington Post*, 13 November 2009, <www.washingtonpost.com/2009-11-13/world/36899222-1-proliferation-nuclear-weapons-abdul-qadeer-khan> (accessed 12 June 2015).
19 Q. Abbas, 'Pakistan's Gwadar Port May Get Special "China" Status', *Daily Mail*, 31 August 2013, <www.dailmail.co.uk/indiahome/indianews/article-2408121/Pakistan's-Gwadar-port-special-China-status.html>; S. Shah and J. Page, 'China Readies $46 Billion for Pakistan Trade Route', *Wall Street Journal*, 16 April 2015, <www.wsj.com/articles/china-to-unveil-billions-of-dollars-in-pakistan-investment-1429214705> (accessed 12 June 2015).
20 'China Agrees to Run Gwadar Port', *Dawn.com*, 21 May 2011, <https://beta.dawn.com/news/630700/China-agrees-to-run-gwadar-port> (accessed 12 June 2015).
21 P. Lee, 'China Drops the Hot Potato', *Asia Times Online*, 28 May 2011, <www.asiatimes.com/atimes/China/ME28Ad01.html> (accessed 12 June 2015).
22 A. Rodriguez and B. Demick 'Could Pakistan Dump the U.S. for "All-Weather Friend" China?', *Los Angeles Times*, 1 October 2011, <http://articles.latimes.com/2011/oct/01/world/la-fg-pakistan-china-20111001> (accessed 12 June 2015).
23 S. Ganguly, *Conflict Unending: India-Pakistan Tensions since 1947*, New York: Columbia University Press, 2001.
24 G. Earl and L. Murray, 'Asian Infrastructure Investment Bank a Challenge for China', *Australian Financial Review*, 20 March 2015, <www.afr.com/news/world/asia/asian-infrastructure-investment-bank-a-challenge-for-china-20150320-1m2yfk> (accessed 20 April 2015); Y. Mao, 'Challenges of the Asian Infrastructure Investment Bank', *Daily Signal*, 28 April 2015, <http://dailysignal.com/2015/04/28/challenges-on-the-asian-infrastructure-investment-bank/> (accessed 29 April 2015); Z. Hongzhou and A. Guschin, *China's Silk Road Economic Belt: Geopolitical Challenges in Central Asia*, Nanyang Technological University: RSIS Publications, 2015, <www.rsis.edu.sg/rsis-publication/rsis/co15099-chinas-silk-road-economic-belt-geopolitical-challenges-in-central-asia/#.VUBWvigXKiY> (accessed 24 April 2015).
25 This asymmetry mirrors the Indo-Pakistani security dilemma, where Pakistan is fixated on Indian security threats, but India sees Pakistan as a lesser concern. An oversimplified

description of the regional security dynamic is that Pakistan worries most about India, India worries most about China, and China worries most about the US.
26 A. Kapur, 'Major Powers and the Persistence of the India-Pakistan Conflict', in T.V. Paul (ed.), *The India-Pakistan Conflict: An Enduring Rivalry*, Cambridge: Cambridge University Press, 2005, pp. 131–55.
27 'Interview with Dr. Zbigniew Brzezinski 13/6/97', in *Good Guys, Bad Guys*, <www2.gwu.edu/~nsarchive/coldwar/interviews/episode-17/brzezinski2.html> (accessed 12 June 2015).
28 W. Burr (ed.), 'China May Have Helped Pakistan Nuclear Weapons Design, Newly Declassified Intelligence Indicates', *National Security Archive Electronic Briefing Book No. 423*, posted 23 April 2013, <www2.gwu.edu/~nsarchiv/nukevault/ebb423>; Khan, *Eating Grass* (accessed 12 June 2015).
29 The Pressler Amendment established that continuing military and economic assistance to Pakistan was conditional and dependent on an annual certification by the president of the US that Pakistan did not possess nuclear weapons. In 1990, President George H.W. Bush was unable to certify that Pakistan did not have nuclear weapons, in the aftermath of a crisis where Pakistan reportedly assembled and deployed nuclear devices.
30 S.A. Kan, *China and Proliferation of Weapons of Mass Destruction and Missiles: Policy Issues*, CRS Report for Congress RL31555, Washington DC: Library of Congress, 11 March 2013, <www.fas.org/sgp/crs/nuke/RL31555.pdf> (accessed 12 June 2015).
31 J. Warrick and P. Slevin, 'Libyan Arms Designs Traced Back to China: Pakistan Resold Chinese Provided Plans', *Washington Post*, 15 February 2004.
32 See Khan, *Eating Grass*.
33 B. Gertz, 'China, Pakistan Reach Secret Nuclear Reactor Deal for Pakistan', *Washington Times*, 21 March 2013, <www.washingtontimes.com/news/2013/mar/21/china-pakistan-reach-secret-reactor-deal-pakistan/> (accessed 12 June 2015).
34 See 'Pakistan's Bin Laden Dossier'.
35 I. Gul, *The Al Qaeda Connection: The Taliban and Terror in Pakistan's Tribal Areas*, New Delhi: Viking Press, 2009; 'Pakistan Taliban: Peshawar School Attack Leaves 141 Dead', *BBC News*, 16 December 2014, <www.bbc.com/news/world-asia-30491435> (accessed 20 January 2015).
36 Goldberg and Ambinder, 'Pakistan'; D.E. Sanger, 'Obama's Worst Pakistan Nightmare', *New York Times*, 11 January 2009.
37 'Hollow Milestone', *Economist*, 23 March 2013, <www.economist.com/news/asia/21574033-democratic-government-completes-full-term-little-applause-hollow-milestone> (accessed 10 December 2014).
38 S. Dasgupta, 'China Gets 40-Year Management Rights on Pak's Gwadar Port, and Access to Arabian Sea', *Times of India*, 14 April 2015, <http://timesofindia.indiatimes.com/world/china/China-gets-40-year-management-rights-on-Paks-Gwadar-port-and-access-to-Arabian-Sea/articleshow/46923252.cms> (accessed 20 April 2015).
39 'Statement of Admiral Michael Mullen, U.S. Navy, Chairman, Joints Chiefs of Staff before the Senate Armed Services Committee on Afghanistan and Iraq', U.S. Senate, Washington, DC, 22 September 2011.
40 M. Wines, 'China Blames Foreign-Trained Separatists for Attacks in Xinjiang', *New York Times*, 2 August 2011, <www.newyorktimes.com/2011/08/02/world/asia/02china.html> (accessed 12 June 2015).
41 B. Riedel, *The Search for Al Qaeda: Its Leadership, Ideology, and Future*, Washington, DC: Brookings Institution, 2008.
42 Gul, *Pakistan before and after Osama*.
43 S.S. Shahzad, 'Al Qaeda Had Warned of Pakistan Strike', *Asia Times*, 27 May 2011, <www.atimes.com/atimes/South_Asia/ME27Df06.html> (accessed 10 January 2015). Shortly after publication of this story, alleging significant sympathy for Al Qaeda in the Pakistani Navy, this reporter was murdered by ISI agents.
44 R. Basrur, T. Hoyt, R. Hussain, and S. Mandal, *The 2008 Mumbai Terrorist Attacks: Strategic Fallout*, RSIS Monograph No. 17, Singapore: S. Rajaratnam School of International Studies, 2009.

45 S. Ganguly and D.T. Hagerty, *Fearful Symmetry: India-Pakistan Crises in the Shadow of Nuclear Weapons*, Oxford: Oxford University Press, 2005.
46 S. Nawaz, *Crossed Swords: Pakistan, Its Army, and the Wars Within*, Oxford: Oxford University Press, 2008, pp. 477–78.
47 D. Frantz and C. Collins, *The Nuclear Jihadist*, New York: Hachette Books, 2007.
48 Goldberg and Ambinder, 'Pakistan'.
49 R.B. Strassler (ed.), *The Landmark Thucydides: A Comprehensive Guide to the Peloponnesian War*, New York: Free Press, 1996, I:76, p. 43.

8 Chinese regionalism
Balancing and constraint in the Shanghai Cooperation Organisation

Alica Kizekova

Introduction

China's ability to employ regionalism within its foreign policy is the subject of this chapter. The numerous assertions of regionalism as a strategic priority are clear and yet the ability to gain outcomes is not. The most recent 'one belt, one road' initiative and grander ideas such as the Asian Infrastructure Investment Bank are at their beginning. The Shanghai Cooperation Organisation (SCO) is older and has weathered a major test of unity. China's challenge is to maintain good relations with an increasingly assertive Russia whilst endorsing Principles of Peaceful Coexistence under the umbrella of its SCO regionalism. This chapter explores China's regionalism since 2008 and discusses the noticeable lack of support for Russia's military actions as well as recognition of the independence of Abkhazia and South Ossetia during the 2008 Russia–Georgia War. Such an enquiry allows an understanding of how effective China's regionalism is and what challenges complicate this strategic priority.

Over the last decade, China has increased its participation in global and regional multilateral organizations as part of its foreign policy. On the regional level, its engagements reach out to several subregions in Asia: Southeast Asia, Northeast Asia, South Asia and Central Asia. With the launch of the periphery policy (*zhoubian zhengce*) or the good neighbor policy (*mulin zhengce*), China gradually joined the Asian Development Bank (1986), the Asia Pacific Economic Cooperation process (1989) and the Association of Southeast Asian Nations (ASEAN) Regional Forum (1994) as well as the nonofficial "Track II" mechanism, the Council for Security Cooperation in the Asia Pacific (1996). Thereafter, China joined the World Trade Organization (WTO), ASEAN plus Japan, South Korea and China, the East Asia Summit, the G20, and other processes such as the Shangri-La Dialogue.

In the ASEAN-led frameworks, China has had a secondary role, and less input in shaping ASEAN's future direction.[1] In contrast, its active leadership in establishing the SCO has given China the opportunity to shape the institutional framework as well as the agenda of SCO consultations with Russia, the Stans (Kazakhstan, Kyrgyzstan, Tajikistan and Uzbekistan), SCO observers and dialogue partners. Therefore, the SCO is an important example of Beijing's regionalization of its foreign policy, and its study reveals much about China's evolving strategic priorities.

The 2008 Russia–Georgia War in the Caucasus was a major test of unity for the SCO as well as for the Sino-Russian relationship. China and the Stans showed minimal support for Russia's military actions and did not endorse the recognition of the independence of Abkhazia and South Ossetia during and after this crisis. Russia demonstrated that it was willing to intervene by using force and supported redrawing the borders in the Caucasus and weakening the North Atlantic Treaty Organization's (NATO) operability in the region, which created unease among the smaller neighboring countries. As a result, China's presence in Central Asia has been viewed as more benign and its position within the SCO has been strengthened.

China's regional goals

China's regional policies are formed with the following principles in mind. One of the core objectives is to harness continuous support for the 'One China Principle' with regard to Taiwan, Tibet and Xinjiang. The United States of America's (US) presence in Asia is another major consideration. China is balancing the US position not by military means, but rather through 'institutional balancing', where it counts on high levels of economic interdependence, and harmonizing economic policies within regional organizations, such as the SCO, in which the US is not a member state.[2] Further, China strives to secure its borders and seize economic opportunities with neighboring states, especially in the energy sector.[3] The result would be increased economic and political influence for Beijing without seeking to directly challenge US global power or Russia's geostrategic interests.[4]

Although China's relationships with Russia and the newly established states in Central Asia are consolidated within the SCO, its formal strategy is still evolving.[5] It is greatly dependent on the policies of the other players, who appear to have either short- or medium-term goals or lack the capacity to sustain predictable patterns in the domestic environment, due to a weak economic base and ongoing political volatility, or a limited capacity to coordinate regional development. After the demise of the Soviet Union, Central Asia became an important arena for cooperation and competition among three major powers: Russia, China and the US. China initially selected a cautious approach to establishing direct links with the newly independent Central Asian states and focused on normalization of its relations with Russia.[6] However, it managed to strengthen its bilateral relationships with all the Stans by signing treaties of friendship and cooperation and improving confidence and mutual trust. Beijing differentiated its relationships with individual countries.

It was primarily interested in neighboring countries: Kazakhstan, Kyrgyzstan and Tajikistan in relation to specification of common borders, and economic and resource potentials. China paid attention to Uzbekistan and Turkmenistan mainly due to their efforts to implement reforms along the lines of the Chinese developmental model,[7] but it initially neglected deeper trade contacts with these states because they did not face ethnic problems (such as the Uighur population fleeing from Chinese authorities to Kazakhstan) that would threaten China's domestic or foreign policies.[8]

Beijing has been particularly concerned with the threat of Islamic fundamentalism and separatism of the northwestern part of the People's Republic of China (PRC), the Xinjiang-Uighur Autonomous Region (XUAR). Historically and ethnically, the population of this region (Xinjiang as 'Eastern Turkestan') is closer to the Central Asian states (viewed as 'Western Turkestan') than to East Asia polities.[9] However, China expects the largely Muslim local ethnic groups to coexist with the Han population in the Chinese cultural space. In order to strengthen the integration of the XUAR, Beijing implemented the Greater North-West development strategy, where Xinjiang plays a strategic role in the transit of energy resources, especially natural gas and oil, from the Central Asian states. China's economic development in these territories and cooperation with the Stans and Russia in curbing spill-over effects of extremism and terrorism are complementary and contribute towards consolidation of China's presence in the region.[10] For this reason, the PRC was willing to develop the Shanghai Five dialogue process into expanded SCO patterns of cooperation.

Shanghai Five dialogue processes

Confidence building among Russia, China, Kazakhstan, Kyrgyzstan and Tajikistan was facilitated by the Shanghai Five (S-5) series of meetings, with the primary focus on achieving disarmament in border areas and building trust among participating nations. Some discussions were at first of a more polarized nature: China versus the Commonwealth of Independent States (CIS) members, rather than truly multilateral meetings.

The first two S-5 agreements[11] had mainly declaratory value, in which there was a shared understanding about nonfirst use of force, and in the case of Russia and China, also the nonuse of nuclear weapons.[12] This was meant to increase confidence among all participants. Russia and China signed a Joint Statement on 19 May 1991, where they agreed not to use force or even threaten one another with force.[13] They further established that they would not sign agreements with a third country that would undermine security interests and the state sovereignty of the other state. Reaffirmation of these declarations was rather symbolic, considering that Russia was capable of retargeting its strategic missiles in twenty minutes, and China's strategic missiles were still, allegedly, targeted at Russia in July 1997.[14] Once the parties agreed on specific regulations in the border areas, they started to pay more attention to the shared security concerns related to the designated 'three evils' of extremism, separatism and terrorism, and the S-5 summits (1998–2000) became more truly multilateral.

From the start, the S-5 states were facing two major limitations in obtaining the best possible outcomes in transparency and verification measures. Transparency requires a full disclosure of defense budgets. Although China published an 'arms control and disarmament' white paper in 1995, the description did not provide information on Chinese defense spending.[15] Through 2011, China was still viewed as downplaying its defence expenditure and the actual defense budget figures were believed to be two or more times higher.[16] Besides transparency, another important confidence building measure is verification. The 1996 Shanghai Agreement does not specify procedures for mutual inspections. The states should carry out their inspections only in instances of great irregularities or major threats.

The final S-5 Summit was a breakthrough, with the attendance of the Uzbek President Islam Karimov. Uzbekistan experienced bombings and incursions from the Taliban-backed Islamic Movement of Uzbekistan in 1999. Since the S-5 elevated its focus on fighting Islamic militants, Tashkent showed an interest in cooperating with the Stans, Russia and China in early 2000. Subsequently, it was suggested that a formal regional organization should be established, subordinate to the authority of the United Nations Security Council (UNSC).[17] This laid the foundation for a more formalized network dialogue between the Stans, China and Russia. These states had improved their military relations and reduced their forces along common borders. Throughout the Shanghai Five processes, participating states acquired a shared understanding of traditional and nontraditional security threats in the region and pledged continued support for regular consultations in the quest for solutions to common security problems. Intensified dialogue through 2000–2001 at the level of defense ministers and foreign affairs ministers, as well as law enforcement officials, prepared this grouping for a more formal structure as the SCO.[18]

The main security concerns for all SCO member states have remained the 'three evils' of extremism, separatism and terrorism. Fear of these threats has been closely connected to protecting internal security, which relates to the regime security and territorial integrity of these states.[19] Elites from the SCO member states hold that the S-5 and the SCO are useful vehicles for harmonizing practices for intelligence sharing. Despite not providing collective security guarantees to SCO member states, the organization became an important forum for states in need of diplomatic support in the event of a security crisis or external criticism of their human rights record.

It was the 2000 Dushanbe Declaration that stressed the importance of respecting internal affairs of other states and their free choice to develop their policies in societal, economic and political spheres. There should be guarantees that no state would intervene under the pretext of humanitarian intervention or suggestions of human rights violations. These principles have been restated on several occasions at annual summits of the SCO. The heads of state also agreed that the cooperation should further encourage a multipolar world and a creation of a "new, just, and rational international political and economic order."[20]

SCO membership and the Sino-Russian driver

The SCO, which was established in Beijing on 15 June 2001, successfully converted S-5 processes into a formal multilateral organization. The SCO is composed of a diverse group of states. These include two global powers, China and

Russia, with influence through permanent memberships in the UNSC and the possession of nuclear weapons, large territories and populations, thereby driving the organization's scope beyond Central Asia. There are also two Stans with regional influence, Kazakhstan and Uzbekistan, as well as two less influential Stans, Tajikistan and Kyrgyzstan. The internal dynamics of the SCO has been compared to "a barometer of the state of Russo-Chinese relations,"[21] where the organizational development appears to be closely linked to the institutionalization of Sino-Russian relations.

Traditional divisions of labor within the SCO are arguably reflected in Russia's security agenda and in China's economic sphere. Russia holds strong historical and cultural ties to Central Asia and these links create a sense of a 'natural' sphere of influence. It is in Russia's interest to use various frameworks, including the SCO, to maintain the status quo in the region. One of the key soft power strategies is the use of Russian language among Russian nationals in the former Soviet republics. In 2007, President Putin signed a decree establishing Russkiy Mir Foundation to promote "the Russian language, as Russia's national heritage and a significant aspect of Russian and world culture, and supporting Russian language teaching programs abroad." In his words, the Russian language creates a "community that goes far beyond Russia itself" and is a "common heritage of many people" and will "never become the language of hatred or enmity, xenophobia or isolationism."[22] In the Eurasian context, Russian is sometimes used as language of interethnic communication, even if used reluctantly, and rarely given formal status as a national language.[23]

Border security is another major consideration. Resolving common border issues with China allowed Russia to focus on more volatile parts of its neighborhood, especially towards the North and South Caucasus.[24] Russia also pays attention to the expansion of NATO to the East. The Putin administration in particular used the SCO to voice its discontent with the continuous presence of foreign forces in Russia's neighborhood during 2004–8. In the words of Vyacheslav Trubnikov, a Russian Deputy Foreign Minister, "I don't think we can be happy with the presence of extra-regional powers whether it is the US, China or some other country."[25] Russia finds the SCO to be a good framework to balance its relationship with the US in Central Asia and at the same time have better control over China's activities in the region. Militarily, it continues to rely on the Russian-led Collective Security Treaty Organization (CSTO). It has been pushing for a greater CSTO–SCO collaboration; however, these contacts have remained rather limited.[26]

Russia has had its differences with the majority of the SCO member states. Initially, Moscow and Tashkent stood united during the expulsion of US forces from Uzbekistan in 2005 until Tashkent restarted its cooperation with Washington.[27] A similar approach was taken by Kyrgyzstan, which was planning not to renew the lease for foreign troops at the Manas Air Base. There were reports that Bishkek had been negotiating a $2.1 billion package of Russian aid.[28] In the end, Bishkek renegotiated a deal with the US government.[29] Kazakhstan's President Nazarbaev questioned Moscow's support of separatist regions of Abkhazia and

South Ossetia during the Russia–Georgia war in August 2008.[30] Astana additionally expressed an interest in participating in the Baku-Ceyhan oil pipeline, which bypasses Russia. The growing differences between Russia and the Stans, along with a gradual divergence of trade towards China, have contributed to the changed dynamics among these states in Central Asia,[31] and in turn have shifted the balance in China's strategic priorities.

All Stans have been interested in obtaining consumer goods from China, while Beijing has negotiated agreements to import primary materials. Apart from energy, China has shown interest in accessing agricultural land; it secured a lease of 2,000 hectares of land in Tajikistan in January 2011. The arable land in this country is limited, and this appropriation of the land for China's use caused discontent among the local population who feared a resettlement of Chinese nationals into Tajikistan to fill the void left by the departure of Tajik citizens for Russia.[32] In exchange for opening up trade links, an initial Silk Road policy delivered $900 million prior to 2013.[33] This was dramatically expanded in October 2013 when President Xi announced in Kazakhstan, China's policy named Silk Road Economic Belt and the 21st-Century Maritime Silk Road. This policy aimed to establish a free trade, transit and hub area. Beijing promised commitments of $40 billion via the New Silk Road Fund.[34] Russia has supported the majority of these projects, especially in setting up a network of telecommunications and transport corridors; however, it opposed the free trade area.[35]

In contrast, China has not fully embraced the idea of coordinating energy policies through the Energy Club, a proposal by President Putin at the SCO Summit in June 2006.[36] Chinese officials have preferred bilateral or 'semi-official' agreements when it comes to energy.[37] They secured contracts with Turkmenistan and Uzbekistan to import oil via pipelines bypassing Russia.[38] Beijing additionally showed an increased interest in security issues and called for more rapid responses towards security threats when it presided over the SCO in 2011–12.[39]

China's strategic reemergence has expanded its operational frontier throughout Central-Eastern Asia, via a network of pipelines that guarantees long-term energy supply as long as the transportation of the gas and oil is protected from destabilizing forces. This development of China's strategic priorities challenges the long-term strategic interests of Russia and the US.

Despite China's increased engagement in security cooperation in Central Asia, Beijing continues to promote noninterference in domestic affairs and objects to participating in any formal military alliances.[40] A military alliance would require more involvement in defense collaboration with the weaker Stans and potential long-term entanglement in local conflicts. China is focused on maintaining regional stability, but chooses other means to this end.[41] The further militarization of Central Asia could easily destabilize the region, which could threaten the realization of economic goals and also distract China from maintaining control over Taiwan's activities in case Taipei decides to challenge the status quo of 'One China' and declare formal independence.[42] However, China perceives SCO 'peace-mission' operations as a means of supporting political stability in Central Asia, thereby ensuring future economic and resource access. In general, these exercises have offered the Chinese People's Liberation Army the opportunity to project power abroad, with some exercises demonstrating the potential ability to protect oil and gas pipelines in the region.[43] These activities, however, are conducted within the context of SCO cooperation and consent of the host states.

Russia has been the primary driver of SCO military cooperation. It exercises a dominant role in the CSTO and the CIS. By connecting the CSTO with the SCO, it has a better chance to coordinate an anti-NATO opposition with the purpose of preventing NATO enlargement to the East and the US installation of the National Missile Defense in Europe. However, both President Putin and his former SCO adviser, the National Coordinator Barsky,[44] stated that the SCO was not a military alliance, but "an organization which can play an important role in promoting development in Asia."[45] Likewise, though Kazakhstan has been an active player in SCO and CSTO exercises, Uzbekistan has not, while Kyrgyzstan and Tajikistan have only small military forces.[46]

The SCO clearly does not aim to become a military alliance in the short and medium term. There has been, however, some contradiction in Russia's commitment to declarations on nonuse of force and noninterference in domestic affairs in other states. The 2008 Russia–Georgia War provides a solid example of this contradictory behavior. Before examining the reaction of the SCO and specifically China to Russia's involvement, the background to this conflict needs to be described.

Beyond the Five-Day War

The origins and significance of the August 2008 war are embedded in the wider geographical and historical contexts of Russia's problematic engagement in the Caucasus. Although the fighting started in South Ossetia, the conflict encompassed other parts of Georgia,[47] and tensions even spread to the Northern Caucasus. Mutual suspicion among all parties had been building up since the early 1990s. The legal-state relations became particularly unclear when the Union of Soviet Socialist Republics (USSR) allowed its autonomous republics to decide freely, by referendum, whether they desired to remain within the USSR or consider their independence. Abkhazia demonstrated its pro-Soviet (and later pro-Russian) orientation quite firmly when, on 17 March 1991, it participated in the referendum and expressed support for remaining within the USSR.[48]

Georgia, on the contrary, did not take part in this referendum, but instead organized an alternative poll to confirm the restoration of the country's independence from the USSR. Abkhazia abstained from the vote and continued to be a part of the USSR until it collapsed in December 1991. On this basis, and with the dissolution of the USSR, the Abkhaz leadership suggested the establishment of a federation, wherein the Georgians and the Abkhaz would be equal. These suggestions were supported by provocative declarations from the Abkhaz nationalist leadership, to which the Georgian side responded with an intervention by tanks on the Abkhaz capital Sukhumi.[49]

The Abkhaz-Georgian war of 1992–93 was a bloody conflict resulting in up to 10,000 lives lost and a quarter of a million refugees, mainly ethnic Georgians.[50]

During the conflict, the Abkhaz received support from the North Caucasus (Chechen fighters) and from the Russian military forces based in Abkhazia. Russia and the United Nations (UN) mediated negotiations between the Abkhaz and the Georgians, resulting in the Moscow Treaty of 1994, which provided a mandate for the oversight of a ceasefire for up to 3,000 peacekeepers from the CIS. The Georgian government desired a multinational UN peacekeeping force, being aware that the CIS consisted mainly of Russian peacekeepers.[51] The UN was embroiled in the Balkans at that time and so agreed to monitor the CIS operations instead. Under these conditions, the UN provided a de facto endorsement of Russia's presence in post-Soviet space.

The Georgian-Ossetian conflict gradually evolved from arguments over the future of South Ossetia and accompanied by legislative conflict, into an armed conflict during the period January 1991 to June 1992. It resulted in an estimated 2,000–4,000 deaths and the displacement of approximately 43,000 people.[52] This localized conflict became a regional concern once the refugees crossed the North-South Ossetian border, and in North Ossetia these refugees became instantly engaged in another dispute, between the Ossetians and the Ingush, which has remained unresolved.[53] This situation directly impacted on Russia's internal security.

Since the 1992 ceasefire brokered by Russia, South Ossetia had existed as a de facto independent state. The Dagomys (Sochi) agreement[54] ordered the formation of a security corridor (Article 1) and the establishment of a Joint Control Commission of the four parties involved in the conflict: Georgia, Russia, and North and South Ossetia (Article 3). The warring parties were ordered to demilitarize the security zone and, in the event of a breach of the agreement, to promptly investigate the incident and commence the restoration of peace and order in the area. This suggests that Georgia agreed to cede some sovereignty over to South Ossetia.

Initially, the structure of the Russia-dominated CIS peacekeeping forces appeared to provide a viable solution, and the agreements, negotiated with Russia's support, determined that the Georgia-Abkhazia and Georgia-South Ossetia conflicts should stop and become so-called frozen conflicts. The international community, however, was focused on the return of internally displaced people and the possibilities of trade relations and energy transport routes through Georgian territory, and clearly overlooked Russia's unwillingness to counter illegal economic activity and support secessionist tendencies in Georgia.[55] From 2004, Tbilisi became more assertive in its policy of achieving internal coherence by employing a soft power offensive of 'charming' the territories into a more democratic and reformed Georgia, and by portraying Russia as the 'creeping aggressor', mainly concerned with maintaining its influence in the South Caucasus and gradually annexing the territories to Russia.

Russia's interests in the South Caucasus go beyond providing a sustainable support for the de facto authorities. Geopolitically, it does not want to lose control over the transportation routes and it aims to constrain the economic and strategic orientation of Azerbaijan and Georgia towards the West. Moscow may have responded to Georgia's increased Western involvement, including construction of the Baku-Tbilisi-Ceyhan pipeline, by disrupting the supply of electricity and gas to Georgia in January 2006 (a claim rejected by Russia, which suggested that extremists or Chechen militants may have sabotaged gas pipelines).[56] Russia also deported Georgian migrant workers in response to Georgia's arrests of four Russian military officers on counts of espionage in September 2006. The severed transportation links and deported Georgian workers would have had a significant impact on Georgia's inflow of money sent by these workers to their families.[57]

The situation became worse after NATO's endorsement of Georgia's membership application in April 2008. During the Bucharest Summit, NATO proclaimed that Ukraine and Georgia would become NATO members and the treaty organization was ready to start an intensive engagement with these applicants (Budapest Summit Declaration 2008). Georgia, Azerbaijan and Ukraine further declared a proactive stance on resolving all frozen conflicts within their respective territories during the GUAM[58] Summit in Batumi in July 2008.[59] At first, Russia followed suit and actively spoke for unfreezing the conflicts. During his last press conference in February 2008, President Putin stated that Russia would not follow the example of the US and Europe and recognize the independent Kosovo. Nor would he endorse the independence of Abkhazia and South Ossetia, thus linking these difference cases. However, a month later, he gained majority support within the State Duma to recognize these two entities along with Transnistria.[60]

In August 2008, tensions between Georgia and South Ossetia escalated into an armed conflict, which climaxed in the Five-Day War between Georgia and Russia. The war started with large-scale violence between South Ossetians and Georgians on 7–8 August 2008. President Saakashvili grew increasingly impatient with his inability to reunite Georgia and responded to numerous hostile acts between the parties prior to the war by launching an attack on Tskhinvali. Some Georgian elites, such as the former Georgian President Eduard Shevardnadze, disapproved of Saakashvili's decision to send forces into South Ossetia. Shevardnadze noted that Georgia had the right to intervene within its territory; however, in his view this attack was a 'mistake' and it was ill prepared.[61]

Russia responded to this incident by launching a counterattack and destroying infrastructure and communications on 8 August 2008. This was the third major conflict between Tbilisi and Tskhinvali, although it was the first time Russia had performed a full scale military engagement in the region since its establishment post-USSR. Moscow named the mission "Forcing Georgia to Peace,"[62] and argued it was preventing a major humanitarian disaster for the Ossetian people. President Medvedev spoke of an "act of aggression" performed by Georgian forces against Russian civilians and peacekeepers. He called upon Russian law and international obligations to "protect the life and dignity of Russian citizens wherever they are."[63] On 9 August, Russian forces crossed the borders to Abkhazia and on the following day, the ground forces were joined by the Russian Black Sea fleet near the Georgian coast of the Black Sea. The Russian air force bombed the Georgian town of Gori (west of Tbilisi). The Russian attacks succeeded in regaining control over Tskhinvali.

This situation displeased China, the organizer of the 2008 Olympic Games, which called for an immediate ceasefire, restraint by all parties and stabilization of the region. Once the Russian troops entered the Georgian towns of Senaki and Zugdidi, the international community started an intensified 'war in words', in which US President Bush spoke about Russia's invasion of the sovereign Georgia and called upon Russia to "respect Georgia's territorial integrity and sovereignty."[64]

The much anticipated Report of the Independent International Fact-Finding Mission[65] on the Conflict in Georgia, established by the Council of the European Union on 2 December 2008, provided findings on the origins and the course of the conflict. It was written by thirty European historical, legal and military specialists. The team, under the supervision of Swiss diplomat Heidi Tagliavini, came to the conclusion that Georgia's intervention in South Ossetia was illegal and Saakashvili's argument that Georgia was only responding to violations by Russia's armed forces was false. The report was also critical of the legality of Russia's involvement in the conflict.

SCO's reaction to Russia's involvement in the South Caucasus

The Russia–Georgia conflict has revealed a divergent response to the crisis between Russia and the other member states. This was the first full-scale military conflict since the establishment of the SCO that required a clear stance from these states. However, the organization cautiously hid behind formulaic statements and encouraged the Russians to resolve the situation in a cooperative and peaceful fashion. The former Soviet republics of Kazakhstan, Kyrgyzstan, Tajikistan and Uzbekistan shared a common fear that a similar harsh approach from Russia could be taken towards them in the event of their disobedience in the future.[66] On the other hand, they ostensibly had the support of a second great power – China – and therefore, the republics were anxiously waiting to see how their Chinese partners would behave.

From the outset, the SCO has promoted itself as the framework that fights against separatism and splitism.[67] It was surprising then, that with this knowledge and adherence to SCO norms, Russia would seek to support the independence from Georgia of the breakaway territories of South Ossetia and Abkhazia. During and in the aftermath of the August 2008 war, the SCO chose a cautious endorsement of Russia over Georgia. It went ahead with the scheduled annual meeting in Dushanbe on 28 August 2008. The subsequent Dushanbe Declaration of the Heads of the Member States of the Shanghai Cooperation Organization voiced "deep concern" with regards to the tensions in South Ossetia and called for a resolution in "a peaceful way through dialogue." The declaration proceeded to highlight "Russia's active role in promoting peace and cooperation in the region" and praised its acceptance of the Six Principles of Settling the Conflict in South Ossetia on 12 August 2008. The SCO member states also restated their "commitment to preventive diplomacy," and expressed their support for the legitimate roles of the UN and the UNSC in conflict prevention (Dushanbe Declaration 2008).[68]

However, there was a clear absence of vocal support for Russia in this war and no sign of condemnation of Georgia for initiating the conflict. This can be interpreted as the member states considering their national interests rather than strengthening their regional cooperation. Moreover, the fact that the SCO refrained from recognizing the breakaway territories of South Ossetia and Abkhazia also demonstrates that the SCO would not support activities that lead to the disintegration of a state. The SCO therefore, adhered to its norms, which reject separatism, but was reluctant to overtly criticize Russia's actions. The Shanghai Convention on Combating Terrorism, Separatism and Extremism stipulates that the annexation of a territory or disintegration of a state is an act that should be punished according to the national law of the parties involved. In Russia's case, it felt obliged to intervene to protect its own nationals in a foreign country. This has been part of a more general aspect in Russian defense policy that seeks to protect Russian interests, citizens and peacekeepers abroad, a concept reinforced by the military doctrines promulgated in October 2009 and February 2010.[69]

The SCO's approach to this matter has demonstrated that it is not an instrument of a single member state. Yet it also showed immaturity on the part of the SCO with regard to the prevention of possible conflicts in the wider region. Thus it is unsurprising that this first large-scale and yet limited conflict between a member state and an external party has been repeated with an ongoing, since April 2014, and larger conflict in Ukraine.[70] However, the question remains as to whether the SCO would become more engaged if there was a conflict between two member states.

China's perspectives

China's muted response to the conflict between Russia and Georgia is the result of a moral and practical dilemma. Morally, China did not back Russia's approach due to the incompatibility with its policies of Peaceful Development and Harmonious World, which revoke the use of force to settle disputes. The escalation of the conflict also coincided with the Beijing Olympics, and China could not afford to send out a mixed message to the world about its benign intentions. This position was made clear by President Hu Jintao during his meeting with Russian President Medvedev on 27 August 2008. President Medvedev informed his Chinese counterpart about the developments in the South Caucasus, to which the Chinese president responded by stating that China was aware of the developments in the region and was "expecting all sides concerned to properly settle the issue through dialogue and coordination."[71] Medvedev reassured Hu that Russia would cooperate with China within the SCO framework to strengthen the peace and stability of the region.[72] China also faced a domestic moral dilemma: supporting the independence of South Ossetia and Abkhazia could provide a green light to those regions within China that had been campaigning for greater autonomy or a clear separation.

From the practical point of view, China viewed this conflict more as a standoff between Russia and the West (underlined by the US-led eastward NATO expansion) than as a simple bilateral conflict between Georgia and Russia. While it sympathized with Russia's discontent at having Western troops approach its neighboring region, it was not ready to be party to another Cold War. China's Peaceful Development has depended on the prevailing international system in both economic and security terms. It would have little to gain from taking a stance that would create tensions with the West and Russia.[73]

One of the greatest concerns for China is its energy insecurity; Premier Wen Jiabao acknowledged that the lack of energy resources is a "soft rib" in the country's social and economic development.[74] Reliance on foreign energy supplies renders China particularly vulnerable. Since August 2010, Russia and China have been connected by an oil pipeline, running from Siberian Skovorodino to China's northeastern frontier, yet China continues to diversify its energy sources and avoids being exclusively committed to an energy agreement with any one country.[75] In exchange for a loan of $25 billon from Beijing, Moscow agreed to provide China with 300,000 barrels of oil a day for the next twenty years. However, analysts have warned that Russia's increasing production of oil will cause a decline in its mature oil fields and may result in an inability to meet China's accelerated energy demands in the long term.[76] Another issue for China may be Russia's supply pricing disputes with other countries, such as its cutting off of the gas supply to Ukraine (with whom Russia now has a larger, escalating dispute). This, in comparison with US, which dominates the energy markets around the globe and operates in the Middle East (the primary source of China's crude oil imports), causes China to be cautious about balancing its needs and maintaining its alliances with regional partners.[77] The SCO, with its principles of noninterference and peaceful resolution of conflicts, represents a safe framework from which China may operate, not least because it enables Beijing to diversify its access to alternative energy suppliers, especially with Kazakhstan and pipelines run through Kazakhstan's territory.

When questioned at the East Asia Security Symposium and Conference in Beijing as to why China did not support Russia in its activities in the 2008 war against Georgia, a prominent Chinese major general responded that China had not clearly understood what Russia's political objectives were prior to the conflict.[78] Had Russia argued that the territories of South Ossetia and Abkhazia were historically parts of Russia's territory and therefore, Russia wanted to reattach these areas to Russia, then, according to the major general, it would have been in line with China's stance on such matters. The Chinese strategists did not understand Russia's support for Abkhazian and South Ossetian independence. The major general concluded that this situation had no impact on the Russia-China relationship or on the SCO's operations in Central Asia. During his presentation at the symposium he admitted that there was still historical distrust between Russia and China, although he acknowledged the positive momentum after the end of the Cold War and posited that eventually the two countries would come to play complementary roles. He also expressed uncertainty of the extent to which the US could manage to contain both Russia and China because their mutual relationship had improved to such an extent on so many levels.

When Russia recognized Abkhazia and South Ossetia, China's Foreign Ministry issued a statement that said:

> China has expressed concern over the latest developments of the situation in South Ossetia and Abkhazia. We understand the complicated history and reality of the South Ossetia and Abkhazia issue. In the meantime, in light of our consistent principle and position on issues alike, we hope to see relevant parties resolve the issue properly through dialogue and consultation.[79]

Chinese caution in its response to the Russia–Georgia war not only stemmed from a policy of opposing secessionism, which could then be mimicked by Tibet and Xinjiang, but also its foreign policy pledge, the Five Principles of Peaceful Coexistence, along with the related New Security Concept.[80] This calls for cooperation, consultation and maintaining peace and stability. Finally, the 2005 formulations of Peaceful Development and Harmonious World, as cited earlier, represented a rising China's pledge to peace rather than provoking further conflict. The latter would be in line with hegemonic transition theory. Rather than unsettling the status quo in a revisionist quest for preponderance, it is in the PRC's interest to help maintain an international system that is conducive to its economic development, including access to stable oil supplies, overseen by the global agenda of the US. This preferred role has been termed 'responsible stakeholder' in the West.[81] In its hope to see an engaged China it complements the Peaceful Development formulation of China's diplomacy. While not entirely in agreement with the US-led system, China has soft balancing options to exercise and need not resort to overtly confrontational ones, nor endorse them in others as a strategic priority.

The aftermath of the 2008 Russia–Georgia War and China's regionalism

In 2008, China and the Central Asian member states of the SCO did not show overt support for the Russian intervention in the Russia–Georgia War and the subsequent recognition of Abkhazia and South Ossetia. Beijing particularly faced a major dilemma; on one hand, it sympathized with Moscow's opposition to NATO's expansion, and on the other hand, it was concerned with endorsing the establishment of states based on ethnicity. Furthermore, it disapproved of the extensive use of force by Russia. In all major declarations that followed, the SCO member states restated their adherence to the principles of nonintervention and territorial integrity. In the aftermath, China succeeded in gaining support from the SCO regarding the, which in the words of the SCO Secretary General, Bolat Nurgaliev, is part of the PRC and therefore any clashes should be dealt with as a "solely internal affair."[82]

The internal balance within the SCO has tilted towards China. The Russia–Georgia conflict did not alter the geopolitical situation in Central Asia in other major ways; however, more attention started to be paid to military and political questions. The SCO, despite its inability to pressure the withdrawal of foreign military forces from the region, not preventing the armed conflict between Russia and Georgia as well as its failure to respond to the crises in Kyrgyzstan in 2010, remained intact and pledged a further expansion of its membership and agenda. After the successful SCO-sponsored conference on Afghanistan attended by the US, European Union, Organization for Security and Co-operation in Europe, G8 and NATO in Moscow in March 2009, the member states showed confidence in the organization's ability to become a significant discussion platform for not only region-related matters, but also global policy issues such as 'international information security'.

On the occasion of the tenth anniversary of the SCO and the Treaty of Good-Neighbourly Relations, Friendship and Cooperation between Russia and China in 2011, Moscow and Beijing elevated the status of their 'strategic partnership' to a 'comprehensive strategic cooperation and partnership'.[83] Moscow and Beijing agreed to coordinate their policies (in multiple areas ranging from missile defense, internet information security, outer space and global warming) in multilateral forums such as SCO, BRICS,[84] G20, and the Russia-India-China mechanism.[85] During the 2012 Summit in Beijing, the SCO heads of state issued a statement opposing the use of force in Iran and Syria. They called for dialogue rather than military intervention in the Middle East.[86] Russia's Foreign Minister, Sergei Lavrov, called the Sino-Russian partnership "irreversible" and conducive to "peace and stability in the world."[87]

In light of the 2014 NATO military withdrawal from Afghanistan, Beijing gives more support to the regional cooperation within the SCO, as a mechanism for enhancing regional security, in order to protect and advance China's economic cooperation and investments in Central Asia. This is a distinct new phase in the evolution of China's strategic priorities. China wants to ensure stability of its western XUAR, which is in close proximity to areas prone to outbursts of violence and vulnerable to possible spill-over from Afghanistan. China is interested in a predictable regional strategic environment that brings stability. To these ends and to advance its national interests, Beijing continues to employ both bilateral and multilateral engagements wrapped in stylized ideas with grand narratives such as a community of common destiny via a belt and road initiative. However, Chinese ideas may not be enough. As this chapter has demonstrated via an enquiry into the SCO, the PRC relies on the SCO member states' compliance with the SCO's principles, especially the nonuse of force and noninterference in domestic affairs. With the SCO China continues to share the driver's seat with Russia, and both states generate initiatives in economic and security areas. The SCO's mechanisms have provided a flexible framework for their evolving Central Asian policies, minimizing the necessity to compete in these spheres, and yet may not be robust enough to withstand more complex international events or have the commitment Beijing's regionalism may require. China's expanding use of regionalism, of an evolving SCO style, and one that places China at the centre as the prominent and initiating power, is thus a continuing strategic challenge and a significant priority for China.

Notes

1 R. Foot, 'China in the ASEAN Regional Forum: Organizational Processes and Domestic Modes of Thought', *Asian Survey*, vol. 38, no. 5, 1998, pp. 425–40.
2 K. He, *Institutional Balancing in the Asia Pacific: Economic Interdependence and China's Rise*, London: Routledge, 2009.
3 S. Harris, 'China's Regional Policies: How Much Hegemony?', *Australian Journal of International Affairs*, vol. 59, no. 4, 2005, pp. 481–92.
4 J.G. Ikenberry, 'The Future of the Liberal World Order', *Foreign Affairs*, vol. 90, no. 3, 2011, pp. 56–68.
5 Z. Huasheng identifies six main priorities for China in Central Asia: (1) border security; (2) combating the 'East Turkestan' movement; (3) energy; (4) economic interests; (5) geopolitics; and (6) the Shanghai Cooperation Organization (SCO), 2007. Z. Huasheng, 'Central Asia in China's Diplomacy', in *Central Asia: Views from Washington, Moscow and Beijing*, New York: M. E. Sharpe, pp. 138.
6 This strategy was especially important due to China's disrupted relations with the West in the aftermath of the Tiananmen Square incident in 1989.
7 B. McCormick and J.H. Ping, *Chinese Engagements: Regional Issues with Global Implications*, Robina, Queensland: Bond University Press, 2011.
8 K. Syroezhkin, 'China in Central Asia: From Trade to Strategic Partnership', *Central Asia and the Caucasus*, vol. 45, no. 3, 2007, pp. 40–51.
9 K. Khafizova, 'Separatism in China's Xinjiang-Uighur Autonomous Region: Dynamics and Potential Impact on Central Asia', *Central Asia and Caucasus*, vol. 19, no. 1, 2003, p. 7.
10 M. Clarke, 'Making the Crooked Straight: China's Grand Strategy of "Peaceful Rise" and Its Central Asian Dimension', *Asian Security*, vol. 4, no. 2, 2008, pp. 107–42.
11 'Agreement on Confidence-Building in the Military Field in the Border Area, Shanghai', 26 April 1996, <http://cis-legislation.com/document.fwx?rgn=3879> (accessed 14 June 2015); 'The Agreement on the Mutual Reduction on Armed Forces in the Border Areas, Moscow', 24 April 1997, <www.fas.org/nuke/control/mrmfba/index.html> (accessed 14 June 2015).
12 Russia and China declared the no-first-use of nuclear weapons against each other and nontargeting of strategic missiles at each other in September 1994. *Fact Sheet: China: Nuclear Disarmament and Reduction of*, Ministry of Foreign Affairs of the People's Republic of China, 27 April 2004, <www.fmprc.gov.cn/eng/wjb/zzjg/jks/cjjk/2622/t93539.htm> (accessed 14 June 2015).
13 Y. Jing-dong, *Sino-Russian Confidence Building Measures: A Preliminary Analysis*, Working Paper 20, Vancouver: Centre for International Studies, 1998, <www.isn.ethz.ch/isn/Digital-Library/Publications/Detail/?ots591=0c54e3b3-1e9c-be1e-2c24-a6a8c7060233&lng=en&id=46425> (accessed 14 June 2015).
14 T. Ming-Yen, *From Adversaries to Partners? Chinese and Russian Military Cooperation after the Cold War*, Westport, CT: Greenwood Press, 2003, p. 92.
15 'China: Arms Control and Disarmament', Information Service of the State Council of the People's Republic of China, Beijing, November 1995, <www.china.org.cn/e-white/army/index.htm> (accessed 14 June 2015); China provided figures for the 1997 defense expenditure in China National Defence, published by the Information Service of the State Council of the PRC in July 1998. <www.china.org.cn/e-white/5/5.3.htm#3> (accessed 14 June 2015).
16 S. Perlo-Freeman, J. Cooper, O. Ismail, E. Skons, and C. Solmirano, 'Chapter 4: Military Expenditure', *SIPRI Yearbook 2011: Armaments, Disarmament and International Security*, <www.sipri.org/yearbook/2011/files/SIPRIYB1104-04A-04B.pdf> (accessed 14 June 2015); A.S. Erickson and A.P. Liff, 'Understanding China's Defence Budget: What It Means, and Why It Matters', *PacNet* 6, Pacific Forum, CSIS, Honolulu,

HI: Pacific Forum, 2011, <http://csis.org/files/publication/pac1116.pdf> (accessed 14 June 2015).
17 R.M. Cutler, 'The Shattering of the Sino-Russian Entente over the Shape of Central Asia?', *Central Asia-Caucasus Analyst*, 2001, <www.cacianalyst.org/?q=node/163/print> (accessed 14 June 2015).
18 M. Nurgaliyev 'Development of the Shanghai Cooperation Organization and Diplomacy of Japan towards Central Asia', *Japan Institute of International Affairs*, <www2.jiia.or.jp/pdf/fellow_report/080317-Marat_Nurgaliyev.pdf> (accessed 30 March 2010).
19 S. Aris, 'Tackling the "Three Evils": the Shanghai Cooperation Organization (SCO) – A Regional Response to Non-traditional Security Challenges or an Anti-Western Bloc?', *Europe-Asia Studies*, vol. 61, no. 5, 2009, pp. 457–482.
20 Dushanbe Declaration by the Heads of State of the Republic of Kazakhstan, of the People's Republic of China, of the Kyrgyz Republic, of the Russian Federation, and of the Republic of Tajikistan, Dushanbe, Tajikistan, Ministry of Foreign Affairs of the Russian Federation, 5 July 2000, <www.ln.mid.ru/Bl.nsf/arh/A69BB7197B47EC174325699C003B5F9D?OpenDocument> (accessed 14 June 2015).
21 S. Aris, 'Russian-Chinese Relations through the Lens of the SCO', *Russie.Nei.Visions*, 34, 2008, <www.ifri.org/sites/default/files/atoms/files/Ifri_RNV_Aris_SCO_Eng.pdf> (accessed 14 June 2015).
22 Russkiy Mir Foundation, 'About Russkiy Mir Foundation, President Vladimir Putin's Address to the Federal Assembly in April 2007', *Russkiymir.ru*, <www.russkiymir.ru/russkiymir/en/fund/about> (accessed 14 June 2015).
23 S. Gradirovsky and N. Esipova, 'Russian Language Enjoying a Boost in Post-Soviet States: Attitudes More Favourable in Georgia, Moldova, and Armenia', *Gallup World*, 2008, <www.gallup.com/poll/109228/russian-language-enjoying-boost-postsoviet-states.aspx> (accessed 14 June 2015).
24 E.A, Hyer, *The Pragmatic Dragon: China's Grand Strategy and Boundary Settlements*, Contemporary Chinese Studies, Vancouver: UBC Press, 2015.
25 V. Skosyrev, *Interview with the Russian First Deputy Foreign Minister Vyacheslav*, 2004; Trubnikov, 'Есть предел уступкам Москвы' ['There Is a Limit to Moscow's Concessions'], *Nezavisimaya Gazeta Daily*, 12 May 2004, <www.ng.ru/world/2004–05–12/1_trubnikov.html> (accessed 14 June 2015).
26 M. Troitskiy, 'A Russian Perspective on the Shanghai Cooperation Organization', in A.J.K. Bailes, P. Dunay, P. Guang, and M. Troitskiy, *The Shanghai Cooperation Organization*, SIPRI Policy Paper 17, Stockholm: Stockholm International Peace Research Institute, 2007, pp. 30–44.
27 B. Pannier, 'Uzbekistan: Military Exercises with Russia Timely for Tashkent', *RFE/RL*, 23 September 2005, <www.rferl.org/content/article/1061630.html> (accessed 14 June 2015); J.C.K, Daly, K.H. Meppen, V. Socor, and S.F. Starr, 'Anatomy of a Crisis: U.S.-Uzbekistan Relations, 2001–2005', Silk Road Paper, Central Asia-Caucasus Institute & Silk Road Studies Program, EurasiaNet.org, 2006, <www.silkroadstudies.org/new/inside/publications/0602Uzbek.pdf> (accessed 14 June 2015).
28 I. Gorst, 'Kyrgyzstan to Shut US Military Base', *Financial Times*, 19 February 2009, <www.ft.com/intl/cms/s/0/2d949bc6-fe62–11dd-b19a-000077b07658.html#axzz2Dreq06OC> (accessed 14 June 2015).
29 J. Nichol, *Kyrgyzstan and the Status of the U.S. Manas Airbase: Context and Implications*, CRS Report for Congress, 2009, <www.fas.org/sgp/crs/row/R40564.pdf> (accessed 14 June 2015).
30 B. Pannier, 'Former Soviet Sphere Shocked into Silence by Conflict in Georgia', *RFE/RL*, 11 August 2005, <www.rferl.org/content/Former_Soviet_Sphere_Shocked_Into_Silence_By_Ossetia_Conflict/1190128.html> (accessed 14 June 2015).
31 J. Lillis, 'Kazakh Energy Profits Give Foreign-Policy Heft', *EurasiaNet*, 19 April 2007, <www.isn.ethz.ch/isn/Security-Watch/Articles/Detail//?ots591=4888caa0-b3db-1461–98b9-e20e7b9c13d4&lng=en&id=53197> (accessed 14 June 2015).

32 S. Blank, 'Revising the Border: China's Inroads into Tajikistan', *China Brief*, vol. 11, no. 14, 2011, <www.jamestown.org/programs/chinabrief/single/?tx_ttnews%5Btt_news%5D=38251&cHash=1c880ed7361f0dc32c7d21caf3ce7055> (accessed 14 June 2015); B. Pannier, 'Tajikistan Agrees to Allow Chinese Farmers to Till Land', *RFE/RL*, 28 January 2011, <www.rferl.org/content/tajikistan_china/2289623.html> (accessed 14 June 2015).
33 S. Peyrouse, J. Boonstra, and M. Laruelle, 'Security and Development Approaches to Central Asia: The EU Compared to China and Russia', *EUCAM* Working Paper 11, 2012, <www.eucentralasia.eu/fileadmin/user_upload/PDF/Working_Papers/WP11.pdf> (accessed 14 June 2015).
34 J. Stokes, 'China's Road Rules: Beijing Looks West Toward Eurasian Integration', *Foreign Affairs*, 19 April 2015, <www.foreignaffairs.com/articles/asia/2015-04-19/chinas-road-rules> (accessed 8 June 2015).
35 Troitskiy, 'A Russian Perspective on the Shanghai Cooperation Organization'.
36 S. Blagov, 'Russia Urges Formation of Central Asian Energy Club', *EurasiaNet.org*, 2007, <www.eurasianet.org/departments/insight/articles/eav110707a.shtml>. (accessed 14 June 2015).
37 Y. Süreyya, 'Chinese energy diplomacy in Central Asia', *Today's Zaman*, 20 October 2013, <www.todayszaman.com/orsam_chinese-energy-diplomacy-in-central-asia_329219.html> (accessed 17 September 2015).
38 E. Petelin, 'China's Energy Monologue in Central Asia', *Security Index: A Russian Journal on International Security*, vol. 17, no. 4, 2011, pp. 29–46.
39 'China Becomes Russia's Top Trade Partner in First Two Months of 2012', *Xinhua*, 7 April 2012, <http://news.xinhuanet.com/english/china/2012-04/07/c_131511784.htm> (accessed 14 June 2015).
40 H. Zhao, 'Central Asia in China's Diplomacy', in E. Rumer, D. Trenin, and Z. Huasheng (eds.), *Central Asia: Views from Washington, Moscow, and Beijing*, London: M.E. Sharpe, 2007.
41 N. Swanström, *China and Greater Central Asia: New Frontiers*, Silk Road Paper, Central Asia-Caucasus Institute & Silk Road Studies Program, 2011, <www.silkroadstudies.org/new/docs/silkroadpapers/1112Swanstrom.pdf> (accessed 14 June 2015).
42 T. Tugsbilguun, 'Does the Shanghai Cooperation Organization Represent an Example of a Military Alliance?', in R.E. Bedeski and N. Swanström (eds.), *Eurasia's Ascent in Energy and Geopolitics: Rivalry or Partnership for China, Russia, and Central Asia?* London: Routledge, 2012, pp. 179–98.
43 M. de Haas, 'The Peace Mission 2007 Exercises: The Shanghai Cooperation Organisation Advances', *Advanced Research and Assessment Group*, Defence Academy of the United Kingdom, 2007, <www.defac.ac.uk/colleges/csrc> (accessed 14 June 2015).
44 K. Barsky, 'Central Asia under the SCO's 'Impermeable Umbrella'', *International Affairs*, vol. 58, no. 4, 2012, pp. 151–63.
45 Putin quoted in Troitsky, 'A Russian Perspective on the Shanghai Cooperation Organization'.
46 Institute for Strategic Studies. *The Military Balance*, 2012.
47 Officially, Georgia has two autonomous republics: Abkhazia (Sokhumi) and Ajara (Batumi). This chapter does not explore the relationship between Georgia and Ajara, which has remained in line with the Georgians.
48 T. Potier, *Conflict in Nagorno-Karabakh, Abkhazia and South Ossetia: A Legal Appraisal*, Leiden: Martinus Nijhoff, 2001, pp. 8–9.
49 T. Goltz, 'The Paradox of Living in Paradise: Georgia's Descent into Chaos', in S. E. Cornell and S. F. Starr (eds.), *The Guns of August 2008*, Armonk, NY: M.E. Sharpe, 2009, pp. 20–27.
50 IISS, 'Georgia: The War in Words', *IISS Strategic Comments*, vol. 14, no. 7, September 2008, <www.iiss.org/publications/strategic-comments/past-issues/volume-14-2008/volume-14-issue-7/georgia-the-war-in-words/> (accessed 14 June 2015).

51 T. Gordadze, 'Georgian-Russian Relations in the 1990s', in Cornell and Starr (eds.), *The Guns of August 2008*.
52 S. Markedonov, 'Caucasus Conflict Breaks Old Rules of the Game', *Russian Analytical Digest*, 45, Zurich: Center for Security Studies, ETH, 2008.
53 B. Rezvani, 'The Ossetian-Ingush Confrontation: Explaining a Horizontal Conflict', *Iran & The Caucasus*, vol. 14, no. 2, 2010, pp. 419–29.
54 Dagomys (Sochi) Agreement (Соглашение о принципах мирного урегулирования грузино-осетинского конфликта), Sochi, 24 June 1992, Ministry of Foreign Affairs Diplomatic Bulletin, pp. 13–14: 31, <www.caucasica.org/docs/detail.php?ID=1329&PHPSESSID=85ce24d286e083a2941a5edb041f4078> (accessed 14 June 2015).
55 M. Laruelle, 'Neo-Eurasianist Alexander Dugin on the Russia-Georgia Conflict', *CACI Analyst*, 3 September 2008, <www.cacianalyst.org/?q=node/4928> (accessed 14 June 2015).
56 N.P. Walsh, 'Georgian Leader Attacks Russia after Gas Blasts', *Guardian*, 23 January 2006, <www.guardian.co.uk/world/2006/jan/23/russia.georgia> (accessed 14 June 2015).
57 It is estimated that approximately 500,000 Georgians worked in Russia, generating roughly US$556 million in 2006. Moscow expelled less than 1% of Georgian migrant workers. *Economic and Political Transition in Georgia*, NATO Parliamentary Assembly, <www.nato-pa.int/default.asp?SHORTCUT=1171> (accessed 14 June 2015).
58 GU(U)AM – Georgia, Ukraine, Uzbekistan, Azerbaijan and Moldova, <http://guam-organization.org/en/node/422> (accessed 14 June 2015). The forum was established in 1997 as GUAM and was renamed GUUAM once Uzbekistan joined the cooperation in 1999; in the aftermath of the Andijan Uprising, Uzbekistan delivered the official withdrawal from GUUAM and the forum was renamed to GUAM in 2005.
59 R. Weitz, 'GUAM and the Georgian War', *CACI Analyst*, 20 August 2008, <www.cacianalyst.org/?q=node/4917> (accessed 14 June 2015).
60 Markedonov, 'Caucasus Conflict Breaks Old Rules of the Game'.
61 'Interview with Eduard Shevardnadze', *Russia Today*, 16 August 2008, <http://rt.com/politics/interview-with-eduard-shevardnadze-2008–08–16/> (accessed 14 June 2015).
62 R. Allison, 'Russia Resurgent? Moscow's Campaign to "Coerce Georgia to Peace"', *International Affairs*, vol. 84, no. 6, 2008, pp. 1145–71.
63 'Statement on the Situation in South Ossetia', *Kremlin.ru*, 8 August 2008, <http://archive.kremlin.ru/eng/speeches/2008/08/08/1553_type82912type82913_205032.shtml> (accessed 14 June 2015).
64 IISS, 'Georgia: The War in Words'.
65 Council of the European Union, *Independent International Fact-Finding Mission on the Conflict in Georgia*, vol. I, September 2009, <www.ceiig.ch/pdf/IIFFMCG_Volume_I.pdf> (accessed 14 June 2015).
66 This applies mainly to the smaller states. Kazakhstan has sought to engage Russia as part of a wider policy of global relationships, while Uzbekistan has been driven back towards Russian cooperation after human rights issues weakened its links with the United States in 2005.
67 The Chinese leadership uses the terms 'separatism' (*fenlizhuyi*) and 'splitism' (*fenliezhuyi*) interchangeably. The difference derives from how the leadership views the intensity of various independence movements within China. Splitism relates to the Dalai Lama's moral support of the Tibetan people at large, while Taiwanese independence or the East Turkestan movement are considered separatism. See the interpretation by S.N. Pandey, *Chinese Counter Terror Intelligence Module – Compatibility to Nov 26 Mumbai Type Terror Attacks*, South Asia Analysis Group, Paper No. 2993, 27 December 2008, <www.c3sindia.org/terrorismandsecurity/447> (accessed 14 June 2015).
68 President of Russia, 'Dushanbe Declaration of Heads of SCO Member States', Events Files, Session of the Council of Heads of State of the SCO, 27–28 August 2008, <http://

archive.kremlin.ru/eng/events/articles/2008/08/205865/205913.shtml> (accessed 17 September 2015).
69 J. Nichol, *Russian Military Reform and Defence Policy*, Washington, DC: Congressional Research Service, 2011, <www.fas.org/sgp/crs/row/R42006.pdf> (accessed 14 June 2015).
70 'President Vladimir Putin Tells West Not To Fear Russia', *BBC News*, 6 June 2015, <www.bbc.com/news/world-europe-33034844> (accessed 8 June 2015).
71 Xinhua News Agency, 'Chinese, Russian Presidents Meet in Dushanbe', *China.org.cn*, 18 August 2008, <www.china.org.cn/international/news/2008-08/28/content_16346413.htm> (accessed 17 September 2015).
72 J. Ling, H. Wang and B. Dai, *Hu Jintao Meets with Russian President Medvedev*, Ministry of Foreign Affairs of the People's Republic of China, 28 August 2008, <www.fmprc.gov.cn/eng/zxxx/t509750.htm> (accessed 14 June 2015).
73 Ibid.
74 J. Wen, 'Attach Great Importance to, and Strengthen Leadership over the Building of a Resource-Saving Society at an Accelerating Pace', *Xinhua*, 3 July 2005, quoted in S.L. Craig, *Chinese Perceptions of Traditional and Nontraditional Security Threats*, Strategic Studies Institute, U.S. Army War College, March 2007, p. 120, <www.strategicstudiesinstitute.army.mil/pdffiles/pub765.pdf> (accessed 14 June 2015).
75 E. Strecker Downs, *China's Quest for Energy Security*, Santa Monica, CA: RAND, 2000; V. Belokrinitskiy, 'Southwesterly Enlargement of Greater China', *Central Asia and the Caucasus*, vol. 45, no. 3, 2007, p. 51; R. Dannreuther, 'China and Global Oil: Vulnerability and Opportunity', *International Affairs*, vol. 87, no. 6, 2011, pp. 1345–64.
76 I. Gorst, 'Russia Opens China Pipeline for Siberian Oil', *Financial Times*, 29 August 2010, <www.ft.com/cms/s/0/dd89374a-b38c-11df-81aa-00144feabdc0.html#axzz1RKc41tEG> (accessed 14 June 2015).
77 'China's Energy Data', U.S. Energy Information Administration, <www.eia.gov/EMEU/cabs/China/pdf.pdf> (accessed 14 June 2015).
78 China Security Symposium, China Foreign Affairs University, Beijing, 22 June 2009, which the author attended. The major general is not explicitly named because the symposium follows the Chatham House rule.
79 Consulate-General of the People's Republic of China in Melbourne, 'Foreign Ministry Spokesperson Qin Gang's Regular Press Conference on August 28, 2008', <http://melbourne.china-consulate.org/eng/fyrth/t509769.htm> (accessed 14 June 2015)
80 *China's Position Paper on the New Security Concept*, Ministry of Foreign Affairs, PRC, <www.fmprc.gov.cn/ce/ceun/eng/xw/t27742.htm> (accessed 14 June 2015).
81 'President Hu Makes Four-Point Proposal for Building Harmonious World', *Xinhua*, 16 September 2005, <http://news.xinhuanet.com/english/2005–09/16/content_3496789.htm> (accessed 14 June 2015).
82 SCO, 'Chronicle of Main Events at SCO in 2009, Information from 10 July 2009', 31 December 2009, <www.sectsco.org/EN/show.asp?id=182> (accessed 14 June 2015).
83 Yu Bin, 'China and Russia Tussle over SCO's Future', *Asia Times Online*, 27 September 2011, <www.atimes.com/atimes/China/MI27Ad02.html>.
84 Acronym for an association of Brazil, Russia, India, China and South Africa.
85 'News Conference Following Russian-Chinese Talks', *Kremlin.ru Archive*, 16 June 2011, <http://eng.kremlin.ru/transcripts/2405> (accessed 14 June 2015).
86 'SCO Leaders Reject Force in Iran, Syria', *RFE/RL*, 7 June 2012, <www.rferl.org/content/sco-summit-rejects-force-iran-syria/24606443.html> (accessed 14 June 2015).
87 'China, Russia Vow to Further Bilateral Ties', *English.gov.cn*, 21 August 2012, <http://english.gov.cn/2012–08/21/content_2208031.htm> (accessed 14 June 2015).

Conclusion

Brett McCormick

In the wake of China's grand coming-out party with the Olympic games, and the rippling financial meltdowns that rocked the Western world, 2008 appears as something of a watershed moment in the progression of China's strategic priorities. The expansion of China's foreign policy concerns – geographically and conceptually – has introduced multiple new routes for analysis. This book has explored new areas of international engagement (e.g., Hoyt on Pakistan), proposed new methods of analysis (e.g., Hyer/Zhang/Hamzawi on domestic factors in foreign policy), illuminated fundamental details in tense current affairs (e.g., Christoffersen on maritime crisis management) and reenvisioned analysis of historical context (e.g., Wilson on strategic culture).

The last few years have witnessed new horizons opening on all sides of China's foreign policy considerations and strategic priorities. The United States of America's (US) drawdown in Central Asia in the post-Iraq, post–Osama bin Laden, post-Afghanistan years has inaugurated new spaces for cooperation, and competition, between China and its continental neighbors. The US 'pivot' or 'rebalancing' to East Asia – combined with an unprecedented surge in territorial disputes across the South China and East China Seas – has challenged every level of bilateral and multilateral regional institution and regime. A decade ago, the *Varyag* was on its way to becoming a floating casino, and now we have the *Liaoning*. A new generation of leadership has taken the reins in Beijing. US Marines are relocating to Guam and Australia. The Trans-Pacific Partnership moves apace with the Asian Infrastructure Investment Bank.

The contents and organization of this book have functioned across three layers. First, the overriding organizational structure is defined by focus on the domestic underpinnings of China's evolving strategic priorities and foreign policy directions (Chapters 1–4), *contrasted* with a focus on the external (i.e., international) drivers and concerns (Chapters 5–8).

Second, within each section we have also endeavored to identify the relative significance of China's continental priorities *contrasted* with maritime priorities. In the first section, Christoffersen's study of maritime crisis management stands in contrast with Su/Cui's discussion of China's Western-leaning center of gravity. In the second section, Granados's review of the shifting significance of China-Japan relations is balanced by Ping's, Hoyt's and Kizekova's analyses of strategic priorities in China's relations with India, Pakistan and Russia, respectively. Finally, half of the chapters emphasize an historical approach to exposing and interpreting shifts in China's strategic priorities (Su/Cui, Wilson, Granados, Kizekova), while half emphasize, instead, a review of current affairs or theory as their main line of approach (Hyer, Christoffersen, Ping, Hoyt).

Our choice of content implies an underlying perspective that regional affairs dominate the evolution of Chinese strategic priorities more so than the China-US balance. This volume has focused on detailed discussion of Chinese foreign policy and strategic concerns since 2008 in accordance with this perspective, rather than a comprehensive updating. For such comprehensive review, we would suggest such excellent works as Robert Sutter's *Chinese Foreign Relations: Power and Policy since the Cold War*, or Marc Lanteigne's *Chinese Foreign Policy: An Introduction*. In terms of overall approach, this volume compares most closely with Suisheng Zhao's *Chinese Foreign Policy: Pragmatism and Strategic Behavior*; Alastair Iain Johnston and Robert S. Ross's *New Directions in the Study of China's Foreign Policy*; and Yong Deng's *China's Struggle for Status: The Realignment of International Relations*.[1]

Zhao's 2004 volume parallels our approach in multiple ways. Just as the chapter by Hyer/Zhang/Hamzawi spelled out in detail, the analysis throughout both volumes reflects the debates between realism and liberalism in both the field of international relations overall, and for the Chinese case specifically. Furthermore, by juxtaposing different perspectives (national, theoretical, methodological), we transcend any need for the sorts of either/or choices demanded of more rigid frameworks. Finally, our volume, much like Zhao's a decade earlier, takes seriously the value of coalescing analysis of current affairs with a broader historical context.

The current volume has a comparable scope to Johnston and Ross's 2006 volume, which was broken into sections on security studies, China and globalization, and Chinese domestic politics. In one form or another, at least half of our chapters directly picked up on issues their work identified as future directions on Chinese foreign policy that would demand further study. They identified the need for continually updating analysis of China's use of force, reevaluation of the offensive or defensive nature of Chinese military strategy, and the likelihood of using force as a tool of diplomacy. For the intervening years between their volume and this one, each of these points has been explored in the chapters by Christoffersen and Kizekova, and the overall issue of Chinese strategy has been productively complicated by Wilson. Johnston and Ross further identified the need to continue study of Chinese attitudes and behavior toward spheres of influence – again well reviewed by Kizekova's examination of China-Russia relations through the Shanghai Cooperation Organisation (SCO), and Ping's examination of China-India relations. Finally, Johnston and Ross pointed to the need for better penetrating the issue of public opinion's impact on Chinese foreign policy, particularly with regard to the individual roles of key leadership – precisely a conclusion of Hyer/Zhang/Hamzawi in their updated review of China's foreign policy process.

The chapters by Su/Cui and Wilson are central to this volume in that they, each in their own way, exemplify the values of using an historical approach to balance analysis of current affairs, while simultaneously demonstrating in stark contrast the widely divergent conclusions to which historical study can point. Wilson's 'myth-busting' emerges from his challenge to discern more accurate patterns of strategic behavior, and question the extent to which *any* aspect of Chinese tradition truly informs contemporary strategy and priorities. Su/Cui, however, build their entire case on the foundation of recognizing a geopolitical logic that has shaped China's strategic priorities across history. The concept of 'strategic culture' that Wilson problematizes is not exactly the same as Su/Cui's concept of an historical 'geopolitical logic' underlying Chinese strategic behavior; it is important to acknowledge the differences between the authors' disciplinary methods. However, these are precisely the types of divergent perspectives from which this multi-author volume seeks to find synergy.

Aside from their fundamental differences concerning the efficacy of applying historical models to current affairs, there is an additional point of contrast in Su/Cui's and Wilson's assessments of 'culture' as a national trait affecting leadership decisions. One of Wilson's conclusions is that culture matters in terms of the *assumptions* Chinese states have made about themselves and others. Specifically, he feels that "the worldview of China's leadership is so conditioned by foreign ideologies" that it is hard to find the assumed continuity with tradition. In direct contrast, Su/Cui's perspective leads them to conclude that "China strategically may need to absorb potentially useful elements from Western civilization, such as democracy," but due to thousands of years of Chinese cultural traditions, it will be difficult to incorporate such foreign elements. In their own ways, both of these points add weight to Hyer/Zhang/Hamzawi's conclusions on the critical need to advance study of the personalities of Chinese leaders, and whatever real or imagined cultural background informs their thinking.

Wilson's chapter also opens patches of analytical ground that many of the other chapters build upon. His observation of how an 'obsession' with an historically construed model of sovereignty is increasingly incongruent with contemporary regional models, and that 'territory matters', bears on much of Ping's study of territorial conflict with India. In a similar way, his conclusion that the 'Near Seas' matter relates to the maritime disputes central to Christoffersen's and Granados's chapters, as does his identification of China's historical willingness to employ gunboats in both war and peace. Finally, his conclusions about how 'size matters' has direct bearing on Kizekova's analysis of the shifting balance between China and Russia in the context of the SCO and Central Asia.

In addition to everything illuminated by the contrast between Su/Cui's chapter and Wilson's, their chapter also lays at the heart of the debate between the 'continental' and 'maritime' nature of China's strategic priorities that permeates this volume. The foundation of Su/Cui's thesis is that China is essentially a land power, and subsequently that "the primary component of China's Grand Strategy is to prioritize the west." They explicitly note the disproportionate number of high-level officials in the current Xi Jinping administration connected to inland provinces. This stands in direct contrast to Christoffersen's assertion that China is shifting "from an identity of land power to maritime power," as explicitly described by Hu Jintao at the 18th Party Congress of November 2012. Where the chapters by Kizekova, Hoyt and Ping illustrate critical elements of continental concern, those of Granados, Christoffersen and to some extent Wilson do the same for the maritime. The full volume makes it clear that this is certainly not an either/or proposition, and that it is more likely the *tensions between* such geographic foci that shape China's strategic priorities, rather than either focus in itself.

Although Kizekova's analysis of Chinese regionalism extends into the present, her historical review of the SCO combines effectively with the predominantly current affairs approach employed by Hoyt and the theoretical approach taken by Ping. For example, Kizekova's perspective locates China's expanding operational frontier throughout Central-Eastern Asia as a strategic *reemergence*. China's interests surrounding long-term pipeline access, when viewed in an historical context, are seen as challenges to Russian and US long-term strategic interests. Alternately, Hoyt's current affairs approach with regard to Pakistan (admittedly peripheral to Kizekova's specific focus) sees contemporary Central-South Asia as a place conducive to shared interests and cooperation. Both agree that after the US and International Security Assistance Force's withdrawal from Afghanistan, a significant new space will open up for Central Asian relations overall. Both also strongly agree that China's foreign policy is, and has been, focused on opening or maintaining markets, rather than military competition or interference in neighboring states' internal affairs. Understanding and assessing China's strategic priorities on the continent clearly requires such an overlapping of the historical, current affairs and theoretical approaches.

On the maritime side, the current affairs focus of Christoffersen's chapter combines effectively with Granados's historical approach. For example, Granados has identified various recurring dynamics governing China-Japan relations, particularly with regard to territorial competition across the East China Sea. Christoffersen's study points to a need for new formal crisis management mechanisms (for managing comparable contemporary disputes), especially in light of ongoing overreliance on 'institutionalized patterns' and 'old-style' processes.

Hyer/Zhang/Hamzawi's chapter has illustrated how various models of analysis connect through both historical and contemporary investigations. They recognize challenges to the neoliberal perspective in how China's rapid economic growth has outpaced acceptance of a new role as a major world power, as also put by Ping. This is immensely helpful for understanding difficulties in making regional institutions work smoothly, as encountered in Kizekova's review of the SCO, or Christoffersen's examination of the Association of Southeast Asian Nations and potential trilateral mechanisms for US–China–Japan, or within the China-India border dispute. Their recognition of how domestic politics and public opinion interact with and interfere with foreign policy decision making, particularly when involving countries like Japan, is a useful tool for better understanding the Diaoyu/Senkaku or anti-Japanese demonstrations issues covered by Granados and Christoffersen. Their conclusions about the effects of leadership personalities on foreign policy have bearing on Christoffersen's observations of enduring 'old styles' of crisis management leadership, and Wilson's complication of enduring 'myths' that explain – or at least are often imagined to explain – strategic leadership decisions.

The two sections of this book were designed to synthesize the domestic and international dimensions of China's strategic priorities. The first section focused on Chinese domestic issues that impact China's international relations. The second section focused on Chinese international issues that impact international relations as a whole. We have aimed to create debate by drawing attention to the overlap of such critical issues. The hope is to generate a synergy useful to both scholar and practitioner. In the preceding chapters we have identified significant new issues that have emerged over the past five to ten years, and illuminated new facets of China's evolving strategic priorities that must be vigorously addressed. Such issues are too important for blindly feeling for the stones. The coming five to ten years will undoubtedly be even more transitional than the previous, and there is naturally much more to be done.

Note

1   R. G. Sutter, *Chinese Foreign Relations: Power and Policy since the Cold War*, Lanham, MD: Rowman & Littlefield, 2012; M. Lanteigne, *Chinese Foreign Policy: An Introduction*, London: Routledge, 2013; S. Zhao, *Chinese Foreign Policy: Pragmatism and Strategic Behavior*, Armonk, NY: M.E. Sharpe, 2004; A. Johnston and R. Ross (eds.), *New Directions in the Study of China's Foreign Policy*, Stanford, CA: Stanford University Press, 2006; Y. Deng, *China's Struggle for Status: The Realignment of International Relations*, Cambridge: Cambridge University Press, 2008.

Index

9/11 116

Abbottabad 114, 116, 122
Abe, Shinzo, Prime Minister 67, 80, 83, 85–7, 89
Aden, Gulf of 17
Afghanistan 101, 104, 106, 114, 119, 121–2, 124–5, 142, 148, 151
  Soviet invasion of 116, 118
Africa 15, 85, 121
Air Defense Identification Zone (ADIZ) 85, 92
Aksai Chin 102, 104, 109, 116
Al Qaeda 121–2
A.Q. Khan 116, 119, 123
Arunchal Pradesh 102, 104
ASEAN 63, 90, 105, 129
  Regional Forum 65, 88, 129
Asian Development Bank 129
Asian Infrastructure Investment Bank 4, 105, 117, 129, 148
Asia Pacific Economic Cooperation 65, 85, 91, 129
Australia *i, xvii*, 3–4, 26, 148

Bangladesh 101, 106, 116, 118
Belgrade, Bombing of Embassy 45, 64
Bilateral, Conflict/Dialogues/Disputes/ Issues/Mechanisms/Relationships/ Security/Talks/Ties 45, 65, 67–71, 73–4, 80, 84–8, 90, 92, 98, 102, 104–5, 116–19, 125, 130, 134, 140, 142
Bond University *i, xv, xvii–xviii*, 3
Bo Xilai 53
Border Dispute (s) 6, 18, 98–100, 103–9
  Agreements 101
  Between China and India, List 101
  Bilateral Joint Working Groups 106

Durand Line 101
Line of Actual Control 102–4, 108–9
McMahon Line 102–3, 108
Negotiations 101
Nine-Dash Line 103
1962 War 98, 102, 108, 114, 116
Solving 106
Territory Disputes 101
BRICS 142
Brinkmanship 64, 122
British India 102–3, 106, 109, 114
  Partition 102–3, 109, 114, 122
Bhutan 106
Bush, George W., President 138

Central Asia 6, 37, 121, 129–31, 133–4, 140–2, 148, 150–1
Century of Humiliation 13, 21, 48, 52, 54, 102–3
China-ASEAN Code of Conduct 63, 89
China's Foreign Policy
  Domestic Politics Model 46
  Dual Approach to Foreign Policy and Public Opinion 51, 52
  Influence of Chinese Leaders on 54–7
  Influence of Interest Groups on 45
  Influence Leader's Personality on 55, 57, 58
  Influence of PLA on 53, 54
  Influence of Public Opinion on 43, 46, 48–52, 54, 57, 58
  Neoliberalism/Liberal Institutionalist Model 43–6
  Neorealism/Structural Conflict Model 43, 44
  Role of Division of Public Diplomacy 49
China's Strategic Culture 8, 9, 18, 19–21
  Good Iron Myth 13, 14
  Great Wall myth 8, 9, 11

Index

Legalists 10
Mao Zedong 13, 14, 18–20
Shiji 9
Spring and Autumn Annals 9
Sunzi *xi*, 8–9, 12–14, 17–20
China, Republic of 33
China Foreign Affairs University *xv*, *xvii–xviii*, 2–3
Chinese Communist Party (CCP) 5, 11, 14, 31, 38, 48–9, 54–5, 63–4, 70–2, 74, 86–7
  Central Committee 38, 64, 70
Clinton, Hillary, Secretary of State 65, 68, 84, 88
CO^2 Emissions 97
Coast Guard 62, 66–9, 73, 81, 83
Code for Unalerted Encounters at Sea 90, 92
Cold War 55–6, 115–18, 140, 149
Colonialism/Imperialism 102–4
  Century of Humiliation 13, 21, 48, 52, 54, 102–3
  Opium Wars 103
Confidence Building Measures (CBM) 70–2
Core Interest 44, 46, 54, 73, 74, 87, 88, 98, 104, 115
Cox, Robert 100
Crisis Management 64–74, 80, 90–2

Dalai Lama 46, 106, 117
Democracy 35, 98, 150
Demographic Transition 105, 108
Deng Xiaoping 47–8, 51, 55–7
Development *i*, 1–2, 4–5, 25–9, 34–9, 44–6, 66, 104–5, 108, 114, 131, 133, 135, 140–1
  Historical 24, 26
  Model 4, 26, 39, 98, 105, 107, 130
  Regional 130
Diaoyu/Senkaku 47, 50–2, 65–74, 80–2, 85, 87–90, 92
  Koga Family 83
  Kurihara Family 83
  Okinawa Reversion Treaty 83
  Rebalancing Policy 84
  San Francisco Peace Treaty 83
  US-Japan Security Treaty 83
  US National Defense Authorization Act 84
Diplomacy *xi*, *xvii*, *xviii*, 4, 12, 15–17, 47–9, 51, 53–4, 74, 91, 117, 138, 141, 149
Durand Line 101

East Asia Security Centre *i*, *x*, *xv*, *xviii*, 2
East Asia Security Symposium and Conference *x*, *xv*, 2, 15, 49, 62, 98, 140
East Asian Summit 65, 91, 129
East China Sea 44, 66, 67, 68, 73, 81, 85–9, 91, 92
  Peace Initiative 89, 91
Economic goods 101
EP-3 incident 53, 64
Ethnicity
  Chinese Minority Groups 33
  Han as Majority Ethnic Group 32
  Han Centralism 33
  Han Dynasty and its People 27, 30, 31
European
  Political Economy 102, 104
  Union 105, 107, 138, 142
Exclusive Economic Zone (EEZ) 80, 86

Five Principles (Panchsheel) Agreement 4, 106–7, 141

Genghis Khan 31
Georgia *xiii*, 129–30, 134–42
Geography
  China as Geopolitically Isolated 24
  China as a Land Power 34, 29
  China as a River-based Civilization 28, 29, 32
  Geopolitical Center of Gravity (Sanjiangyuan) 25–8, 32, 34, 29
  Grand Unification of China 25, 31, 32, 33
  Great Development of the West 35
  Importance of Water in Geopolitics 27, 28
  Kunlun-Center Theory 29
  Loess Plateau and Dawn of Chinese Civilization 28, 29, 31, 32
  Northwest China's Historical Importance 30, 31, 34
  Role in Geopolitics 24–7
Geopolitical Logic as a Graphical Code (103:) 33–6
  Importance of Naval Power 34
  Northwestern Region 39
  Three Rivers (3) 34
  Western Barrier (1) 33, 36
Global Political Economy 3, 6, 97–9, 103
  Definition 99
Global Times 53
Governance 17, 34, 74, 97–9, 108, 124–5
Great Power 4–6, 44, 46, 58, 97–8 138

Definition 99
  Revisionist 46, 99, 107, 141
  Statecraft 6, 97, 100, 103, 107–9
Group of Two (G2) 81, 91
Group of Eight (G8) 142
Group of Twenty (G20) 129, 142
Guam 86, 148
Gwadar, Port of 105, 117, 121

Han Dynasty 9–11, 27, 29–31
Haqqani Network 121
Harmonious World 4, 139, 141
Hegemony 4, 10, 44
Himalayas 26–7, 33–4, 36, 38
Hong Kong 47, 71, 107
Hu Jintao, President 63, 65, 139, 151
Human Rights (HR) 45, 50, 58, 97, 104, 108, 132

Import Substitution Model 98
India *xii*, *xvii*, 6, 26, 38, 97, 114, 142, 149–51
  Analysts 118
  British 102–3, 106, 109, 114
  Border 98, 101
  Constitution 102
  Creation 101
  Democracy 98
  Development 98, 105, 114, 125
  Growth 103
  Indo-China War 98, 102, 108, 114, 116
    McMahon Line 102–3, 108
  Indo-Pakistani Tensions/War 114, 117, 118, 121
    Kashmir 101–2, 104, 109, 115, 121
  Political Economy 103
  Public perception 98
  Revisionist 107
  Security 115–17, 119
  Structural Power Capacity 99–100, 104–5
  Territory Disputes 101
  Visits to 102
Indian Ocean 15–16, 114, 117, 121
Industrial Revolution/Industrialize 1, 4, 27, 37, 98, 103, 105
Infrastructure 100, 116, 137
  Bank 4, 105, 117, 129, 148
  Civil-military 63
  Development Model 98
  Public Goods 105
  Strategic 10
International Atomic Energy Agency 119

International Security Assistance Force 106, 114, 151
Iran 106, 117, 123, 142
Ishihara, Shintaro, Governor 83, 89
Islam 106, 114–15, 122–3, 131–2

Japan 5–6, 8, 15–17, 19, 31, 47–8, 50–2, 60, 65–75, 80–92, 105, 121, 129, 148, 151
  US-China Dialogue 68, 69

Kashmir 101–2, 104, 109, 115, 121
Kazakhstan 129–31, 133, 134–5, 138, 140
Kerry, John, Secretary of State 84
Korea 10, 14, 16, 18, 44–5, 69, 73, 85–6, 90–1, 106, 115, 123, 129
Korean War 20
Kyrgyzstan 129–31, 133, 135, 138, 142

Lancang River 26, 34, 38
Leadership 11–12, 20, 43–5, 47–9, 53–5, 57–8, 63–4, 67, 70, 74, 87, 90, 98, 102, 108, 115, 123, 129, 135, 148–52
Leading Group for Maritime Security 72, 74
Leading Group on Coastal Defense 70
Lenin (ism, ist) 14, 18–19, 21, 48, 72
Libya 17, 116, 119, 123
Line of Actual Control (LAC) 102–4, 108–9

Macau 107
Malacca 15, 17
Mao Zedong 13–14, 18–20, 47–8, 51, 55–7, 102
Marines US 86, 148
Maritime Strategy 62, 63, 68, 74
Maritime Agencies 62, 63, 67, 69, 72, 73
  Chinese Coast Guard 62, 69, 73
  Fisheries Law Enforcement Command 62, 73, 85
  Maritime Safety Administration 62, 73
  State Oceanic Administration 73, 83
Marx (ist, ism) 21, 32, 48, 56–7
McMahon Line 102–3, 108
Medvedev, Dmitry, President 137, 139
Middle Power *xvii*, *xviii*
  Definition 99
Ministry of Foreign Affairs (MFA) 3, 15, 49, 66, 71–3
Ming Dynasty 10–11, 14–17, 31, 34, 82
Modi, Narendra, Prime Minister 98, 102

156 Index

Mujahideen 116, 118
Multilateral, Engagements/Forums/
　　Mechanisms/Organizations/
　　Regimes xvii, 65, 74, 125, 129,
　　131–2, 142
Myanmar/Burma 11, 38, 105, 106

Nepal 105
Nine-Dash Line 103
Nixon, Richard, President 116, 118
North American Free Trade
　　Agreement 107
North Atlantic Treaty Organization
　　(NATO) 106, 114, 116, 130, 133,
　　135, 137, 139, 141–2
Non-aligned Movement 107
Nontraditional Security Threat/Issues 68,
　　103, 108, 132
Nuclear Weapons 98, 101, 104
　　Brinksmanship 122
　　Nuclear Non-Proliferation Treaty 119
　　Pressler Amendment 115, 118
Nye, Joseph 86–7

Obama, Barack, President 50–1, 65, 81,
　　84, 86–8, 90–1
Oil 37, 66, 74, 97, 105, 121, 131, 134–5,
　　140–1
Okinawa 85–6
　　Reversion Treaty 83–4, 87
Olympics 50, 139
One Belt One Road 117, 129
Open Door Policy 35, 107
Osama bin Laden *xiii*, 6, 114, 116, 122,
　　125, 148

P5+1 106
Pakistan *xiii*, *xviii*, 6, 38, 101–2, 104–6,
　　109, 114–15, 120, 124–5,
　　148–9, 151
　　Abbottabad 114, 116, 122
　　China Relationship 116–17
　　Domestic Politics 114–15, 120
　　Gwadar 105, 117, 121
　　India relationship 114–15, 121–2
　　Inter-Services Intelligence 122
　　Musharraf administration 123
　　Nuclear Program 115–16, 118–20, 123
　　Territorial Disputes 101, 109
　　Terrorist Groups 114–15, 120–2
　　US Relationship 106, 115–16
Peaceful Rise/Development 4, 15, 74,
　　138, 140
People's Daily 53, 85

People's Liberation Army (PLA) 14, 47–8,
　　53–4, 63–4, 66, 72–3, 84, 98
Persian Gulf 114, 121
Philippines 8, 48, 70
Population (s) 1–2, 11, 14, 17, 20, 28, 32,
　　49, 97–9, 103, 105, 107–8, 120,
　　125, 131, 133–4, 149
Power(s) 4, 11–13, 17, 30, 44, 49, 54,
　　58, 69, 82, 89–92, 104, 107,
　　123, 135
　　Balance of 4, 55, 103, 105
　　Continental 21
　　Decentralized 35, 66
　　Economic i, 2, 4, 15–16, 25, 35, 44,
　　　47, 114, 121, 124–5, 130–1, 134,
　　　140, 151
　　Extra-regional/Outside 105–6, 114,
　　　120, 133
　　Global i, 2–4, 50, 130, 132
　　Great 4–6, 44, 46, 58, 97–8 138
　　　Definition 99
　　　Revisionist 46, 99, 107, 141
　　　Statecraft 6, 97, 100, 103, 107–9
　　Hard 12
　　Imperial 10, 35
　　Initiating 142
　　Land 34, 39, 62, 150
　　Loss of 105
　　Major 45–6, 55, 81, 130, 151
　　　Definition 45
　　Maritime/Naval/Sea *vxiii*, 4, 15–16, 34,
　　　44, 62–3, 74, 103, 150
　　Middle *xvii*, *xviii*
　　　Definition 99
　　Military 4, 47
　　Mystical 31
　　Personal 55–6
　　Political 12, 30
　　Relative 99
　　Revisionist 46, 99, 107
　　Rising/Emerging 44, 47–8, 114
　　Small 99, 101, 106
　　　Definition 99
　　Soft 12, 133, 136, 141
　　State/National/Domestic 10, 12,
　　　58, 97
　　Structural 6, 99, 105
　　Super 50, 55
　　Western 15, 33–4
　　World 46, 48, 50, 151
Public Goods 4, 10, 101, 105, 109
Public Opinion *xii*, 5, 43, 45–6, 48–52,
　　54, 57–8, 66–7, 98, 149, 151
Putin, Vladimir, President 133–5, 137

Qing Dynasty 10, 14, 17, 33–4, 82

Rebalance (ing) 39, 81, 84, 91
Revisionist Power 46, 99, 107
Russia 6, 28, 37, 105–6, 129–42, 149–51
Ryukyu Islands 83, 86

Sea Lines/Lanes of Communication (SLOC) 68, 88, 114, 117
Security xvii, 11, 21, 28, 39, 49, 52, 54, 67, 88, 91, 100, 104, 115–16, 120, 123, 132, 134, 136, 140
  Agenda 133
  Assistance 119, 125
  Border 133
  Challenges 114
  Chinese National Security Elite 8
  Coastal 17
  Collective 132
  Collective Security Treaty Organization (CSTO) 133, 135
  Common/Shared Interests 65, 131, 132
  Core Security 17
  Council for Security Cooperation in the Asia Pacific 129
  Dilemma 44, 114
  Dynamic 114
  East and West 39
  Environment 80–1, 115
  Food 38
  Global/systemic 101
  Information/Cyber 85, 142
  Internal 132, 136
  Insecurity 11, 54, 80, 86, 140
  Maritime 68–70, 72, 74, 80
  Military 45
  National 36, 38
  National Security Commission/Council 64, 68, 70, 74
  National Security Strategy 80
  New Security Concept 4, 107, 141
  Nontraditional *xvii*, 68, 103, 108, 132
  Nuclear 120, 123, 125
  Organization for Security and Co-operation in Europe 142
  Perceptions/Perspectives of 86, 115
  Politics of 28
  Regime 132
  Regional 45, 115, 118, 120, 125, 142
  Sea Lane/Lines, SLOC 17, 68
  Services/Forces/Assets 115, 122, 124
  Studies 20, 149
  Territorial Assurance 100–1, 104

United Nations Security Council 52, 132
US-China Security & Economic Dialogue 65
US-Japan Security Treaty 83–4, 86–8
US–Japan Treaty of Mutual Cooperation and Security 85
Zero-sum 124
Self-determination 104, 108
Shanghai Cooperation Organization (SCO) *xiii*, 6, 106, 129, 130–5, 138–42, 149
Shangri-La Dialog 129
Shi, Myth of (control of battlefield conditions) 17
Silk Road, Economic Belt/Maritime Silk Road 134
Simla Convention 99
Singapore 117
  Global Dialogue 68
Sino-Japanese
  Japan-China High-Level Consultation on Maritime Affairs 68, 69
  Japan-China Maritime Search & Rescue Cooperation 68
Sino-Japanese Friendship Association 70
Six Party Talks 45, 106
Small Power 99, 101, 106
  Definition 99
Socialist State Directed Market Capitalism 98
Social Media 45, 50–1, 57
South Asian Association for Regional Cooperation 106
South China Sea 34, 44, 47, 62, 63, 65, 67–9, 80, 85, 87, 88, 90, 103
South East Asia Treaty Organization 116
Sovereignty 11, 44, 47, 49, 52, 54, 56, 82, 84, 87, 89, 90–2, 99–100, 107–9, 131, 136, 138, 150
  Mutation of, Revision of 107–8
  Peace of Westphalia, system 33, 100–4, 109
  Security 100
  Special Administrative Regions 107
  Special Economic Zones 107
  Territorial Assurance *xii*, 100–2, 107–8
Soviet Union (USSR) 35, 47, 107, 115, 130, 135, 137
Sri Lanka 105
State Commission of Border and Coastal Defense 63
Statecraft *xii*, *xviii*, 17, 20, 97–101, 103–5, 107–9

158 *Index*

Based approach 97, 100
Definition 99
Domestic 101
Global 105
Great Power 6, 97, 100, 103, 107–9
Middle Power *xvii*, *xviii*, 99
Small Power 99, 101, 106
State Oceanic Administration (SOA) 73–4
Strategic Studies, Definition 4
Structural Power 6, 99, 105
Sun Yat-Sen 33
Sunzi *xi*, 8–9, 12–14, 17–20
Syria 123, 142

Taiwan *xviii*, 4, 8, 16–17, 34, 36, 39, 44, 47, 50, 58, 68, 80–3, 85–7, 89–91, 107, 130, 134
Tajikistan 129–31, 133–5, 138
Taliban/Tehrik-e-Taliban Pakistan (TTP) 114–16, 118, 121–2, 125, 132
Tang Dynasty 14, 24, 27, 29–31
Terrorism *xviii*, 6, 85, 103–4, 106, 114–15, 121–2, 124–5, 131–2, 139
Turkmenistan 130, 134
Turmoil, Political 35, 105, 108
Theory *xii*, *xviii*, 2, 18, 100, 149
    Critical *xii*, 6, 99–100, 102, 107–9
    Kunlun-Center 29
    Hegemonic Transition 141
    Liberalism (neo) *xii*, 44, 105, 149
    Mercantilism (ist) 98, 103, 105
    Problem solving 6, 56, 100, 102, 104–5, 108–9
    Realism (neo, ist) *xii*, 13, 43–4, 55–6, 98, 104–5, 149
    Sanjiangyuan 28
    Strategic 20
Tibet 5, 11, 24, 33, 36–9, 87, 98, 104–5, 130
    Qinghai– Railway 36, 105
    Qinghai-Tibet Plateau 24, 26–7, 36
    Government-in-exile 104
Trans-Pacific Partnership 148

Uighur/Uyghur 46, 69, 120–1, 131
Ukraine 137, 139–40
United Nations 71, 85, 136
    Convention on the Law of the Sea 103
    Security Council 52, 132

United States of America i, xii, xiii, 3, 26, 44, 62, 64, 80, 84, 89–91, 97, 105, 107, 114, 130, 135, 140–2, 148–9, 151
Afghanistan 106, 114, 118–19, 122, 124–5, 151
Central Asia 133
China 85, 87–8
    Bilateral 84
    Cooperation 114, 120–4
    Crisis management 64–74
    Military Maritime Consultative Agreement 65
    Rapprochement 47
    Shared Interests 115, 117–19
Coast Guard 73
Department of State 66
Diaoyou/Senkaku 81–3
India 114
Japan 65–6, 68–9, 71, 73–4, 80, 86–7
Marines 86, 148
Mediating role 68, 91
Naval War College xvii, xviii, 73
Pakistan 106, 114–16
Rebalancing Policy 84
Status of Forces Agreement 82
Uzbekistan 129–30, 132–5, 138

Vietnam 8, 10–11, 16, 48, 70, 116, 118

Wen Jiabao, Premier 38, 52, 66, 68, 140
World Trade Organization 45, 129

Xi Jinping, President 98, 102
Xinjiang 33, 36–7, 39, 80, 87, 105, 130–1, 141

Yang Yi, Admiral 68
Yangtze River 26–8, 34, 37
Yasukuni Shrine 51–2, 69, 80, 85
Yellow River 9, 26–32, 34, 37–9
Yongle Emperor 15–16

Zheng He *xi*, 8, 15–17
Zheng He Myth (China's peaceful rise) 15–17
    and China's gun-boat diplomacy 15–17
Zhou Enlai, Premier 47, 51